ADVOCACY AND POLICY CHANGE EVALUATION

ANNETTE L. GARDNER
AND CLAIRE D. BRINDIS

ADVOCACY AND POLICY CHANGE EVALUATION

Theory and Practice

STANFORD BUSINESS BOOKS

AN IMPRINT OF STANFORD UNIVERSITY PRESS

STANFORD, CALIFORNIA

Stanford University Press
Stanford, California

Special discounts for bulk quantities of Stanford Business Books are available to corporations, professional associations, and other organizations. For details and discount information, contact the special sales department of Stanford University Press.
Tel: (650) 725–0820, Fax: (650) 725–3457.

Printed in the United States of America on acid-free, archival-quality paper.

Library of Congress Cataloging-in-Publication Data

Names: Gardner, Annette L., author. | Brindis, Claire D., author.
Title: Advocacy and policy change evaluation : theory and practice / Annette L. Gardner and Claire D. Brindis.
Description: Stanford, California : Stanford Business Books, an imprint of Stanford University Press, 2017. | Includes bibliographical references and index.
Identifiers: LCCN 2016039746 | ISBN 9780804792561 (pbk. : alk. paper) | ISBN 9781503602335 (ebook)
Subjects: LCSH: Political planning—Evaluation. | Policy sciences—Evaluation. | Social advocacy—Evaluation.
Classification: LCC JF1525.P6 G37 2017 | DDC 320.6—dc23
LC record available at https://lccn.loc.gov/2016039746

CONTENTS

SEVERAL factors have fueled the need for skilled evaluators who can design appropriate evaluations to meet diverse stakeholder needs: increased foundation interest in supporting advocacy and policy change (APC) initiatives to achieve systems change; evaluation of democracy-building initiatives worldwide; and diffusion of advocacy capacity beyond the traditional advocacy community (such as service providers). Evaluators have met these needs with great success, building a new field of evaluation practice, adapting and creating evaluation concepts and methods, and shaping advocate, funder, and evaluator thinking on advocacy and policy change in all its diverse manifestations. The field will only continue to grow and evolve.

This book is designed to build on this groundswell of evaluation thought and practice and to be insightful and instructive. We combine the plethora of concepts, definitions, designs, tools, empirical findings, and lessons learned thus far into one practice-focused and easy-to-use resource. This book addresses the varied evaluation needs of stakeholders by presenting a wide array of options specific to evaluating advocacy and policy change initiatives. It also addresses the challenges associated with evaluation practice, such as the complexity and moving target of the context in which advocacy activities occur and the challenge of attribution issues and identification of causal factors.

There are several academic and practical reasons for developing this book. Current advocacy and policy change evaluation practice lacks a deep understanding of the existing research and models from the political science, public policy and nonprofit management disciplines, including organized interests, influence, agenda setting, media, and models of the policy process. Consequently, evaluators often do not incorporate a robust, theory-based foundation into their evaluation practice, limiting their effectiveness in designing advocacy and policy change evaluations and informing stakeholder learning. Increased understanding of core principles and scholarly research will enable evaluators to make themselves heard more broadly and to contribute to the knowledge base of political representation, influence, and systems change.

At the practical level, this book provides useful, real-world examples of developing appropriate evaluation designs and applying the findings to advocacy practice and decision-making. Our review of available resources is broad and deep and includes an examination of relevant evaluation strategies, as well as an analysis of the findings from the 2014 Aspen/ UCSF APC Evaluation Survey of tested evaluation designs and data-collection instruments. Completed by 106 members of the American Evaluation Association (AEA)[1] and evaluators of advocacy and policy change initiatives of all types, our understanding of actual APC evaluation practice has been greatly expanded by the results—advocacy tactics evaluated, evaluation strategies used, and detailed information about gaps in the APC evaluation field.

Additionally, throughout the book, we describe and compare six evaluation cases that speak to the diversity of advocacy and policy change evaluations, including a range of evaluation designs, conventional and unique evaluation methods, and approaches to informing advocate and funder strategy. They were identified by individual Aspen/UCSF APC Evaluation Survey respondents as being conducted in the past five years and containing an interesting methodology or significant lesson. A primary reason for developing the six cases of evaluation practice was to surface design models in a variety of advocacy and policy contexts. It is helpful to see how evaluators of advocacy and policy change initiatives mix and match different methods and link them to evaluation questions and a theory of change and/or logic model while being mindful to re-

---

1. The twenty-three-item survey was administered electronically in May 2014 by the Aspen Planning and Evaluation Program to the 585 members of the Advocacy and Policy Change (APC) Topical Interest Group (TIG) and 1,000 randomly selected members of the American Evaluation Association. The survey was completed by 106 evaluators, a 7 percent response rate. The response rate of APC TIG members was 9 percent. All respondents had been involved in evaluating advocacy and policy change initiatives within the last five years.

source constraints and a quickly evolving context. How evaluators balance stakeholder information needs that may go beyond strategic learning early on while addressing challenges to validity, such as an evolving initiative, small sample size, and limitations in resources may be the "art" of advocacy and policy change evaluation. All six initiatives were sponsored by philanthropic organizations or nonprofit public charities and speak to funder willingness to invest in different strategies to achieving a policy change as well as commitment to achieving long-term systems change, and include: (1) the *Initiative to Promote Equitable and Sustainable Transportation (2008—2013)* was funded by the Rockefeller Foundation Board to support adoption of policies for equitable and sustainable transportation options largely through the reauthorization of the Federal Surface Transportation Bill in 2009 and through support of commensurate state policies in key, influential states; (2) the United Nations Foundation provided support for the *Let Girls Lead program (2009—present)* to create a global movement of leaders and organizations advocating for adolescent girls' rights. The Let Girls Lead initiative strengthens the capacity of civil society leaders, girl advocates, and local organizations to promote girl-friendly laws, policies, programs, and funding in Guatemala, Honduras, Liberia, Malawi, and Ethiopia; (3) Oxfam funded the *GROW Campaign (2012—present),* a multinational campaign to tackle food injustice and to build a better food system that sustainably feeds a growing population, and it included a six-month campaign targeting World Bank policy on large-scale land acquisition; (4) the Pew Charitable Trusts launched campaigns in Canada and Australia targeting regional and locally based land-use planning processes, as part of its *International Lands Conservation Program (1999—present)* to conserve old-growth forests and extend wilderness areas; (5) funded by ClearWay Minnesota, the *Tribal Tobacco Education and Policy (TTEP) Initiative (2008–2013)* provided resources and assistance to five tribal communities to pass or expand formal and informal smoke-free policies while increasing community awareness of secondhand smoke; and (6) *Project Health Colorado (2011–2013),* a public-will-building campaign was launched by the Colorado Trust to engage individuals and organizations in a statewide discussion about health care and how it can be improved. By encouraging people across the state to be part of the solution, Project Health Colorado believed it would make a difference in how decisions are made about health care. (See Appendix A for detailed descriptions of these six cases.)

To examine the similarities and differences in designs, methods, and data collection instruments, we compare two different evaluation cases in Chapters 3, 4, and 5. Our pairing of cases is intentional, choosing to compare evaluations that were done at about the same time in the program process. In Chapter 3, we compare designs of two end-point evaluations, the Initiative to Promote Sustainable and Equitable Transportation and the Let Girls Lead program. In Chapter 4, we compare two midpoint evaluations, the GROW Campaign and the International Land Conservation Program. Last, in Chapter 5, we compare two multiyear evaluations, the Tribal Tobacco Education and Policy (TTEP) Initiative and Project Health Colorado. While there is significant diversity in the six evaluation cases' policy objectives, advocacy tactics, and contexts, there are similarities in purpose, design, methods, conventional and unique instruments, the evaluator role, and use of evaluation findings.

A three-part "pracademic" framework is used to increase utility of the book for evaluators, advocates, and funders. The first two chapters tilt toward the academic and describe concepts and models from the policy sciences and nonprofit scholarship that can be used to help evaluators navigate the deep and many times turbulent public policy waters and develop a theory of change. The remaining five chapters focus on the "meat" of the evaluation design, applicable methods, and recommendations for advancing individual and collective evaluation practice. Second, our "pracademic" approach applies to each chapter, and we lay out concepts and models in the first half of the chapter and finish with a discussion on actual evaluation practice, specifically the findings from the Aspen/ UCSF APC Evaluation Survey and the six evaluation cases. The three parts are: (1) useful theories and conceptual models; (2) appropriate designs, methods and measures; and (3) getting to wisdom and advancing individual and collective advocacy and policy change evaluation practice. Each chapter builds on the previous chapter although each is designed to be unique and to address specific evaluation needs. For example, evaluators who are new to advocacy capacity and/or policymaking will find

Chapters 1 and 2 about theoretical underpinnings useful in developing sound evaluation questions.

That being said, while this book is intended to expand on prior advocacy and policy change evaluation guides and to serve as a comprehensive resource for evaluators, advocates, and funders, it is not intended to be an evaluation textbook for beginning evaluators. A basic understanding of evaluation is assumed. It should also be noted at the outset that this book does not promote one framework or evaluation design over another. Instead, it is intended to be a "cookbook," providing a variety of strategies and measures that have been used in the field and applied to a wide array of advocacy and policy change evaluation issues.

PART 1: USEFUL THEORIES AND
CONCEPTUAL MODELS
Evaluators will benefit from grounding their practice within a robust understanding of advocacy and policy change, including scholarly research about what we know and do not know about the policymaking process and individual and collective action. The primary goal of Part 1 is to expand evaluator capacity to use applicable concepts and models, such as the policy stage model of policymaking to frame evaluation designs. We also look across disciplines and seek commonalities as well as gaps in knowledge that challenge evaluation, such as the lack of a single definition of advocacy. Evaluators who ignore these foundational components of their evaluation practice are at risk of overlooking critical aspects of advocacy and policy change initiatives, such as the advocacy activities postpassage of a policy, which are not so transparent. They are also at risk of having a limited understanding of the perspectives and strategies of advocates, decision-makers, and funders important in the planning and implementation of advocacy and policy change initiatives.

In Chapter 1, we review the public policy concepts and definitions important to evaluation practice, including models of policymaking process and the venues where policy is made. In Chapter 2, we describe advocacy in the broadest sense, particularly the myriad types of advocates— individuals, organizations, and groups—and their attributes, as well as the many strategies and tactics that advocates use to build a constituency for change and influence policymaker support. In both chapters, we try to strengthen the link between theory and practice and provide real-world examples as well as suggestions for incorporating a concept or model into an evaluation design. We also describe the policy and advocacy contexts in the six evaluation cases to illustrate the diverse scenarios that evaluators may encounter—international, national, state, regional, and local, as well as policy issues—health, transportation, land-use, food security, human rights, and gender equity.

PART 2: APPROPRIATE DESIGNS, OUTCOMES,
AND METHODS
In Part 2, we shift from the academic perspective to the design and implementation of advocacy and policy change evaluations. We use a macro-to-micro approach, starting with recommendations for developing an evaluation design followed by suggestions for selecting and/or developing specific methods and outcomes. Second, we use the findings from the Aspen/UCSF Survey about advocacy and policy change evaluation practices to illustrate evaluation designs at different points in an advocacy and policy change initiative as well as the ways that evaluators mix and match their methods.

In Chapter 3, we review the evaluation strategies important for designing advocacy and policy change evaluations, including the evaluation purpose, knowledge of the context, rigor, and working with stakeholders. We also describe several challenges (and possible solutions) to advocacy and policy change design, some of which are contextual (such as lack of transparency) and some of which are methodological (such as initiative complexity and uncertainty). In Chapter 4, we discuss conventional and unconventional or unique evaluation methods that have been specifically developed for advocacy and policy change initiatives. While we are mindful to the evolving and complicated nature of an advocacy and policy change initiative, we advocate developing and working with a program theory of change and/or logic model. In Chapter 5, we review the unique, off-the-shelf instruments that have been used by the field, such as those reported in the peer review literature and/or frequently mentioned by survey respondents, and we describe their intended focus, use, and limitations. In each chapter we compare and contrast two evaluation cases to illustrate the points described in the narrative as well as provide useful designs, strategies, and tools.

PART 3: LEVERAGING WISDOM FROM THE FIELD
In Part 3, we shift from evaluation practice to opportunities and challenges for advancing the field of advocacy and policy change evaluation. Recognizing that APC evaluators are diverse and conduct other types of evaluation, as well as come from different backgrounds, we recommend leveraging the wisdom and knowledge of seasoned APC evaluators and creating a "community practice" through continued sharing and networking.

In Chapter 6, we revisit partnership-based evaluation principles and describe the possible roles that may be afforded to evaluators by advocacy and policy initiatives—educator, strategist, and influencer. Unlike evaluation of stable programs that have a specific intervention, evaluators of advocacy and policy change initiatives may find themselves in the position of informing decision-making and being a potent voice for change. We also discuss the Aspen/UCSF Survey findings on the key uses of recent evaluations and describe evaluation products and processes developed by the evaluators of the six evaluation cases. In Chapter 7, we identify gaps and discuss new frontiers in evaluation practice, including suggestions for strengthening individual evaluation practice, or what we call "mindful evaluation." Second, with input from our partners at the Aspen Institute and other longtime advocacy and policy change evaluators and funders, we make recommendations for advancing the field, such as expanding the geographic focus of APC evaluation, continuing to build capacity among those evaluators committed to working in this arena, and supporting the sharing of designs, methods, and lessons learned, assuring that evidence is used in the next generation of efforts to improve the lives of those most often left behind. Furthermore, building a strong network among the APC evaluation community also helps to assure that evaluation techniques will be incorporated sooner and more effectively, thus accelerating learning and wisdom across a variety of evaluation stakeholders. Second, we believe there is a place for evaluators in the scholarship on advocacy, public policy, and nonprofits, and we describe areas and topics that would benefit from APC evaluation findings and methods.

In sum, this book taps into knowledge from other disciplines, relevant evaluation concepts, and the works of the APC evaluation community to strengthen advocacy and policy change evaluation practice. Our intention is to create an enriched understanding of advocacy and policy change that can be used to inform future evaluation practice. We reflect on individual and collective evaluation practice to address the current challenges raised by advocacy and policy change initiatives, as well as advance APC evaluation theory and design.

That said, we have been humbled by the enormity of our task: the advocacy and policy change evaluation arena is broad and deep, and in all likelihood we have overlooked a relevant model, idea, or perspective. While we have both worked in the international arena and with underserved populations, our understanding of policy, policymaking, and advocacy has been largely shaped by the U.S. context. So as not be too United States-centric, we have used examples that are present in most settings, such as access to health care and human rights issues, as well as examples of specific policies that are more widely known.

The overall tone and philosophy of this book is to provide both a supportive guide while taking a "critical friend" perspective, sharing information on specific strengths and gaps to advance the field of APC evaluation. We recognize that it is an emerging field that learns and builds upon a collective history of evaluation practice, while also building its own identity and recognition. The results are well worth the effort. Through focusing the evaluation lens on the increasing importance of advocacy in addressing the issues of disparities, equity, and social justice and the well-being of global communities, APC evaluation is becoming a prime vehicle for effective learning and the shaping of future advocacy and policy change strategies and tactics.

ACKNOWLEDGMENTS

AT a time that the field of advocacy and policy change (APC) evaluation is reaching a critical point in its young development as a recognized area of evaluation concentration, it is important to recognize the critical actors that have played such a vital role in shaping this body of work, as well as their commitment to its advancement. This book has greatly benefitted from the input of many experienced advisors, many who have also persevered in this area since the APC movement began taking shape in the early 2000s through the efforts of a networked collaborative of like-minded evaluators and private and public funders. Many of their tools, toolkits, and wisdom are sprinkled throughout the book; clearly, without their insights and generosity of spirit and support of this emerging field, this book would not have been written. While there are too many visionary pioneers to identify by specific name but whose work is included throughout this book, there are some individuals we want to warmly acknowledge for their substantive contributions to this book. Julia Coffman deserves special recognition for building the base and developing evaluation planning frameworks and tools, and for sharing evaluation best practices. Other noteworthy individuals include the reviewers of individual chapters: Jenifer Cartland, Sue Hoechstetter, Tom Kelly, and Laura Roper. The partnership with the public and private sponsors of advocacy and policy change initiatives and their evaluations has been the lifeblood of this ongoing collaborative, including the Atlantic Philanthropies, the California Endowment, the Annie E. Casey Foundation, the Colorado Trust, and many, many others. Thanks to them, the experiences of advocates and their efforts are increasingly visible and are informing others.

We are extremely grateful to the Aspen Institute's Aspen Planning and Program Evaluation team, headed by David Devlin-Foltz. We feel very fortunate to have worked with David, Suzanna Dilliplane, Robert Medina, and Angbeen Saleem, to design, launch, and analyze the 2014 Aspen/UCSF APC Evaluation Survey, the results of which have guided us well, and which are integrally described throughout the book. Their wealth of experience in this arena, as well as a commitment to advancing the APC evaluation field in many creative ways has helped to bring great breadth and depth to this book. We also express our deep gratitude to the American Evaluation Association (AEA) and for the current and former leadership of the AEA Advocacy and Policy Change Topical Interest Group for their support and assistance in administering the Aspen/UCSF Survey. The 106 respondents to the survey, APC evaluators from all "walks of life," deserve a warm thank you for their willingness to share their experiences, suggestions for strengthening evaluation practice, and perceptions of field strengths and weaknesses.

We thank the evaluators and funders of the six evaluation cases for generously sharing their experiences and insights with us, including Carlisle Levine (Let Girls Lead), Jewlya Lynn (Project Health Colorado), Glenn O'Neil (Oxfam GROW Campaign), Jared Raynor (Initiative Promoting Equitable and Sustainable Transportation), Sheri Scott (Tribal Tobacco Education and Policy [TTEP] initiative), and Edward Wilson (International Land Conservation Campaign). These cases, woven throughout the book, represent another foundational anchor, providing real-life experiences with implementing a variety of APC evaluation efforts. Through these varied cases, readers gain the capacity to further understand the range and diversity of evaluation topics and their contexts, the high commitment to supporting advocacy and policy change, as well as the dedication and hard work of advocates and evaluators worldwide to improve the lives of others and heal the environment. We salute the advocates, as well as the evaluators, who provided such valuable insights into their sometimes chaotic, but enormously important endeavors on behalf of individuals, communities, states, regions, nations, and the environment.

We want to acknowledge the supportive partnership with the editorial staff at Stanford University Press, particularly Margo Beth Fleming, for her wonderful expertise as a coach and supporter, whose dedication to the birth of this book provided vital energy to us as authors. Our copy editor, Hollie Quinn, deserves special recognition for her critical eye and phrasing that make books like this more compelling. We also deeply acknowledge the professional reviewers of this book, Julia Coffman and Michael Quinn Patton. We also want to acknowledge the significant role played by our parents, Donna and Murray Gardner, and Lucy and Walt Dale, in guiding us and deeply valuing our many endeavors over the years on behalf of people whose voices are often silent. Finally, and perhaps most importantly, we thank our families, Charles and Ian Simons and Ralph Brindis, and our sons and their wives, Seth Brindis and Stephanie Reich and Daniel and Amalia Brindis Delgado, for their continued support and encouragement, as well as their commitment and dedication to advocacy throughout their lives.

ILLUSTRATIONS

Part 1

Useful Theories and Conceptual Models

CHAPTER 1

POLICY AND POLICYMAKING
Making a Difference

INTRODUCTION

Policy and policymaking permeates and shapes our daily lives, from man-dating funding for public schools to regulating the disposal of hazardous materials. No one is untouched by public policies, and when well thought out and implemented, they are potent vehicles for social betterment. The policy process and its outcomes are the raison d'etre of government and a lens on the ongoing debate about the nature of societal problems and ap-propriate solutions. Public policymaking is also increasingly viewed as a venue for individuals, organizations, and groups to intervene and achieve system-wide change that heretofore was limited to the privileged few. But engaging in policy change, be it organizing a community to act on its own behalf or examining the implementation of a newly minted measure, bill, or budget, is a daunting undertaking under any circumstance. Under-standing the challenges as well as opportunities for change are necessary first steps to designing a successful advocacy and policy change (APC) evaluation. In this chapter, we review the scholarship on public policy and describe the concepts that are important to advocacy and policy change evaluation practice, including the nature of policy change. We focus on public sector policymaking or decisions made by federal, state, local, and municipal governments, be it laws, regulatory measures, or funding priorities though many of the same principles apply outside of the public sector.

Through a tailored review of public policy scholarship, we aim to provide a handy reference for evaluators who are new to the policymaking process, and/or evaluating it and wanting for a bird's eye view. While theory building is outside the purview of many advocacy and policy change evaluations, evaluators can still use theory to understand a complicated policy venue: the type of policy, models of the policy change mechanism, and the different policymaking venues. Be forewarned, this is a changing and somewhat chaotic arena, with vague boundaries and a weak theoretical foundation. Characterizing the steps that a policy goes through before it becomes law is not a particularly difficult task. However, understanding the political actors and institutions and their roles and relationships at each stage of the decision-making process is a different matter since they are less transparent and possibly in flux as environmental factors change, such as a change in administration. (Please note: These models and definitions speak primarily to U.S. public policymaking. However, we are intentionally broad in our inclusion and description of these concepts since many political systems share the same components of government, elections, organized interests, and a decision-making process.)

With this groundwork laid, we provide recommendations for incorporating policymaking concepts and models into evaluation practice. While incorporating a policy change model into an evaluation design can be challenging since stakeholders may have competing theories of change, some policy frameworks, such as the policymaking stage model, can be readily adapted to many different types of evaluations in different contexts. This and other models will be described in this chapter. As with many other types of evaluations, articulating and facilitating a shared understanding of the assumptions about the policymaking process is key in setting the parameters of an advocacy and policy change evaluation.

Last, to ground this discussion to the reality of policymaking, we tap into the findings from the 2014 Aspen/UCSF APC Evaluation Survey completed by 106 APC evaluators, as well as describe and compare the real-life policy issues that were targeted by advocates in the six advocacy and policy change evaluation cases that were developed for this book.

While not representative of the universe of policy arenas and issues, the cases illustrate the diversity of policy types, geographic levels of decision-making, and venues where policymaking takes place.

WHAT IS POLICY?

There is no one definition of "public policy," and it can be narrowly or broadly defined. For example, one classic political science definition, "Public policy is whatever governments choose to do or not to do" (Dye 2002, 1), is too broad to be of use to evaluators. It belies the complexity of the actual decision-making process. It also overlooks the role that values play and that in many cases, policymaking is deciding which values will prevail, such as whether responsibility for implementation of a new program should be done at the federal or state level or left to the private sector (Kraft and Furlong 2010). Political scientist Thomas Birkland (2001, 20) provides a list of attributes that are commonly used to define policy and that is more helpful for framing an advocacy and policy evaluation design:

- Policy is made in the public's name.
- Policy is generally made or initiated by government.
- Policy is what government intends to do (is purposive) on behalf of the public.
- Policy is what the government chooses not to do.
- Policy is interpreted and implemented by public and private actors.

These attributes—the how, what, and where policy is made—and their application to evaluation practice are described in the next sections.

THE POLICYMAKING PROCESS

We look to the political science arena for models that we believe will help evaluators develop a more robust understanding of the policymaking process and the contextual factors that shape it. As explained by political scientist Thomas Dye (2002), these models describe a distinct way of thinking about policy, but they are not mutually exclusive and they can be combined to explain a policy's trajectory. These models overlap in that they focus on representation, as well as the distribution of power and likelihood of incremental or radical policy change. They explain how public and private institutions, organized interests, and policymakers interact to produce and implement policies. In their broadest sense, they characterize the nature and role of individuals and groups, the role of information and beliefs in decision-making, the level of action, and activities at various stages of the policy process (Schlager and Blomquist 1996). Increasingly, public policy models take a systems approach and detail the relationships among these components and provide evaluators with a foundation on which they can base a theory of change as well as develop a sound contextual analysis.

The most encompassing model describes the policy process as a set of stages or the "policy cycle" (hereafter referred to as the "policy stage model") framework. While not a perfect description of the policymaking process, we suggest that all evaluators incorporate aspects of this model into their evaluation design, particularly in the development of a theory of change and/or logic model. Drawing on the literature, we have created an annotated stage model that describes the opportunities for evaluators to better understand the policy landscape as well as key activities and events that can be incorporated into an APC evaluation logic model. Originally premised on the application of systems theory to explain the policy process, the stage model is a chronological rendering of interdependent stages in the policymaking process. Collectively, the stages are the subject matter of the policy studies arena within political science, and the goal is to study the procedures and processes by which policy is made (Theodoulou 1995; Dye 2002). Each of these stages has its own body of scholarship and research questions, with some attracting more attention than others.

Stage 1, *Problem Recognition,* is the stage when the public makes demands for government action, and policy problems are recognized by policymakers as requiring action. If recognized as legitimate, problems, such as global warming, workplace safety, or equity issues, then become issues. At this stage, it is important to determine who identifies a problem, the role of public opinion and the media, and the nature of the problem, such as whether it is a new problem (say, a crisis), or broad and systemic (say, lack of employment opportunities). Polling information, media coverage, and policymaker communications are useful for understanding the history, context, and saliency of the problem to the public, advocates, and decision-makers. It is also helpful to understand the length of time it takes for a problem to reach a critical point and policymaker acknowledgement that action is justified. It is a worthwhile investment in effort since in all likelihood the debate and voices raised at this stage will have a ripple effect and shape the remaining the stages.

Stage 2, *Agenda Setting*, is considered the "make or break" stage, and if problems do not make it on the policy agenda, the process stops there. During this stage, an issue is given serious consideration by policymakers, launching the search for a policy solution. It is useful to specify who identifies the issues that gain policymakers' attention, such as professional associations, the media, decision-makers, influential individuals, as well as the mechanism for narrowing the set of issues that policymakers will act on. Additionally, issues that are kept off the agenda are worth noting, such as those like strict gun control that are opposed by powerful private sector interests.

Stage 3, *Policy Formulation*, is the development of acceptable policy proposals to address the problem(s) identified during Stage 1 by interest groups, policymakers, and think tanks. It is the stage when policy analyses are conducted to determine the relative merits of one policy over another with the intent to improve policies. This stage provides detailed information on the understanding of the causal sequence between the problem and the policy solution.

Stage 4, *Policy Adoption*, is the act of selecting which policy proposal will be enacted into law by decision-makers or the courts. It is also the stage of *Policy Legitimation* or the process of building support for adoption, including bargaining, competition, persuasion, and compromise. A policy's progress can be tracked as it winds its way through hearings, voting, and signing.

Stage 5, *Policy Implementation*, is when a bill becomes a law and is translated into guidelines or rules and regulations by bureaucracies. New legislation, such as agency activities and public expenditures, is implemented through public programs and involves federal, state, or local government. This stage provides information on the legal and technical aspects of a policy and a blueprint for action that can be monitored and used in assessing achievement of policy goals. Recently, there has been increased use of implementation science to assess Stage 5 since a poorly executed policy may be the same or worse than no policy at all. This is also a stage where there is the possibility of greater equality of representation across advocates, such as the public comment period and participating on agency committees. However, the evidence on legislative and administrative lobbying at the federal and state levels in the United States suggests that while lobbyists of all types are very active during Stage 5, business interests dominate both arenas (Boehmke, Gailmard, and Patty 2013).

Last, Stage 6, *Policy Evaluation,* is the systematic evaluation of a policy—its actual impacts, costs, and whether or not it achieved its intended results. It is an opportune time to assess whether or not policy was implemented as intended and with the necessary resources and system capacity to fulfill the policy's intent. The objective is to inform policymakers on whether or not they made the right choice as well as the effects of the policy, and should be familiar territory to APC evaluators. Standard evaluation design principles apply, but the context poses particular challenges, such as government concerns about negative findings and limited use of findings by decision-makers and government agencies (Dye 2002). Evaluator Carol Weiss (1999) and other evaluators describe the interface between evaluation and public policy and the limited avenues and opportunities for educating policymakers. While the information-rich environment and the confluence of interests and ideology precludes full consideration of evaluation findings by policymakers, there is still the opportunity to play more than a symbolic role and educate decision-makers and the public on a policy's impact.

The literature suggests high agreement about the stages of the model to the extent that these are the primary stages, though even this varies somewhat, such as having *Agenda Setting* as Stage 1, instead of *Problem Identification.* There are also suggestions for expanding the stage model further, such as adding a new Stage 1, *Building Advocacy Capacity,* to describe the groundwork that is developed prior to the identification of a problem (Brindis, Geierstanger, and Faxio 2009).

There are issues with the stage approach that evaluators should be mindful of. Political scientists Hank C. Jenkins-Smith and Paul A. Sabatier (1994) point out that the model may be "descriptively inaccurate" for policies that go through the stages in a different order or bypass one or more stages. For example, the role of media in influencing public and policymaker opinion may straddle Stage 1, *Problem Recognition,* and Stage 2, *Agenda Setting.* Or, depending on the saliency and conflict surrounding an issue, the media may be active at all stages. For example, the 2010 Affordable Care Act, or Obamacare, attracted widespread public and policymaker attention and figured prominently in the media pre- and postpassage. Additionally, these stages correspond to decision-making points, but not all initiatives advance to a decision. Critics also argue that a stage approach is purely descriptive and not a causal model that explains why something happens or when something is likely to happen.

However, while not a perfect characterization of how policy is crafted, the stage model is nonetheless a descriptive and flexible heuristic. At a minimum, we recommend that you align your policy issue with the stage (or stages) of the model and examine the scholarship for that particular stage. For example, if you are looking at advocacy postpassage, focus on the policy implementation and policy evaluation literature. Second, examine the analytical aspects of the stage model that can inform your situation, in particular the *Policy Formulation* and *Policy Evaluation* stages, when policy analyses are likely to be undertaken and can provide detailed information on policy options and the likelihood of policy sustainability (Chelimsky 2014). These are also the stages that APC evaluators are well positioned to improve the quality of a policy or program.

Last, the stage model is also useful for identifying decision points that are opportunities for advocates to make themselves heard, such as during the public comment period. These decision points also represent evaluation opportunities. For example, assessing the level of funding allocated to a policy during the *Policy Implementation* stage may reflect the political savvyness of the advocacy community, as without sufficient resources, the policy passage may remain largely a paper tiger. Advocates are highly knowledgeable of the policymaking process and its opportunities, making it even more important that evaluators familiarize themselves with the decision points of the process.

Policy Change Models

Increasingly, in APC evaluation practice, it is important to give some thought to the models that characterize the change aspect of policy change, particularly when developing a theory of change. A policy can undergo significant change as it winds its way through the decision-making process and may not resemble its original form by the time it is adopted. However, upon closer examination, we see that this is really a much more nuanced discussion. Policy change may be incremental and consist of small changes in existing policies or passage of noncontroversial policies. Described as "muddling through" by political scientist Charles E. Lindblom (1979), the incrementalism model explains why policies are rarely terminated. Nor are radically new policies passed. This is due in part to the stability of a policy arena, a desirable feature, but it is also reflects the difficulties in bringing about more radical change. Overlapping policy jurisdictions, contested problems and solutions, policymaker reluctance to support new and potentially risky policy shifts, and ideological stalemates, particularly in market-oriented systems all act as significant impediments to reform. U.S. health care reform and the passage of the Affordable Care Act was a lesson in incrementalism (and patience), taking forty-plus years to pass. Immigration reform has proceeded slowly as well in the United States.

While a useful approach to studying the small steps that lead up to a policy change, the incremental model lacks a strategic orientation to policy change and does not account for the radical reforms that do take place or need to take place, such as climate change policy. Moreover, policy change can at times be swift and result in transformative change. This can be due to events, conflict, and economic crises, such as the 9/11 attacks and the 2008 Great Recession. There are a few models that describe this sudden form of policy change, including the "cyclical" model, such as the shifting back and forth between privileging public interests (government expansion) over private interests (minimal government intervention) every thirty years. Alternatively, there is the "backlash" or "zigzag" model, such as increased spending on welfare programs following a period of increased spending on fiscal stimulation. Last, there is "punctuated equilibrium" model and the occasional radical departures from stable periods of small-scale policymaking to a large-scale policy change (Baumgartner, Jones, and Mortenson 2014). Derived from evolutionary biology theory to explain the sudden appearance (or disappearance) of species, the punctuated equilibrium model can help evaluators develop a heightened awareness of the circumstances that may set the stage for large-scale policy change, such as a sea change in the political actors and their alliances, as well as an increase in media opportunities that moves an issue onto the national agenda (Stewart, Hedge, and Lester 2008). Dramatic policy change may also be impacted by emerging evidence or policy solutions that appear to have better traction and viability.

Alternatively, there is the "no change" model, such as policy gridlock and decision-maker failure to achieve a policy change due to ideological differences, disagreements among political actors, or intractable problems. It can happen in an issue area and/or at a level of government and can have serious repercussions (Kraft and Furlong 2010). The inaction of the U.S. Congress during the Obama administration has had a negative effect on public perceptions of government and individual decision-maker accountability. The positive version of the "no change" scenario is continued support for a program, particularly in public spending. For example, the U.S. Congress maintained annual funding to nonprofit community health centers during the early 2000s—a major win at a time when state budgets were being slashed.

Incremental, radical or transformative, and no change models are important for characterizing a policy's potential advancement or failure. Savvy advocates will familiarize themselves with the policy landscape and factor this into their advocacy strategies. Likewise, evaluators that are able to tether their evaluation design (particularly the logic model and outcomes) to a change process will be able to more accurately characterize an advocacy and policy change initiative, documenting both its anticipated and unanticipated outcomes.

Other useful models characterize discrete activities or aspects of public policymaking, such as the "rational choice" models whereby policy is shaped by the interaction of context and the rational actions of groups and individuals. A well-established area of inquiry, these models are useful for comparing different policy arenas and understanding decision-making in different contexts, such as the role of the administrative agencies in supporting and/or executing a policy. They are helpful for portraying government as a system that changes over time and reacts to environmental factors, and they have evolved to include cultural norms, relationships, and jurisdictional authority (Theodoulou and Kofinis 2004). For example, the Institutional Analysis and Development (IAD) framework focuses on how institutional arrangements and their governance systems affect the allocation of resources, such as interstate and water agreements (Nowlin 2011). Another model is Institutional Rational Choice posited by Elinor Ostrom whereby rational political actors change the institutions, arrangements, and rules, increasing the likelihood of achieving their desired policy goals (Schlager and Blomquist 1996).

A long-standing approach to understanding how policy is made is to focus on the individuals and groups who dominate the policymaking process or the "who" in Harold Lasswell's (1951) classic political science definition of politics: "Who gets what, when, and how." But "who" could include many types of political actors—groups, organizations, government agencies, individual decision-makers, communities, and the public—many of which are described in Chapter 2. There are the group models whereby policy results from group interactions and multiple competing interests. Referred to as "pluralism," there may be more opportunities for new groups to form, though some groups may carry more weight than others, such as the business sector, unions, and trade associations. The relative influence of each group in large part determines which policy option will prevail. At the other end of the group spectrum, there is the "elite" model where a privileged few, namely the rich and powerful, make policy. The opportunities for less-resourced and/or influential advocates are limited. There is a tendency to exclude outsiders; at its worst, it is cronyism. This model could apply to an emerging policy arena as well as a new democracy where a small group holds hegemonic authority and political voices are still establishing themselves. Another group model is "corporatism" or political systems where organized interests, such as professional associations, business, the military, unions, or citizen groups, are part of the decision-making and implementation process, not just advocates. This model helps characterize the nature of the relationship that advocates have with government and the extent to which they are insiders and partners. Fueled by efforts to decentralize and/or privatize government functions in developed countries, corporatism is an increasingly important element of a political system (Theodoulou 1995).

Particularly informative to the APC evaluation community has been John Kingdon's "policy windows" model, also referred to as the Multiple Streams (MS) Model (Kingdon 1995). It specifies the opportunities afforded to advocates to champion their policy agenda when there is a confluence of streams of problems, politics, solutions, participants, and choice opportunities during the *Agenda Setting* stage. The policy window is the opportunity afforded to policy entrepreneurs to move a proposal out of the primeval soup where it has been gestating and onto government's agenda, and is considered by many political scientists to be the most critical stage for advancing the policymaking process. The model speaks to the opportunities afforded to advocates as well as a change mechanism that can be integrated into a theory of change. Recent versions of this model include identifying policy windows later in the *Policy Formulation* and *Policy Implementation* stages, as well as expanding the policy stream to include institutions (Nowlin 2011).

For evaluators who are focusing on coalitions or networks, the Advocacy Coalition Framework (ACF) provides a multifaceted model of policy change that emphasizes the role of learning and changes in belief systems to explain policy change (Jenkins-Smith and Sabatier 1994). It is useful for characterizing the like-mindedness among a coalition of allies and coordinated activity over a longer period of time than that described in the policy stage model, or several decades. Evaluators can look further upstream for the antecedents to a policy change, including identifying the key stakeholders and the core beliefs that support a policy change later on. Moreover, they can understand the dynamics of policymaking over time, an improvement over the older static political science descriptions of policy communities, such as "iron triangles," or closed, tightknit relationships between organized interests (Birkland 2001).

Because policy change may not necessarily be due to direct advocacy, it is important to not limit one's focus to traditional models of political action. The Deliberative Democracy Model shifts attention from institutions and actors to the role of informed dialogue in shaping decisions (Dryzek 1996). Similar to consensus-based decision-making, there is the intentional inclusion of as many voices as possible and emphasis on evidence-based decision-making. While more likely to occur in a representative democracy, the model can be used to describe policy situations where research is key to identifying problems and formulating solutions. Another emerging area, the Narrative Policy Network (NPF), looks at policy-oriented learning and how narratives or policy stories are transmitted and interpreted by political actors when making policy choices (Nowlin 2011).

More recently, policy scholars are focusing on the barriers to making truly informed, rational decisions. Scholarship in other arenas, such as behavioral economics and neurobiology, is providing new models premised on peoples' hardwired desires and behavior. For example, emotional triggers, such as the willingness to conform to a group's preferences, even when it means voting against one's interests, may play a more significant role than originally thought (Smith and Larimer 2013). While there is no prevailing model, the scholarship on decision-making is good food for thought and can help with the development of a robust theory of change.

Given the opaque nature of some policy arenas, it can be challenging to select a particular model that best characterizes how a particular policy is being crafted. Political scientists Stella Theodoulou and Chris Kofinis (2004) offer a pragmatic approach or using the policy stage approach to developing an understanding of the overall structure of the policy process and then incorporating other models to deepen your understanding of the dynamics of policymaking. Each model represents a unique and sometimes competing understanding of policymaking and should be explored with funders and advocates, who may have a very different understanding or no model at all. While it may require some exploration of the literature and discussions with stakeholders early on, it is an effort worth undertaking and one that will strengthen the alignment between the advocacy and policy change initiative and the evaluation design.

This grounding of the evaluation design in one or more of these models will also benefit the evaluation stakeholders. The results of the Aspen/UCSF APC Evaluation Survey indicate the second most highly rated gap (48 percent, or "very significant") was *poor understanding of advocacy and policy change processes by funders and/or grantees.* If not addressed, this gap has the potential to create a misalignment in stakeholder information needs and the purpose of the evaluation. One approach is to ask stakeholders—advocates, funders, and policymakers—how they think policy is made and what the underlying mechanisms of change are. This should be done early on as part of the development of a program theory of change and/or logic model or as part of the analysis of contextual factors. If there is not a shared understanding, there is an opportunity to have a dialogue with stakeholders on different models and seek consensus on the model that best describes a policy change process (Stachiowak 2013).

Additionally, it is useful to seek the perspective of someone who has an historical understanding of a particular policy and how it has evolved, be it a policymaker, agency staff, researcher, or other evaluators. A significant percent of Aspen/UCSF Survey respondents (25 percent) indicated that *limited expertise among evaluators in the policy or issue area of the advocacy initiative under evaluation* is a "very significant gap." Documentation, such as government reports, legislative tracking services, and the public policy peer review literature can be enormously helpful here. At a minimum, APC evaluators should develop their own understanding of change and an appropriate model of policymaking. Simultaneously, they should consider informing the understanding of others, as necessary, in the policy arena they are evaluating.

TYPES OF POLICIES

Evaluators can use several basic categories of policy types to increase the alignment of the evaluation design with the attributes and dynamics of a particular policy. While there is some debate about the extent to which these frameworks mirror the complex reality that confronts advocates and decision-makers, they continue to be the basis of policy analysis and scholarship.

Since public policy is about making decisions, policies can be categorized by *type of decision.* All public policies are formerly approved legal actions and include: laws passed by Congress or state legislatures to govern behavior (such as requiring people to purchase automobile insurance); executive orders signed by the president to manage the federal government (such as to wage war); and judicial rulings that change the interpretation of existing law (such as the U.S. Supreme Court's 2014 decision to make the state Medicaid expansion optional under the Affordable Care Act). Knowing what kind of decision is being championed or promulgated provides insights into a policy's purview and the likely advocate strategy. For example, the passage and the implementation of laws provide advocates with many points of access, including targeting the public, legislators, and the media. Influencing a U.S. Supreme Court decision, by contrast, is a stretch for many advocates in terms of expertise and resources though important nonetheless.

Another useful way to classify policies is based on *policy outputs* and the type of benefits they confer on society. Political scientist Theodore Lowi (1964) developed two classifications, with some policies being considered "distributive" (providing benefits to a specific group of people through the budgeting process, such as spending on roads) or "redistributive" (transferring resources from more affluent groups to less-well-off groups, such as aid to poor communities). These policy outputs provide tangible (or material) benefits to people, with the latter characterized by more conflict since they typically reflect class differences and require less powerful interests to prevail over more powerful, affluent interests. There are other types of classifications of policy outputs that may provide useful ways to frame a specific policy. One example is whether or not a policy provides a "collective good," such as funding for national defense or public health. Another example is to ask if a policy conveys a "private good" (also referred to as "privatization"), whereby a private company provides services for which consumers pay. Policies may also be classified as "nonmaterial" policy outputs such as regulatory laws that are intended to influence the behavior of specific groups or individuals through the use of sanctions or incentives, such as ensuring workplace safety. Or a policy may be procedural in that it specifies how something will be done, such as educational policies that are shaped by federal policy and establish requirements at the state level.

The *government budget* and public agency spending processes are where these financial policy outputs and competing interests are most visible. While a federal government shutdown is a major media event, state-level spending, where state budgets are more vulnerable to an economic downturn is no less contentious. Additionally, each dollar spent by government has a behind-the-scenes story, be it an allocation formula that is tied to demographic changes, the willingness (or unwillingness) to backfill and compensate for decreased funding during lean times, or tethering of funding to unsustainable sources of funding, such as tobacco settlement funds. Evaluators may not need to do a cost-analysis, but they do need to be mindful of the political dimensions of the dollars that make up nearly every policy decision.

Policies also can be classified by the *ideology* they represent and characterized as either liberal or conservative. In the United States, the distinction is typically used to describe the role of government and whether it is a means to an end (the liberal perspective) or is too big and counterproductive (the conservative perspective). However, the reality is that policy does not fall readily into one or the other bailiwick. Still, it is helpful to know where on the ideological spectrum a policy lies and who is likely to benefit. For example, the debate about building the Keystone Pipeline between the Alberta, Canada, tar sands and the Gulf of Mexico spans conservative and liberal interests, such as potential environmental dangers, business interests, as well as efforts to try to make the United States less dependent on external petroleum.

In sum, there are multiple conceptual classifications and frameworks that can serve as a foundation for understanding policymaking in your context. Think about tailoring a framework to your project without losing sight of three key attributes: the intended role of government; the policy outputs; and the benefits to the public, such as programs, services, and funding. Naming a policy by type of benefit is a good first step to understanding its potential course of action and where and how advocates are likely to participate in the policymaking process. Last, consider whether or not some classifications help strengthen the link between the advocate perspective and the evaluation design. Is there an ideological conflict that precludes agreement by stakeholders and that will slow down or stall some types of policy reforms?

POLICYMAKING VENUES

The venues where policy is made—government and its institutions, levels of decision-making, and the topical areas—provide opportunities for advocates to participate in the policymaking process and for evaluators to observe advocacy in practice. For many advocates, showing up to be physically present is one of their key tactics, including organizing protest marches, bringing constituents to meet their representatives at the federal and state capitals, or providing testimony to elected officials.

It is important to recognize *government* as the site of policy change and the venue with the greatest capacity to address public problems. It exercises authority over a group of people and gives legitimacy to policies (also referred to as the "power of the state"). It behooves evaluators to be familiar with the different types of government and how they establish the terms under which policy is made. There are differences in governments based on who holds decision-making authority, ranging from a democracy where government officials are elected by a majority of the people, to a dictatorship where one person holds power by dint of force. Second, governments have different branches of government and policymaking processes, which can make it either easy or difficult for policymakers to act and are predictive of a government's ability to achieve its objectives.

Governments also have different power structures, and relations vary between branches of government and the federal, state, and local levels, such as decentralized taxing authority. Referred to as "federalism" in the United States or the sharing of authority among the federal and state government, the question of decentralizing (or centralizing) responsibility, particularly funding responsibility, can greatly constrain or facilitate policy action. At one level, decentralizing authority to states and localities allows for policymaking that reflects the capacity, problems, and historical antecedents of a particular level. However, it can also exacerbate inequities among states and localities. In the United States, there are significant structural differences across states, such as the use of the initiatives and referendums process whereby citizens can vote to approve or repeal measures or propositions (Dye 2002).

Moreover, government is a system within a system, and it is heavily influenced by socioeconomic attributes, such as the distribution of capital and ownership of property, influence of religious institutions, the wealthy elite, and the military, and the importance of the public good versus individual interests. These environmental factors determine in large part the degrees of freedom within a government system, as well as shape the relationships among political actors and advocates.

Once the structure and composition of a government has been identified, it is useful to clarify *how government exercises authority,* or what is referred to as governance. This too can vary by geography and level of government, as well as be narrow or broad in focus, including dictating the terms of the economy, resolving conflict, and ensuring social well-being. Knowing the internal rules of government and the public and private actors, the customs, capacity, processes, forms of involvement, and scope provides insights into the prepassage stages of the policymaking process.

Knowledge of the *bureaucracy* that is responsible for the executing and administering of policies or policy implementation is central to understanding the extent to which a policy postpassage is likely to have teeth and achieve its goals. While hierarchical and highly organized, bureaucracies at all levels, even at the client-level, or what is called "street-level bureaucracy," may have significant discretion in interpreting and applying a policy (Lipsky 2011). Nor are government bureaucracies impervious to influence, or to what is referred to as "agency capture." Bureaucrats will also have their own political agendas as well as seek to protect or expand their budgets. However, they have technical expertise in the writing of rules and regulations and deep understanding of the policy arena. They are potent partners in understanding the content of the policy and its potential reach.

While the *legislature* is the traditional venue for making and passing policy, other venues, such as the *executive branch* and *agencies* charged with crafting the rules and regulations, provide opportunities for advocates to have a voice. For example, in the United States, organized interests of all types target both the legislature prepassage and the administrative agency responsible for implementing the policy (Boehmke, Gailmard, and Patty 2013). Additionally, advocates working on behalf of vulnerable populations and/or those involved with issues such as environmental justice, immigration reform, abortion, and compensation for personal injuries, may find the courts a useful venue for policy change.

The *level* at which policy is made—federal, state, regional, county, and municipality—plays a role in shaping the advocacy universe and its tactics but less so than the policy issue itself. The scholarship, albeit limited, suggests there are limited differences in representation and organized interests may be active at either or both levels. And these venues may vary from one level of government to another, with each level having its own bureaucracy, decision-making processes, and political actors (Boehmke, Gailmard, and Patty 2013). For example, decentralization in responsibility for funding and provision of social and health services, such as HIV/AIDS, mental health, and homeless services from the federal government to state and local governments in the 1990s has resulted in increased advocacy at the state and local levels. The findings from the Aspen/UCSF APC Evaluation Survey suggest that APC evaluators are versatile and are able to conduct evaluations at multiple levels or: national (50 percent); state (54 percent); regional (22 percent); and local (county, city, neighborhood; 36 percent).

Policymaking is also situated in particular *topical areas*: economics and budgeting, health care, welfare, education, energy, and the environment. These areas have a different composition (and possibly a different configuration) of public and private stakeholders and different economic and political issues, and they are referred to as "subgovernments" or "issue networks." While their importance and influence varies by policy arena, there is some evidence that their membership is expanding to include the public (Kraft and Furlong 2010). For example, the health policy arena experienced a large increase in interest groups when President Clinton tried to pass health care reform legislation in the early 1990s (Weissert and Weissert 1996).

Whether or not there are fundamental differences to how policymaking takes place in each area is an interesting question. All U.S. policymaking uses the same rulebook, but one cannot assume the rules are applied the same way or stay constant over a period of time. The policy issue itself may create differences in the policymaking process, such as climate change, which has been classified as a "wicked problem par excellence" and has an exceedingly long time horizon before the effects of policy will be observed (Huitema et al., citing Jordan et al. 2011, 179). Ideological differences and leadership turnover can propel a policy area forward or stall it until a new administration takes over. For example, raising the minimum wage or immigration reform may well be impacted by waves of policy action and inaction, reflecting political pressures that are increasingly polarizing. Evaluators need to be mindful of a policy area's distinctive history and its attributes.

Not surprisingly, the majority of respondents from the Aspen/UCSF Survey—approximately 60 percent—report that they work in the area of health policy, including health care, public health, and diseases and disorders, followed by education (39 percent) and community improvement/ economic development (31 percent). Health policy is undeniably the "big gorilla" and one of the most congested and complicated policy arenas, particularly in the United States, where it has been fueled by health care reform debates as well as the sector's tremendous impact upon the American economy. The private foundation presence is significant, many of which have devoted significant resources to advocacy capacity building and specific advocacy campaigns internationally, nationally, and locally. (See Table 1.1.)

The survey results also show that APC evaluators as a whole are involved in upwards of seventeen policy arenas, though to differing degrees. These results also point to policy arenas where we might anticipate future growth, such as the fields of energy and the environment, where the pressure to act is likely to intensify as the effects of global warming escalate. APC evaluators should be vigilant and make the case for greater attention to evaluation. Moreover, individual APC evaluators are involved in more than one policy arena, and there is great potential for working across policy borders since evaluation models and methods are fairly flexible and policy areas are increasingly interconnected. For example, the lens of health disparities and social determinants of health bring to light the interrelationship between education level, economic status, and health outcomes.

Identifying and observing a policymaking venue(s) greatly increases

Table 1.1. Focus of Aspen/UCSF APC Evaluation Survey
Respondents: Key Policy Areas

Policy Areas	*Percent of Survey Respondents That Focus on a Policy Arena*
Health	58%
Education	39%
Community Improvement/Economic Development	31%
Food, Agriculture and Nutrition	30%
Civil and Political Rights	26%
Youth Development	24%
Improved Governance	22%
International, Foreign Affairs and National Security	21%
Energy and Environment	13%
Disabilities	12%
Housing and Shelter	11%
Science and Technology	9%
Arts, Culture and Humanities	9%
Immigration	8%
Public Safety, Disaster Preparedness and Relief	6%
Legal-related	4%
Recreation and Sport	1%
Other	16%

(Note: Individuals could indicate more than one category in which they participate.)
Source: Aspen Planning and Evaluation Program, The Aspen Institute

evaluator understanding of a particular policy and its contextual factors, and it is an opportunity for collecting data, such as the number and type of participants, the presence of the media, and the information provided by advocates. The policy venue may or may not be transparent. Some policies may have limited public involvement, such as the behind-the-scenes intentions of government under a new administration. A helpful way to identify policymaking venues is the traditional *Big P small p* distinction where *Big P* policies are formal laws, rules, and regulations enacted by elected officials, while *small p* policies are organizational guidelines, internal agency decisions, or memoranda. If you know what kind of policy is being crafted, you can identify the institution(s) and decision-makers responsible for shepherding a particular policy.

Policies are often a part of a *policy universe* and interact with other policies, such as in intergovernmental systems where federal policies shape state-level legislation. The reverse is true, and localities and states may serve as incubators of innovative policies that trickle upwards and influence national policymaking. Policies may also cross national borders, or what is called "policy transfer," and the learning by one political system of another system's policies, procedures, and administrative structure (Mossberger and Wolman 2003). In the United States, there has been extensive study in the diffusion of policies across state lines and the factors that impede or facilitate adoption, sometimes verbatim, by state lawmakers (Walker 1983). Using Everett M. Roger's (1995) "diffusion of innovation" model and theories on internal determinants, political scientists have developed a robust body of scholarship to explain why policy adoption occurs in some settings and not in others. In short, while we think of policymaking in terms of a single policy, the reality is more complicated and knowing a policy's lineage and its place in a network of policies are important for developing a sound contextual analysis.

Last, don't lose sight of the *contexts*—social, environmental, economic, and cultural—that influence a policy arena, its networks, and dynamics. We are witnessing tremendous change globally and locally, as evidenced by the dislocation of large numbers of people from the southern hemisphere, extreme weather, acts of terrorism targeted at everyday activities, and technological advances that are transforming the sharing of information and mobilization of individuals and communities.

EVALUATION PRACTICE: SIX EVALUATION CASES

Our six evaluation cases speak to a range of local, state, national, and international policymaking scenarios that may be encountered by evaluators. Except for Project Health Colorado, a statewide public-will-building campaign, five of the initiatives focused on passing specific policies in the areas of health, the environment, gender equity, and transportation. The Tribal Tobacco Education and Policy (TTEP) Initiative focused on the passage of local smoke-free policies, such as smoke-free casinos, in five tribal communities. The GROW Campaign is a multinational campaign to tackle food injustice issues and to build a better food system that sustainably feeds a growing population. It also included a six-month campaign targeting World Bank policy on large-scale land acquisition that was intended to be a unifying element within Oxfam in which all affiliates could participate. The International Lands Conservation Program targeted regional and local policies to maintain biodiversity in Canada and Australia. The Initiative to Promote Equitable and Sustainable Transportation targeted the reauthorization of the 2009 Federal Surface Transportation Bill as well as equitable and sustainable policy options at the state level. Last, the Let Girls Lead model supports a network of advocates to promote girl-friendly laws, policies, programs, and funding in Guatemala, Honduras, Liberia, Malawi, and Ethiopia.

While the emphasis was on the passage of public policy in most of these initiatives, there are some notable exceptions. Project Health Colorado followed on the heels of the passage of the Affordable Care Act and was a strategy to strengthen decision-making on health care. None of the initiatives focused solely on one-time policy wins and included a combination of advocacy strategies. Nearly all of the initiatives spanned multiple years, except for the GROW Campaign's World Bank Land Freeze Campaign, which was a six-month-long campaign, demonstrating funder and advocate maintenance of effort, a critical aspect of most policy change initiatives.

All of the initiatives targeted different levels of government and institutions—international, federal, regional, state, and local government—with some initiatives targeting one or more levels of policymaking at the same time. For example, the Initiative to Promote Equitable and Sustainable Transportation targeted federal and state policymaking simultaneously. Additionally, while some initiatives had international or national goals, much of the advocacy and policy work was at the local level in all of the cases.

As described in their evaluation reports, all of the initiatives demonstrated achievement of some or all of their advocacy and/or policy change objectives. In the two initiatives with an advocacy-capacity-building component—Let Girls Lead and the Tribal Tobacco Education and Policy (TTEP) Initiative—grantees also achieved some policy gains, including passage of girl-friendly policies and local smoke-free policies. While more concerned with the successful implementation of the Affordable Care Act and shaping public opinion on health care access, Project Health Colorado reached more than twenty-five thousand people in-person by street teams, community members, as well as staff, with some participating in volunteer trainings, community forums, story collection, and sharing.

The policy gains were not what were desired in some cases, but they were significant all the same. For example, the GROW Campaign World Bank initiative did not result in the six-month freeze on large-scale land acquisition, though there were changes in World Bank policies and regulations, with inclusions of land rights in the World Bank safeguards review.

Nor did a campaign necessarily go in the anticipated direction in some cases. For example, the International Lands Conservation Program had a spillover effect among policy venues, with the opportunity to apply the 50/50 concept to protecting forests to Australia policymaking, though this proved less feasible than in Canada. Additionally, the Federal Transportation Reauthorization Bill passed as the evaluation findings were being developed for the federal component.

In short, a broad range of policy and policymaking evaluation scenarios are possible. Nothing from the six cases suggests there are policy arenas or issues that do not lend themselves to an advocacy campaign. Nor is one policy arena, namely, health, garnering all the resources and attention of funders. This is good news for evaluators, although as we discuss later in Chapter 6, many campaigns and advocacy initiatives go un- or underevaluated or have insufficient funding to develop in-depth findings and/or inform stakeholder learning and practice.

CONCLUSION

Policy and politics shape our daily lives and future in fundamental ways, such as ensuring clean drinking water, paying for roads and infrastructure, strengthening public education, and so forth. The policymaking process is an opportunity for people from all walks of life to partner with decision-makers to improve social and environmental conditions. However, as we have explained in this chapter, the policy process can be long and difficult and many bills fail to make it through the process the first time or even a second or third time—if ever. Additionally, as demonstrated by the Project Health Colorado evaluation case that focused on building public will, there may not be an obvious policy win to mark the success of an advocacy initiative. Or, the definition of a policy win may change as the effects of a policy become known at a later time, or if there is a major change in the political landscape, such as a sea change in ideology.

While the complexity of the policy process is sometimes daunting, we urge evaluators to understand and embrace the complexity (and chaos) that characterizes public policy. Having an understanding of the dynamic and complicated nature of the policymaking process based on existing and emerging models and scholarship creates a reality check for evaluation designs, such as whether to hold advocates responsible for securing passage of a piece of legislation or monitoring the implementation of a policy to assure fidelity to the law's requirements. Evaluators should also strive to understand the historical and substantive dimensions of a policy or policy arena. Not only will this policy acumen strengthen evaluation design, but also it will strengthen the partnership with advocates who may or may not be very knowledgeable of the policy process and political actors. Last, as exemplified by our six evaluation cases, evaluators can anticipate a range of policy change scenarios—international, regional, state, and local, public and private—as well as high or low involvement in the policymaking process. Policymaking models provide the means for quickly making sense of an unfamiliar and complicated landscape.

Next, we take a close look at the many types of advocates that evaluators are likely to encounter—individuals, organizations, coalitions, and communities—and the many ways they strive to be heard and influence policy outcomes.

CHAPTER 2

ADVOCACY
Influencing Decision-Making

INTRODUCTION

The "who" of public policymaking—decision-makers, government, institutions, public and private advocates, and the public—are integral to the "how" and "what" of policymaking. Depending on the political system, these political actors, their relationships, and their influence can be varied and complex, particularly as new voices emerge. Some of these voices represent constituents whose voices may have previously been marginalized or new constituents who come to the policy issue later, but who nevertheless bring a powerful voice to the issue, such as the technology sector's emerging commitment to environmental issues.

Considered a critical means for expanding democracy, this broad swath of political actors, whom we call "advocates," bring to bear their influence prior to and/or during the policymaking process. Their strategies and tactics are increasingly recognized for their potential to achieve lasting systems change. Foundations, public agencies, and nongovernmental organizations have marshaled significant resources to ensure that advocates' voices are heard and that they are able to navigate the policy arena. However, without thoughtful evaluation, advocacy strategies are unlikely to result in the policy mobilization and impact that they intend; those who seek greater social justice will be thwarted in their efforts unless they more fully understand what is effective in creating social change.

Here, we ask and answer three simple questions that have complicated answers: What is advocacy? Who are advocates? What do advocates do? We look across three areas of study (political science, nonprofit organizations, and advocacy capacity) to unearth useful concepts and models that derive from decades of study. Additionally, we draw on public policy scholarship on advocates and the tools of their trade. By tapping into a significant body of knowledge about influence, power, and advocacy organizations of all types, evaluators will gain a robust understanding of concepts that can provide them with insights in the face of a particular program or intervention. A useful assessment requires a savvy evaluator who can recognize and understand the players and power dynamics that traditionally have been the realm of the political scientist.

Second, we describe the universe of advocacy tactics that are currently being assessed by advocacy and policy change (APC) evaluators. Many of them are traditional forms of advocacy, such as lobbying and being involved in the electoral process. However, there are several tactics that focus on mobilizing and organizing communities more broadly, which may never result in policy change in the conventional sense. Our aims are to support a shared understanding of these tactics as well as to help identify the key components of advocacy and policy change initiatives that lend themselves to evaluation.

Last, we provide thumbnail descriptions of the advocates and their advocacy strategies and tactics from our six evaluation cases, providing a reality check and the advocacy scenarios evaluators are likely to encounter.

WHAT IS ADVOCACY?

"Advocacy" is commonly understood as championing or supporting a cause or policy goal (Obar, Zube, and Lampe 2012). This seemingly uncomplicated definition, however, takes on different meanings depending on whom you ask. While representing the preferences and interests of all citizens is a common theme, the political science perspective focuses on how political groups mobilize resources, how groups function, and whether or not they have an impact. Advocates understand their activities in more practical terms of how to best use tools to achieve desired policy goals. Nonprofit researchers examine organizational capacity and the role of advocacy in different types of organizations. Evaluators look at advocacy through the lens of program evaluation and are bound less to academic theory than to the information needs of funders and advocates themselves. They all observe the same phenomenon, but they have a different relation to it and different objectives. To strengthen the crosswalk between these perspectives and help evaluators develop a more nuanced definition, we look at advocacy and its tactics through each lens, noting differences and similarities.

Political Scientists

Political scientists typically focus on the group aspect of advocacy, both as a way to explain how policy is made and as a vehicle for expanding representation and strengthening democracy. Both interpretations have waxed and waned as new models of policymaking have emerged and scholars have debated the desirability of group participation, particularly if it is primarily more affluent groups that prevail. However, scholars have made significant inroads into dissecting interest groups, understanding why individuals and institutions join them, and how they exert influence on the policymaking system at the federal and state levels (Baumgartner and Leech 1998). Additionally, characterizing the interface between groups and government has provided useful information about strategies that influencers bring to bear, be it by applying pressure through the legal system, bargaining to achieve results, or acting collectively with advocacy allies (Heinz, Nelson, and Salisbury 1993).

"Group" is defined broadly in the political science literature and includes the less organized collectives, such as coalitions and social movements. However, the primary focus has been on interest groups or the public and private organizations that attempt to directly influence decision-making. Political scientists are unresolved about the question of interest group impact or power, which may be due to the difficulties of studying influence, such as a discerning attribution in a crowded policy arena. If five organizations lobby for a local tax and it passes, who gets the credit? Or, is it a reflection of a coalition that has been more successful than any one actor working alone? There is also the perennial concern that more and new voices have not fulfilled the expectations of pluralists who posit that multiple groups competing for public resources is a good thing.

Interestingly, the word "advocacy" is not typically used in the political science arena, let alone included in *The Concise Oxford Dictionary of Politics*. Instead "political voice" comes closest, defined as "any activity undertaken by individuals and organizations that has the intent or effect of influencing government action—either directly by affecting the making or implementation of public policy or indirectly by influencing the selection of people who make these policies" (Verba, Schlozman, and Brady 2012, 38).

Advocates and Nonprofits

There is a rich and growing body of literature on the advocate perspective and how individuals and organizations develop advocacy capacity and achieve a desired policy change. There are "how to" books, workshops and courses targeted to advocates on conducting different types of advocacy, such as working with the media. Focused primarily on strategy and tactics, these resources provide insights into how advocates think about their options for engaging in the policymaking process—their terms and definitions, assumptions on how policy change is achieved, and understanding of the political context.

More recently, advocacy is perceived as a role that anyone can play and should play, driven in large part by the growing use of advocacy by nonprofit organizations. Nonprofits that traditionally have not had a strong formal political voice but have a longtime relationship to government and/or represent clients, populations, or communities are attracting policymaker attention and extending their political voice (Smith 2010). "Advocacy" figures prominently in the nonprofit literature and is less concerned with mobilizing a group's membership and is more focused on supporting organizational planning, developing advocacy expertise in specific areas, and expanding fundraising. It is understood as a set of activities or role that organizations undertake as their primary or secondary function on behalf of a collective interest (Jenkins 1987).

The news on nonprofit advocacy capacity is encouraging. In the Alliance for Justice's 2015 assessment of the advocacy capacity of 280 nonprofits, nearly 40 percent of respondents said they engage in advocacy, as well as service delivery (30 percent), and community building, development or organization (20 percent). Nonprofits also look to partners to conduct advocacy in areas where they are weaker, such as litigation, media relations, and ballot measures. The ability of nonprofits to partner with others as part of a coalition or network has gained funder attention and support, and it is increasingly a focus of the APC evaluation community (McClure and Renderos 2015).

Evaluators

Evaluators of advocacy and policy change initiatives tend to frame advocacy within the context of program evaluation and the identification of outcomes, measures, and sources of data. Efforts have been made to use some political science concepts in the areas of agenda setting, and the policy stage model described in Chapter 1 has been used in advocacy and policy change evaluation guides and frameworks to develop a program logic model and/or characterize advocacy tactics. Evaluation exhibits a close alignment with the nonprofit arena and its focus on organizational capacity, since many evaluations have been conducted on behalf of foundations that support nonprofit advocacy capacity.

Presently, there is no one definition of advocacy that has been widely adopted by advocacy and policy change evaluators. The APC evaluation community has proffered similar and overlapping definitions of advocacy, with most broadly focusing on the activities—education, mobilization, legal action, lobbying—that have a specific target, be it policymakers, the public, or the media. For example: "Advocacy is a tactic for achieving social or policy change, such as framing the issue, developing alliances, gathering and disseminating data. The impact of advocacy efforts provides the essential infrastructure that leads to policy change and, subsequently, to social change" (Reisman, Gienapp, and Stachowiak 2007, 14).

In sum, political scientists, advocates, and evaluators share similar objectives of changing public and policymaker perceptions, expanding participation in the debate of problems and policy options, and influencing policy decisions. However, they have a different relationship to and definition of advocacy and its practice.

Given that "advocacy" can mean different things to different people, what is an evaluator to do? One possibility is to define it in the broadest sense so that it is not tethered to a particular perspective, policy arena, or locale. While there is some wisdom to taking the broad approach, as one evaluator in the international arena argues, "Each organization will have its own nuanced definition of advocacy" (O'Flynn 2009, 1). Evaluators are well advised to resist the impulse and not adopt a textbook definition that may have no alignment with the values and beliefs of those carrying out advocacy. To increase the alignment in evaluators/stakeholder definitions of "advocacy," it is important to acknowledge the possibility of different stakeholder understandings of "advocacy" in your situation and discuss these differences during the evaluation design phase. We also suggest considering what the literature has to offer to develop and then adopting a definition that is appropriate for the context. For example, in a context where the goal is to expand mental health services for a specific client population, the definition of advocacy might draw on examples of documented behavioral health advocacy and specify on whose behalf these activities are being undertaken.

Also, consider including the goal of the advocacy initiative in the definition of "advocacy" and indicate whether the policy goal is to pass or repeal a bill or measure, or even working toward implementing a law with fidelity and adequate resources. By combining the means with the ends, the definition of advocacy can then become core to evaluation design.

WHO ARE ADVOCATES?

It is not always easy to identify the advocate in a policy arena or advocacy campaign, as these landscapes can be noisy and crowded. There are typically multiple positions represented on a policy issue, making it more difficult to achieve a desired policy gain. And advocates come in all shapes and sizes, as we describe below. Or the policy space may be closed off to broader participation and allow only a select few—the wealthy elite, the military, or elected officials—to participate. However, it is important to clearly determine who is representing a position or a cause in developing the evaluation design. To clarify who is and is not an advocate, we look to common definitions of "advocate":

- a person who argues for or supports a cause or policy;
- a person who works for a cause or group; and/or
- a person who argues for the cause of another person in a court of law.

We are less interested in the last definition, although the legal system is an important means for exerting influence in the policy arena. The first and second definitions are better aligned with how we think of an advocate and his or her role, either as someone who actively tries to persuade others to act or is affiliated with an organization or group with the same intent. However, these definitions are not really enough to inform an evaluation design, so we suggest the following rules of thumb when identifying advocates and their positions:

Everyone can be an advocate. Regardless of how we define advocacy, everyone has the capacity (though not necessarily the freedom) to make his or her wishes known, from the parent who seeks funding for his or her child's school to a community that is opposed to commercial development. Moreover, research suggests that the number and diversity of advocates is increasing, or what has been referred to as the "advocacy explosion" (Berry 1997). This broader understanding nudges us to consider all voices and to not overlook hidden or silent voices, including those committed to maintaining the status quo or even to eliminate previous policy gains.

Who counts as an advocate depends on the context. That is, we need to be mindful of the historical conditions that shape the political context. The model of representation and inclusion of the public within the policy process determines in large part who can be an advocate. For example, in the United States, groups and organizations have been considered bedrock forces of American politics, a perspective that dates back to the 1700s when Alexis de Tocqueville argued that political groups were the means for increased representation. This is not the case everywhere, such as countries in the early stages of democracy building, where group action has traditionally been less prevalent. However, efforts such as the student protests in Taiwan in 2014 showed stirrings of political action in nontraditional settings. Some argue that this "wildfire" has been the result of the Internet, which has brought images of new tactics to populations not previously organized.

There are individual, organization, and group advocates. The reality in many counties, states, and national governments is that individual and group advocates coexist though the combination and/or influence of each varies by policy issue, historical precedence, and cultural norms.

Using these rules of thumb, we suggest the following micro to macro framework to help identify whom the advocates are in your particular situation.

Individuals

The individual advocate is a shape-shifting political actor. The place of the individual in politics and policymaking is not fixed and is determined by societal norms that define the rights of the individual, the tendency for individuals to associate with others, and recognition of individual diversity. Moreover, individuals can be more than one type of advocate. An experienced policy director may also be an influential policy entrepreneur or an elected official at some point in his or her career. It is a fluid role, but there are some individual advocates who are likely to be part of the advocacy community for most policy issues, specifically citizens, policymakers, lobbyists, policy directors, policy entrepreneurs, policy champions, bellwethers, and elected and appointed officials.

While their involvement may be episodic and/or far removed from the policy process, a *citizen's* political clout should not be underestimated. Citizenship confers rights and responsibilities that in and of themselves exert significant influence. In addition to asserting their right to vote, calls for increased civic engagement and strategies for engaging citizens through grassroots mobilization efforts make citizens formidable advocates alone and together (Putnam 1996).

However, some types of individual advocates are more involved in the policymaking process than others (also known as "insiders"), particularly policymakers, lobbyists, and policy directors, and their roles deserve special recognition in an evaluation design as they can serve as key informants both in helping to shape evaluation questions, as well as in providing vital insights later on.

It is essential to include the *policymakers* in your cataloging of individual advocates in your evaluation context since they are very influential advocates as well as being the primary targets of advocates. The term "policymaker" typically refers to elected public officials (such as legislators or the board of supervisors) who are directly responsible for crafting policy. Their close proximity to the policymaking process makes them a ready point of access and target of influence. For example, advocates can provide information about a particular problem (such as Fact Sheets) and participate on committees to develop rules and regulations. Many of their decision-making activities, such as public comment periods, are also opportunities for advocates to present their case. Policymakers also exhibit multiple types of behaviors and actions, many of which can be documented, counted, and monitored, including increased understanding of an issue, support for a specific policy, and increased political will or the willingness to achieve a change.

In reality, other elected and nonelected actors can be policymakers, including lobbyists and people seeking political office. *Public officials*, such as government officials and bureaucrats who are not elected to office, are also sensitive to public opinion, providing a point of access for advocates of all types. Though access to these individuals can be difficult, these policymaking insiders can provide information on successful advocacy tactics and behind-the-scenes information on the context of a particular policy and policy arena.

While *lobbyists* typically act on behalf of a variety of organizations, such as unions, corporations, or public sector agencies, they are a distinct category of actors whose role may go well beyond trying to influence decision-maker support for or against a specific bill or measure, such as networking and conducting research. In the United States, the lobbying activities vary by policy stage and policy venue (issue, level of government) though the definition of lobbying remains the same. While viewed with some suspicion for improper conduct and influence peddling, the lobbyist population and its role continues to expand in many countries. Although much of the APC evaluation in the United States has shied away from lobbying because of restrictions in foundation support for lobbying, the presence and effectiveness of lobbyists and their tactics should not be ignored. Their venues and tactics are not so different from those of advocates who do not engage in formal lobbying. Also, international funders are less shy about supporting lobbying and U.S. funders are supporting 501(c)(4) organizations, which can engage in lobbying. For example, most of the $70.3 million contributed by the Atlantic Philanthropies to support immigration reform was in the form of 501 (c) (4) funding, affording advocates more options than 501(c) (3) organizations (Morariu, Athanasiades, and Pankaj 2016).

Private and public sector organizations, such as professional associations, public agencies, and service providers, may have a dedicated *policy director* who is responsible for a variety of advocacy activities. Lobbying may or may not be part of this person's position description, but political acumen is a must. Their research activities may add credibility and stature to their organization and position him or her as the "go to" person for information and advice about a particular policy issue. A knowledgeable player, evaluators are well advised to seek out these people for information.

Other Influential Individuals: Policy Entrepreneurs, Policy Champions, and Bellwethers

This last category speaks to individual advocates who influence policy-making in less direct but important ways nonetheless. Think of them as roles or "hats" that could be worn by any of the individual advocates listed above. Originally conceived as a way to distinguish between advocates, *policy entrepreneurs* are advocates who are willing to invest considerable energy and resources and have political connections and savoir-faire to secure a policy win (Kingdon 1995). More recent characterizations speak to their ability to make policy change occur and/or introduce and diffuse innovation into the policy arena (Mintron and Vergari 1998).

A hat that is worn primarily by elected or appointed officials, *policy champions* have the ability to directly promote or affect policy and are points of contact for outside groups (Mahoney and Baumgartner 2015). The Aspen Institute (2010) has identified three categories of champion traits: (1) demonstrates interest and awareness of a policy issue; (2) promotes awareness and understanding by delivering positive statements about a policy issue, for instance; and (3) advocates for improved policy and practice, for example, by sponsoring legislation. Increasingly, "champions" is being used to describe an increasingly diverse group of influential individuals, such as journalists, celebrities, service providers, and consumers, with whom advocates are being encouraged to partner in orchestrated strategies (Roma and Levine 2016).

Less directly involved in supporting or passing legislation, *bellwethers* are influential individuals who intentionally track policy issues and whose knowledge of the current and future policy agenda carries weight with others. Not limited to a particular type of person or organization, these players are useful to evaluators in that they are knowledgeable about a specific policy issue, as well as its likely outcomes. Elected and nonelected public officials may be bellwethers and carry significant political weight, as well as have tenure, creating stability and certainty in their decision-making capacity.

Organizations

The readily observable actors in a policy arena are organizations, of which there may be many kinds, some of which play multiple roles. For example, we are seeing more service providers in the health and human services arena hire a policy director to engage in advocacy. While organizations are the easiest type of advocate to discern in a crowded policy arena, they may or may not be the most potent voice. For example, restrictions on lobbying can greatly restrict an organization's reach. Additionally, organizations are typically part of a community of advocates and rarely act in isolation. For many evaluators, organizations will be the typical unit analysis, particularly in initiatives that seek to expand organizational advocacy capacity. The key organizations to include in your mental model of the advocacy context are government agencies, political parties, nonprofits and nongovernmental organizations, and the media.

Because its role is to provide public services and be accountable to its citizens, *government* plays a fundamental role in mobilizing advocates and defining their positions and roles. In many instances, advocates are the voice for a government agency, expanding public awareness and support for a particular issue, policy, or regulation. For example, the public comment period provides a means for advocates to bring to bear information that a short-staffed agency may not be able to muster. The drafting of rules and regulations postpassage is another opportunity for advocates to participate on agency committees to hammer out the sometimes arcane but important details about how a law will be implemented. However, this partnership can tilt the other direction, with outside interests having too much influence, such as contracting with one service provider to the exclusion of others (Birkland 2001). The point here is that just because government agencies are not your typical advocate, they are an important player in any advocacy community.

While *political party* influence may also ebb and flow, depending on the political milieu (such as when one party controls both the House and Senate in the U.S. Congress), their role in influencing public opinion and forming the long-term policy agenda should not be overlooked. It is important to know whether a policy has bipartisan support or if there is strong opposition by one or both parties to an advocate's position. For example, federal budget decisions can be particularly divisive for ideological reasons (such as expanding health insurance coverage) and securing support for a more ideologically neutral expenditure (such as federally subsidized community health centers) may be a desired course of action.

The adoption of advocacy tactics by *nonprofit and non-governmental organizations (NGOs)* that historically have not had a political voice (such as service organizations), accounts for a significant portion of the growth in advocacy organizations since the 1960s (Baumgartner and Leech 1998). Not all of these organizations should be considered newcomers to advocacy and policy change. Many nonprofits have provided public services for years and are considered important partners in a particular policy arena. Nonprofit advocacy strategies and tactics are not too dissimilar from those of traditional interest groups, such as trade associations (Andrews and Edwards 2004). The results from Alliance for Justice's 2015 assessment of the advocacy reach of 280 nonprofits indicate most were involved in state advocacy (83 percent), followed by local and federal advocacy (76 percent and 58 percent, respectively). They reported their highest capacity in administrative and legislative advocacy and their lowest capacity in ballot measures, electoral and litigation (McClure and Renderos 2015). Similarly, in the international arena, international and local NGOs play a lead role and engage in a variety of advocacy strategies and tactics to address human rights abuses, ensure access to basic resources, strengthen land rights, and so on (Kelly 2002).

Less visible but potentially very influential are the variety of *think tanks*, the private sector, media, and nonprofits that conduct research and analyses on specific problems, policy areas, and individual policies. Their research may be at the request of government or other political actors that seek to strengthen their understanding of any issue or explore policy options. Think tanks can be international, national, and/or local. They can be stand-alone organizations such as the Rand Corporation or a department within an association, university, or industry (Theodoulou and Kofinis 2004).

Evaluators will find the *media* to be an important node of inquiry in many advocacy and policy change initiatives, fueled in part by the emergence of new forms of media, such as the growing use of social media by advocates to facilitate civic and collective engagement (Obar, Zube, and Lampe 2012). The scholarship on the media's role in expanding public and policymaker awareness and support of a particular issue is vast, but the findings are mixed. While the media is generally thought of as being a key source of political information and may play an important role in focusing attention on emerging problems and agenda setting, cause and effect are not clear. Is the media the source of ideas and information that leads to greater attention of a policy issue, or is the media a useful means for policymakers to make their case and shape public support? Or both? Regardless, advocates are working with the media and learning how to frame and communicate their issues, educating policymakers and possibly shaping public opinion. The scholarship suggests that these efforts can be worthwhile and the media does affect policy outcomes (Theodoulou and Kofinis 2004).

Groups

Advocacy groups ranging from organized communities or coalitions of organizations to informal, diffuse collectives, such as the public, networks, or social movements, are considered one of the most potent forces for change in the policy process, although the actual influence of groups has been questioned by those who posit that better-resourced interests usually prevail (Schlozman, Verba, and Brady 2015). An increasing number of groups do not necessarily translate into better policymaking; whether financially or on other counts, some groups are more powerful than others. However, the research on political groups provides nuanced information about group type, such as membership versus nonmembership groups, their activities, and organizational structure, much of which can inform evaluation practice.

Unlike individual actors, identifying and describing key advocacy groups may be a little more challenging—there are many different types and they may be involved on an episodic basis. Advocacy groups are typically defined as external and separate from government though the line between the two can be blurred. For example, there are associations of decision-makers, such as the U.S. National Governor's Association, which play an advocacy role. Additionally, groups may form networks and only engage in advocacy work as one of their many activities, adding to the difficulty in identifying group advocacy tactics and trying to determine attribution in an advocacy initiative. We describe the key groups that evaluators are likely to encounter in their evaluation context: the public, interest groups, networks, coalitions, and social movements. There are some important structural differences, such as whether they have a membership and act on behalf of member desires, or if they advocate as a distinct organization versus an amalgamation of organizations.

The aggregate of individual citizens at the national, state, or local level, the opinions and preferences of the *public* matter a great deal to elected officials. While opportunities for public participation in the policymaking process vary by country, their actions can be multifaceted and persuasive. In the United States, the public is regularly polled on its attitudes and options. People can express their opinions in writing and/or speaking to government officials and the media. They can vote in elections and on initiatives and referendums. However, as political scientists Michael Kraft and Scott Furlong (2010) point out, only a fraction of the public may actually get involved in the policymaking process and voice their opinion, let alone take an interest in public affairs. Disempowerment, distrust of government, and a history of low public involvement can dampen public involvement unless it is directly affected, such as the terrorist attacks of

September 11, 2001, or the Great Recession of 2008. While a diffuse, amorphous, and potentially dynamic group, public opinion poll data and media coverage of public opinions are valuable sources of information on the problems that occupy a public's attention and the direction that policymaking is likely to go.

The most studied of all the group types in the U.S. political science arena, *interest groups* go by many names, including "organized interests" and "pressure groups." They are different from other types of political groups in that they represent a particular defined interest and tend to exert their influence on Congress, state legislatures, and even the Supreme Court. There are different types of interest groups, many of which are highly experienced and have long tenure in a policy arena (Birkland 2001). The better-known ones are trade associations that have a profession for which they seek policy gains, while also providing benefits, such as the American Medical Association (AMA). Their membership base enables them to engage in a variety of advocacy activities, including lobbying at the federal, state, and/or local levels. Public interest groups are organizations that represent an entire society and not just a membership, such as environmental and human rights groups. There are special interest groups that have a strong economic interest, such as organized labor or business groups. An interest group can be a voluntary association and include a diverse array of organizations, such as corporations, charitable organizations, or civil rights groups. They may or may not have a membership requirement, and there are some differences in function and degree of influence by county and country. Last, unions, which represent particular classes of workers, engage in collective bargaining over wages, benefits, and working conditions for their membership. Interest groups of all types are potent agents of change before, during, and after the policymaking process. They may engage in investigative journalism, grassroots organizing, and bringing legal action to change policy. They also typically engage in lobbying activities at the state and federal levels, providing information on their position and testifying at legislative committee meetings (Kraft and Furlong 2010).

Because they are a critical aspect of the U.S. policymaking universe, the role of interest groups in shoring up or undermining democracy is a perennial question for scholars. Their influence in the United States has been purported to wax and wane, particularly with the decline in blue-collar jobs and relatively weak job growth in the private and public sector post-2008. Regardless of their actual influence, interest groups, their tactic—organizing and mobilizing their members, lobbying, and bringing their economic clout to bear—have been well documented by level of government and by state. For example, they are required to report their lobbying activities under the U.S. Lobbying Disclosure Act (LDA). Additionally, there are many state-by-state and longitudinal analyses in the political science literature that are useful in mapping the universe of informal political actors.

Policy venues have their own *networks*, which are also referred to as "policy subgovernments" and "issue networks" in the political science arena, and are comprised primarily, though not exclusively, of elected officials, government agency representatives, and organized interests. These informal settings have traditionally not included the public, but they are increasingly the sites of communication and sharing of information, an opportunity for advocates to gain access to other political actors while educating others on their issues and position. These networks are also a source of information on the technical details of a policy issue and the policy proposals that decision-makers are likely to consider (Kraft and Furlong 2010). More recently, "networks" has come to refer to loosely affiliated organizations that share a common policy goal but that lack a formal structure, and which are increasingly being seen by U.S. foundations as a lever for policy change. As we will describe in Chapters 4 and 5, APC evaluators are developing frameworks and instruments to characterize the roles, communications, and outcomes of specific networks.

Sometimes referred to as "policy communities," *coalitions* are groups that coalesce into a larger entity that has the opportunity to increase its resources and become a formidable force in the policy arena. This simple definition belies the complexity of the interaction among these groups, which is compounded by their potentially decades-long involvement in a particular policy arena. Fueled by funder support for coalition approaches to system change in complex arenas, scholarship in coalition formation and functioning has gained traction, particularly the Advocacy Coalition

Framework, which describes the policy process as the competition between coalitions and the likelihood of a policy change when these groups
are aligned (Jenkins-Smith and Sabatier 1994).

Community action can be a potent and vital vehicle for change, particularly in low-income and marginalized communities. Supporting and
evaluating community-organizing initiatives experienced a resurgence of
activity in the United States in the mid-2000s, with the aim of shifting
the existing power bases to community members. Using the principles
developed by Saul Alinsky in the early 1970s of nonviolent, creative engagement, the Occupy Wall Street and the Black Lives Matter movements are examples of strategies to unite people and focus attention on
social problems and imbalances in power. The emphasis is on challenging
top-down decision-making and uniting the disempowered or bottom-
up decision-making. At the practice level, tools emphasize a creative approach to organizing and rational discourse and include music, guerrilla
theater, strategy, and leadership development (Si Kahn 2010). In these
situations, the advocate may be a partner or a facilitator versus playing a
lead role, and advocacy activities tend to focus on the upstream activities
of the policy change model, such as advocacy capacity building, community mobilizing, outreach and education, policy analysis, media advocate,
and possibly social protest (Stachowiak 2013).

Last, a less organized group, *social movements* tend to be big, more
informal, and include all types of individuals and collectives. They are
an important means for expanding participation in the policy process.
But, their size may be less important than their potential for creating a
sea change in the way people think about the policy agenda. Take, for
example, the civil rights movement in the 1960s, and more recently the
Occupy Wall Street movement. Social movements may be bigger than
the other group types, but they tend to be episodic and wane as their
relevancy and/or success declines.

In short, an advocacy community can be crowded and complex. It is
also dynamic as leaders and organizations come and go and as a policy
issue advances from problem to policy. It is helpful to clarify the roles of
these different types of advocates, their positions on a particular issue,
and whether or not they are acting alone or with others. There are frame-

works that can help you distinguish the policy actors and their advocacy roles. For example, political scientists Michael Kraft and Scott Furlong (2010) distinguish between the "formal government institutions" that make public policy and the "informal actors" that work with and/or influence institutional actors, including the public, interest groups, policy subgovernments, and issue networks. Getting oriented early and collecting descriptive information on the advocacy community and its key players, or partnering with someone who has this insider perspective will be invaluable in the long run. As we describe in Chapter 4, there are ways to map the universe of advocates and characterize their relationships, giving evaluators a leg-up in understanding the political and cultural context.

WHAT DO ADVOCATES DO?

Motivated by pressing problems that threaten the well-being of our communities—global warming, social and political unrest, environmental degradation, national and global security, economic insecurity, epidemics such as Ebola and the Zika virus to name a few—advocates are making themselves heard using a variety of means. They are holding governments accountable for their most vulnerable populations and strengthening the rights of women, children, the elderly, low-income populations, and increasingly the environment and its other inhabitants. Savvy about the policymaking process and navigating the political arena, advocates are bringing to bear a variety of advocate strategies and tactics, including targeting their advocacy further upstream and educating the public on issues, securing policy victories, and working with agencies to ensure successful execution of policies.

Advocacy activities are perhaps the most thoroughly researched and documented aspect of advocacy practice, and there are a few models that can be used to navigate the complex universe of advocacy strategies and tactics. In this section, we take a macro to micro approach to describing advocacy, starting with conceptual frameworks from the literature that can help clarify the impacts of advocacy on policymaking and finishing with categories and types of advocacy tactics.

Concepts and Frameworks: Politics, Power, and Influence

Characterizing the *politics* or discussions and debates between groups and individuals on an issue, policy, or program is an important aspect of any evaluation design. While an evaluation of a program to curb emissions may not be directly concerned with advocacy capacity or policy change, in all likelihood in this era of increased concern with global climate change, it embodies opposing points of view and powerful political actors. The lessons learned by considering politics or "Who gets what, when, and how?" in a comprehensive program evaluation can be bountiful, not only for those in the midst of advocacy efforts, but others in parallel and future struggles (Lasswell cited by Theodoulu and Cahn 1995, 2). The conflicts that can arise from differences in people's beliefs, values, and attitudes can play a significant role in facilitating or impeding policymaking (Kraft and Furlong 2010). Increasingly, APC evaluators are documenting the political culture of an advocacy and policy change initiative and the way people think about government and the political process, such as the rights of the individual, liberal or conservative values, reproductive rights, equality, and property rights. Reviewing media coverage and documentation on a policy issue as well as informant interviews can reveal whether or not there is conflict, the types of conflict, and how these conflicts are resolved or managed, such as an ideological divide along party lines that might undermine passage of significant reforms.

No analysis of advocacy would be complete without some reflection on *power*, a multifaceted concept that has been defined and categorized in multiple ways to explain the unequal distribution of power among political actors, why some issues make it on to the policy agenda and not others, and characterize the different forms that power can take. This has great relevance in developing countries where newer advocates are trying to gain access in the face of huge economic or cultural challenges. Other models of power exist, such as the holding of power by actors. Do political actors have power over, with, or within? Additionally, power can be characterized as diffuse, limited, or cumulative. It is additionally helpful to know whether power compels or prevents (Birkland 2001). All these typologies are helpful in describing the power dynamics that are part of nearly every policy and advocacy scenario.

Additionally, success in crafting and passing policy may be a question of the type and amount of *influence* that political actors have. An elusive concept, we know what influence is when we see it, but it defies ready definition. Sometimes conflated with power, influence comes in different shades of gray and can be exerted in multiple ways to "politically motivate an institution's or organization's decisions in a certain direction" or more simply put: "changing minds" (Tsui 2013; Parrish 2008). Manipulation, mobilization, persuasion, coercion, inducements and use of financial and political resources, the threat or use of physical force—all are different types of influence that can be wielded to shape an agenda or determine a policy outcome (Theodoulou and Kofinis 2004; Dahl 1991). It may or may not be distributed equally among individuals, groups, and institutions. Nor do more voices necessarily translate into an equal amount of influence in the decision-making process. For example, advocates that play an insider role, such as government policy advisors who are tasked with providing input on a problem or policy may have a great deal of influence, more so than community organizations, operating outside the policymaking system. Ultimately, government wields the most influence because it is responsible for making public policy. In many ways, assessing policy change is about assessing how much influence advocates can bring to bear in wooing government officials and pushing their issues to the forefront of the policy agenda.

ADVOCACY TACTICS

In our experience, knowing the advocacy strategy and tactics that are being used in your evaluation context is absolutely essential for determining the focus of the evaluation and selecting appropriate methods. Evaluators should detail the universe of tactics undertaken by advocates—when they use them and the capacity required to undertake them early in the evaluation—being mindful to the diversity of advocacy and policy change initiatives. Some initiatives focus exclusively on developing organizational or individual capacity to do one type of advocacy, such as working with the media or conducting community organizing. Other initiatives focus on developing overall organizational capacity to undertake multiple advocacy tactics, such as adding experienced staff to extend an organization's involvement over time and across multiple policy issues. Finally, some initiatives focus on deploying a specific strategy or tactic, such as a multistate communications campaign on the benefits to the public of tobacco cessation programs.

Unfortunately, the scholarship on the influence or effectiveness of specific tactics is not clear-cut. Direct personal contacts with decision-makers is perceived by advocates and decision-makers alike to be one of the most effective tactics, but other research suggests that maintenance of effort, tenure, credibility, and the specific context carry more weight than a particular tool or approach (Baumgartner and Leech 1998). Moreover, barriers to participation in the U.S. political arena have persisted if not increased since the great recession of 2008. The uneven distribution of resources, namely, money, tends to tilt the balance of power toward more affluent interests in profound ways (Schlozman, Verba, and Brady 2012). However, evaluators will find the scholarship on the effectiveness of advocacy tactics more generally, as well as specific tactics, helpful for articulating program outcomes.

The political science focus on interest groups has resulted in a rich compendium of advocacy activities across different types of advocacy organizations from which to draw, increasing the rigor of evaluation instruments. A good portion of this literature has focused on lobbying, but over time, these tactics have expanded to encompass the use of new approaches, such as social media, educational activities (including hosting policy forums), and targeting tactics to new policy arenas and/or venues where decision-making takes place, such as social justice advocacy, which focuses on the root causes of economic and other inequities. Based on this literature and efforts by advocacy and policy change evaluators to catalogue the universe of advocacy tactics, we worked with the Aspen Institute and developed the following list of commonly used tactics. (Please note, while the scholarship on advocacy tactics suggests the growth in new forms of advocacy has been slow, that doesn't mean that our list won't be missing a new tactic by the time this book goes to press.) In addition to helping evaluators develop a detailed program theory of change, this list is intended to foster a common understanding of advocacy activities and improve the generalizability of evaluation findings. It is also intended to foster a shared understanding of advocacy activities between advocates, funders, and evaluators. Do not assume advocates take a textbook approach to naming and defining these tactics or have a common understanding among themselves. There may be some differences by topic, nationality, demographics, or geographic location.

To organize our list, we cluster advocacy strategies and activities by four types of purposive change: mobilizing citizens and uniting advocacy allies; expanding public and policymaker awareness; influencing policymaker support; and researching and monitoring policy. Not all of these activities directly target a specific policy, such as community organizing, and many are steps toward increased participation in the policy process, such as gaining media coverage of a particular problem that later finds itself on the policy agenda. This list is not intended to mirror actual advocacy practice. Some activities fit under two or more categories, such as providing testimony, which can educate decision-makers while also influencing their support. Additionally, some tactics might be defined as "strategies" and include a number of smaller discrete tactics. Last, this list assumes some degree of individual and organizational advocacy capacity and does not speak to facilitating factors, including: resources (money, staffing); a strong constituent or membership base; supportive leadership; organizational planning skills; content expertise in a specific policy arena; and personal relationships with decision-makers and members of the community (Kimberlin 2010). (Please see Table 2.2 for a list of individual advocacy tactics, their definitions, and their targets.)

Mobilizing Citizens and Uniting Advocacy Allies

A multifaceted approach that is important for building a base of support to ensuring successful passage of a policy proposal, funders have been very active in supporting these grassroots tactics worldwide. Many of these tactics are also referred to as "collective action," and they focus on bringing people together to achieve a specific goal, such as mobilizing an association's membership to write their congressional representative. These initiatives can be transnational, such as enforcement of laws prohibiting human trafficking, as well as local, such as mobilization of community groups to provide housing to the homeless. Key tactics include civic engagement, coalition building, community organizing, canvassing, holding protests or demonstrations, and building social movements.

Expanding Public and Policymaker Awareness
Advocates can educate the public and decision-makers, using a variety of means, such as media coverage, policy forums, and conducting research on policy proposals. In the international arena, there has been an emphasis on recognizing the voices of oppressed peoples in educational approaches targeting the public (Friere 1970). Additionally, the global focus on social justice and equal access to human rights, such as economic security and health care serves as a rallying point for many advocates. Typical advocacy tactics include public awareness campaigns, public will campaigns, media advocacy, and election-related advocacy.

Influencing Policymaker Support
While these tactics tend to be more visible when a policy is in play, targeting policymakers and other influential political actors is really an ongoing undertaking. These activities are both a means to cultivating support as well as cementing a relationship with decision-makers that can be useful later on. The most studied and most controversial of these tactics is lobbying and attempting to influence legislation by communicating with government officials involved in the decision-making process (U.S. Internal Revenue Service). But it isn't the only tactic. Other potentially influential tactics targeting policymaker support include influencer/influential education, policymaker education, champion development, political will campaigns, and testifying at legislative or agency hearings.

Researching and Monitoring Policy
As a set of activities that requires technical expertise in conducting research as well as reviewing and commenting on laws, policies, budgets, and procedures pre- and postpassage, this is an area that is experiencing growth. Established advocates and new advocates, such as nonprofits, are bringing this expertise in-house or contracting with think tanks and academic institutions, increasing their understanding while establishing themselves as an informed and credible voice. These activities include

policy analysis and research, model legislation, ballot measures, regulatory feedback, budget monitoring, and litigation.

In sum, advocates have many options though many of these tactics will not be needed or even be appropriate. Tactics may be ongoing, episodic, or deployed one time. Some are stand-alone tactics, such as an education campaign, while others are combined with one or more tactics, such as a cover-the-waterfront approach to securing passage of a specific piece of legislation.

Advocacy and the Policymaking Process

To map the advocacy universe and its dynamics, we suggest referring to the policymaking models that were described in Chapter 1. As described in Table 2.1 below, the policy stage model is particularly useful and allows evaluators to compare advocacy tactics across stages, as well as to identify where advocates target their efforts. For example, professional interest groups that have a large membership and dedicated staff may be active in all five stages, while a less established or resourced organization may only have the person power to raise policymaker and public awareness of a particular issue during one stage. Additionally, the focus of a stage will determine which advocates are more likely to be active than others, such as the limited role of think tanks in stages that do not have an analytical focus. Last, noninstitutional actors, such as the public, will have limited access to the stages where policymakers engage in deliberation about policy proposals and voting on individual policies.

There are some shortcomings to using this framework to guide evaluation design. Advocacy tactics may not readily correspond to a particular stage, such as expanding organizational advocacy capacity. Given this situation, evaluators might want to develop a framework that overlaps with the policy stage approach but incorporates additional prepassage stages that are helpful for evaluation design, including: an early *institutional capacity* and *leadership development* stage during which organizations (1) develop their own policy content and advocacy skills, (2) conduct strategies planning, and (3) build meaningful and strategic alliances, prior to launching advocacy activities (Brindis, Geierstanger, and Faxio 2009); a *mobilization and maintenance* stage and increased willingness and abil-

Table 2.1. Stages of Policymaking Process, Potential Advocacy
Activities, and Influential Advocates

Stages and Advocacy Activities	Influential Advocates
Stage 1. Problem Recognition: Advocacy efforts are focused on educating and encouraging appointed and elected officials to recognize the compelling nature of the policy issue, increasing their motivation to act, such as policy forums, in-person meetings, and media advocacy.	Public, Interest Groups, Lobbyists, Media,
Stage 2. Agenda Setting: Advocacy tactics concentrate on determining which issues will occupy the attention of decision-makers, such as securing media coverage and influencing public opinion.	Public, Interest Groups, Lobbyists, Media
Stage 3. Policy Formulation: Decision-makers and other stakeholders actively advocate on its behalf of a policy proposal to achieve the remaining stages, such as providing information about policy impacts on target populations.	Interest Groups, Lobbyists, Media, Think Tanks
Stage 4: Policy Adoption: Advocates and decision-makers build support for adoption, including bargaining, competition, persuasion and compromise.	Interest Groups, Lobbyists, Media
Stage 5. Policy Implementation: Advocates work with agencies to draft rules and regulations or engage in other tactics to influence decision-maker support, such as protests, and ongoing monitoring of policy implementation.	Interest Groups, Lobbyists, Media
Stage 6. Policy Evaluation: Advocates work to sustain public interest and attention, with hopes of ongoing support for the implemented policies, such as partnering with advocacy allies and educating new policymakers. Decision-makers seek information on the effectiveness of their policies.	Interest Groups, Lobbyists, Media, Think Tanks

Sources: Theodoulou 1995; Lowery and Brasher 2004; Theodoulou and Kofinis 2004.

ity to represent a particular interest; and an *interest community* stage and interacting with the existing and new members, some of which may be allies, while others are opponents (Lowery and Brasher 2004). An additional postpassage state, or the *shifting the long-term priorities and resources of political institutions* stage, will help illuminate an organization's capacity to maintain its advocacy focus over the long-term (Andrews and Edwards 2004).

Of course, it is the policy milieu that will determine what stages to focus on. If the initiative focuses on prepassage stages such as *mobilization and maintenance* and *agenda setting*, you may not need to focus on the latter stages, such as participation in *policy implementation* and developing rules and regulations. For advocacy initiatives that are targeted to a specific policy, you may want to "take the long view" and monitor the evolution of advocacy tactics pre- and postpassage of a law, for example, including the *policy maintenance stage*. Be forewarned, as we explained in Chapter 1, few policies are signed into law the first time around, particularly at the state and federal levels, extending the time it takes to achieve a desired policy change to several years. Furthermore, once a law is passed, additional attention is needed to assure it is implemented with fidelity. Alternatively, an advocacy initiative may be ongoing or not target a specific policy, such as working with the media during every stage. It is useful to document the ebb and flow of specific advocacy tactics across the stages and examine advocate flexibility, technical acumen, and maintenance of effort (Gardner, Geierstanger, Nascimento, and Brindis 2011).

Another useful framework is to organize advocacy by the branches of government where advocacy takes place. For example, efforts to influence those policymakers who work with laws, public programs, or court decisions are referred to as "policy advocacy." "Legislative advocacy" are advocacy activities that target the legislative branch, such as lobbying. "Administrative advocacy" activities are an effort to influence the development of regulations, executive orders, and other executive branch vehicles, as well as enforcement of the law. Last, "legal advocacy" (also referred to a "litigation advocacy") activities use the judicial branch to influence policy though litigation (Ezell 2001). The research on lobbying suggests that advocates focus on more than one venue at a time depending on the attributes of the policy issue (Boehmke, Gailmard, and Patty 2013).

In the next section, we provide a reality check and see which tactics are more likely to be used than others, providing guidance on what evaluators can anticipate though this is a moving target. Second, to illustrate the diversity in advocacy initiatives, we discuss the advocates and the advocacy undertaken in the six evaluation cases.

EVALUATION PRACTICE: ADVOCACY TACTICS
EVALUATED

As described in Table 2.2 below, the Aspen/UCSF APC Evaluation Survey findings indicate that APC evaluators focus primarily on communication, education, and research tactics targeting the public and/or decision-makers, including *public awareness campaigns* (59 percent), *policy analysis and research* (55 percent), *media advocacy* (48 percent), *influencer/ influential education*, such as government officials (48 percent), and *policy- maker education* (46 percent). Not surprisingly, upstream advocacy tactics that may or may not have a policy change as a goal figure prominently in APC evaluation practice or *coalition building* (59 percent) and *community organizing* (52 percent). This may explain why other tactics that are integral to the policymaking process were rated lower in focus or *regulatory feedback* (21 percent), *budget monitoring* (20 percent), and *model legislation* (18 percent).

Last, activities that stray dangerously close to lobbying figure less prominently in APC evaluation, such as *political will campaigns* (32 percent), *lobbying* (25 percent), and *voter outreach* (7 percent). This narrower slice may reflect the perspective of the funder—especially private foundations in the United States whose tax requirements require that grant- ees not engage in direct lobbying efforts.[1] For evaluations outside of the

---

1. In the United States, there are private and public foundations, with each having different restrictions on lobbying. Public foundations get their support from many sources and may engage in limited lobbying and make grants earmarked for lobbying. These limits are calculated two ways: the "501(h) Expenditure" test and the "Insubstantial Part" test. Private foundations receive their support from a single individual, family, or corporation, and they may not lobby or provide funding for lobbying except to public charities that lobby (Alliance for Justice 2015).

United States, lobbying-related activities are often part of an advocate's toolkit.

The message here is that although evaluators do not focus on all advocacy tactics equally, APC evaluators still need to be prepared to evaluate a broad range of advocacy strategies and tactics to be informative to stakeholders. On average, survey respondents indicated that they focus on upwards of six advocacy activities, speaking to the need to have sufficiently broad content and methodological expertise that can be applied in different policy arenas, to upstream, prepassage tactics, and across the stages of the policy change model.

EVALUATION PRACTICE: SIX EVALUATION CASES

Similar to Chapter 1, we bridge the gap between theory and practice and illustrate the advocacy strategies and tactics that evaluators may encounter with the six evaluation cases. While this is an "apples and oranges" comparison and these cases are very different campaigns with different objectives, they speak to key areas where APC evaluators are likely to focus their efforts. For the *Tribal Tobacco Education and Policy (TTEP) Initiative*, each of the five tribes developed its own advocacy strategy—a core health equity issue in that change has to come from the community. Advocacy tactics, such as adopting smoke-free policies in public buildings and educating decision-makers, were targeted at elected officials, commissioners, and department heads. Messaging, coalition building, and community ownership of change were targeted at the community level. While Oxfam led the *GROW Campaign* in many national contexts, it was run by coalitions of allies and partner groups. Oxfam undertook a broad range of activities including: lobbying; direct advocacy to decision-makers in the public and private sectors on policy reforms; public mobilization through online and offline activities; generation of media coverage with a range of media outreach strategies; research; and development of policy briefs. In addition, for the World Bank Land Freeze Campaign, there was a video project with the rock group Coldplay as well as social media actions and stunts. The *International Land Conservation Initiative* campaigns in Canada and Australia relied on multiple advocate groups, scientists, policymakers, government agencies, as well as corporations

Table 2.2. Advocacy Activities and Their Targets

Advocacy Activities	Definition, Scope	Target	Percent of Aspen/UCSF Survey Respondents that Focus on Tactic
Mobilizing Citizens and Organizing Advocacy Allies			
Civic engagement	Increasing individual involvement and motivating them to improve the quality of civic life	Individuals, Public	Not asked
Coalition building	Unifying advocacy voices by bringing together individuals, groups, or organizations that agree on a particular issue or goal, such as field operations	Individuals, Public, Interest Groups, Nonprofits	59%
Community organizing (also referred to as community mobilization)	Creating or building on a community-based groundswell of support for an issue or position, often by helping people affected by policies to advocate on their own behalf	Individuals, Public	52%
Canvassing	Conducting telephone polls, focus groups and public opinion polls to assess public views and attitudes on problems and policy issues	Public	Not asked
Protests or demonstration	Mobilizing rallies, marches, and civil disobedience	Individuals, Public	6%
Building social movements	Creating or expanding a loose collection of groups and individuals that seek to change an understanding of an issue	Public, Interest Groups, Nonprofits	Not asked
Expanding Public and Policymaker Awareness			
Public awareness campaigns	Raising recognition among the general public about a policy issue or position, such as a messaging campaign	Public	59%

Table 2.2. Advocacy Activities and Their Targets (continued)

Advocacy Activities	Definition, Scope	Target	Percent of Aspen/ UCSF Survey Respondents that Focus on Tactic
Public will campaigns	Influencing the willingness of a non-policymaker target audience to act in support of an issue or policy proposal	Public	36%
Media advocacy	Influencing coverage in the media, which may include, but is not limited to broadcast television, radio, print and online newspapers and magazines, blogs, and social media; may be paid or earned	Media, Policymakers	48%
Voter outreach	Conveying an issue or position to specific groups of voters in advance of an election (voter outreach, hosting a candidate debate, and educating candidates); voter registration and get-out-the-vote, and encouraging citizens to vote	Public, Policymakers	7%

Influencing Policymaker Support

Lobbying	Efforts to influence specific legislation or support or oppose a ballot initiative	Policymakers	25% (in the U.S. context)
Influencer/ influential education	Informing individuals identified as key influencers over decision-making about an issue or policy position	Policymakers, Influentials	48%
Policymaker education	Informing, advising, or briefing decision-makers about the technical aspects of an issue or position, and about its broad or impassioned support	Policymakers	46%
Champion development	Cultivating high-profile individuals, including policymakers, to adopt an issue and publicly advocate for it	Policymakers, Influentials	36%

Table 2.2. Advocacy Activities and Their Targets (continued)

Advocacy Activities	Definition, Scope	Target	Percent of Aspen/ UCSF Survey Respondents that Focus on Tactic
Political will campaigns	Influencing the willingness of policymakers to act in support of an issue or policy proposal	Policymakers	32%
Requests for advice	Providing written technical advice or testimony at legislative or agency hearings	Policymakers	Not asked
Researching and Monitoring Policy			
Policy analysis and research	Systematically investigating an issue or problem to better define it or identify possible solutions	Policymakers	55%
Model legislation	Drafting legislation consistent with an advocacy position on a policy issue for dissemination to policymakers	Policymakers	18%
Regulatory feedback	Providing comments on and suggested improvements to specific policy regulations	Policymakers	21%
Budget monitoring	Tracking the government's budget allocations or spending on particular policies	Policymakers	20%
Litigation	Using the judicial system to move policy by filing lawsuits or civil actions	Courts	2%

Sources: Aspen Planning and Evaluation Program, The Aspen Institute; Alliance for Justice 2015; Coffman and Beer 2015.

and trade associations operating in, and dependent on, the boreal forest. Similar campaigns took place in both countries—a combination of tactics, including leveraging science-based arguments for the value of land conservation, empowering Indigenous communities to assert their rights over native lands, and cultivating strong relationships with key decision-makers from across the political spectrum. *Project Health Colorado* supported fourteen grantees from Colorado, many of which were new to advocacy and represented multiple sectors, including advocates, education and research, leadership, community mobilizing, providers, public education, and public health. Grantees undertook diverse activities while working together using a common message framework to advance public will on health care access. The initiative also included a paid media and mobilization campaign, a social media strategy, volunteer trainings, community forums, and story collection and sharing. Under the *Initiative to Promote Equitable and Sustainable Transportation*, there were seventy-four federal-level grants that strengthened the capacity of transportation advocates, thirty state-level grants that focused on several issues (with a large emphasis on laying the groundwork for revised federal policy), and twenty-one grants focused on communications demonstration projects, and search and technology grants. Advocacy tactics included: research and policy analysis; communications and framing the debate; organizational capacity building; program/project support; coalition and diverse partner development; and funder-to-funder meetings. Last, the *Let Girls Lead* program focused on individual advocacy capacity development and the creation of a global movement of 110 leaders and organizations advocating for girls. Fellows undertook a range of advocacy tactics that varied by country and included: experts communicating with policymakers; policy implementation analysis; broad public education; marches; and adolescent girls and boys meeting with local officials.

Using our four categories of advocacy tactics, we see there are many parallels with the Aspen/UCSF Survey findings. All initiatives included tactics to *expand public and policymaker awareness*, targeting both audiences though they used different modes of communication. For example, the use of media figured prominently in the Project Health Colorado campaign and the GROW World Bank Campaign. Second, except for

Project Health Colorado, all the initiatives sought to directly *influence policymaker support* using a variety of tactics, including the use of lobbying in the case of the World Bank Initiative. Three initiatives included *research and monitoring policy* in their portfolios of advocacy tactics: the World Bank Initiative; the Campaign to Promote Equitable and Sustainable Transportation; and the International Lands Conservation Program. *Mobilizing citizens and uniting advocacy allies* figured prominently in two initiatives—the International Lands Conservation Program and the Initiative to Promote Equitable and Sustainable Transportation—both of which are broad policy issues and include many stakeholders.

The primary difference between the survey findings and the cases is one of emphasis: five of the six cases focused on policy change, and consequently there was higher evaluator engagement in areas like policymaker education and lobbying. A second observation is that all of these campaigns included a combination of advocacy tactics. In addition to having content expertise about a specific policy issue, evaluators need to understand individual advocacy tactics and their relation and importance to other tactics. Resource constraints may limit evaluator ability to assessing only those tactics which are of highest value or interest to stakeholders, a difficult situation if a goal is to inform advocacy practice more generally.

CONCLUSION

We end this chapter on an upbeat, but cautionary note. Advocates and advocacy in all shapes and sizes have flourished in recent years and will continue to do so in the future, contributing to a significant knowledge base that can inform evaluation practice. Notwithstanding the expansion of advocacy on behalf of marginalized or silent voices and the potential for increased representation, there are significant cultural, economic, and systemic barriers to leveling the policy playing field in the near future. Nor, as we have described above, does advocacy even in its narrowest sense lend itself to easy examination. Tactics may change unexpectedly or be assembled into toolkits, which make it difficult to assess effectiveness. However, evaluators can turn to a variety of frameworks and definitions to characterize advocates and their strategies and tactics before, during, or after a policy change initiative. Evaluators can undertake this exciting work with a sense of perspective, as well as an understanding of what to do and on whose behalf.

Our six cases suggest that while the focus may be on a particular advocacy strategy, such as a public-will-building campaign, the reality is that multiple tactics will be brought to bear, expanding advocacy capacity while doing advocacy. Also, the many and diverse grantees in the six cases corroborate the complex advocacy universe described in the literature. Anticipating and being prepared for the many possible advocacy evaluation scenarios may be difficult, but as we discuss in Chapter 3, there are many solid options for making sense of this complicated landscape and designing a rigorous and informative evaluation.

Part 2

Appropriate Designs, Outcomes, and Methods

DESIGNING ADVOCACY AND POLICY
CHANGE EVALUATIONS

INTRODUCTION

Evaluating advocacy and policy change (APC) initiatives is less daunting than it was in the 2000s, buoyed by a growing number of tailored
evaluation how-to guides and evaluator willingness to share instruments
and lessons learned. APC evaluation can also draw on the pioneering
works of policy evaluators, such as Eleanor Chelimsky and Carol Weiss,
as well as the evaluation field's discussions about the role of context, cultural competence, applicability of experimental designs, and approaches
for strengthening evaluation design. Existing and emerging evaluation
approaches, such as developmental evaluation, empowerment evaluation,
and appreciative inquiry, are particularly helpful for orienting the evaluation design and framing the evaluator/stakeholder relationship. In this
chapter, we lay out some guidelines for designing APC evaluations, focusing on evaluation strategies that are particularly applicable in advocacy
and policy change settings. Since APC evaluation is still expanding its
frontier, we take a pragmatic approach to evaluation design and consider
a range of approaches: monitoring; developmental, formative, and summative designs; deductive and inductive approaches; and quantitative and
qualitative methods.

Lest the reader think that developing and executing an appropriate evaluation design will be smooth sailing, in all likelihood this will

not be the case. Challenges abound, and we have included a list of the primary threats to APC evaluation design along with some suggestions for addressing or at least tempering their effects. An advocacy campaign rarely stays the course and is heavily influenced by political and policy conditions, such as unexpected shifts in alliances or media coverage of an unforeseen event. However, some things remain constant, such as the legislative calendar and stable policy networks.

Last, we describe actual APC evaluation designs, including the findings from the Aspen/UCSF APC Evaluation Survey findings on design strategies and a comparison of two evaluation case studies, *Let Girls Lead* and the *Initiative to Support Sustainable and Equitable Transportation*, to illustrate the diversity in evaluation designs, challenges addressed, and useful strategies.

IDENTIFYING THE EVALUATION STRATEGY

APC evaluators have developed a solid collection of templates and ways to frame methods and tools for evaluating an advocacy and policy change initiative, guided by policy change models as well as other related frameworks, such as developmental evaluation, appreciative inquiry, and empowerment theory. For example, PolicyLink's *Getting Equity Advocacy Results (GEAR)* helps advocates, organizers, and their allies track the results of equity campaigns. It includes benchmarks, methods, and tools and is organized around four principles: Build the Base; Name and Frame the Equity Solutions; Move the Equity Proposal; and Build, Advance, and Defend. Another approach is the *Advocacy and Policy Change Composite Model* developed by APC evaluators and evaluation staff representing multiple foundations. Its strength lies in providing a template that lays out components of an APC initiative, including policy goals (the stage model of policy change), individual tactics, interim advocacy and policy outcomes, and longer-term impacts, such as improved services. It also provides a comprehensive set of advocacy tactics and their definitions, as well as potential interim outcomes, such as changes in political will and public awareness. The difference between these frameworks is one of emphasis: most have a similar set of evaluation methods and tools in common.

In the international arena, Jim Coe and Juliette Major of the Overseas Development Institute (ODI) (2013) organize popular evaluation methods by four dimensions of an advocacy initiative: (1) strategy and direction and the strength of an initiative's program theory of change; (2) management and outputs or monitoring and assessment of advocacy tactics; (3) outcomes and impact and the extent to which change has occurred; and (4) understanding causes or why an advocacy initiative succeeded or failed. Another framework in the international arena, but which has applicability more broadly, is the *Institute for Development Research (IDR) framework*, which recommends that advocacy work should be measured against three criteria: (1) policy or changes that result from influencing decision-making structures; (2) civil society and the strengthening of civil organizations to continue to advocate and participate in decision-making; and (3) democratic space or expanding civil society involvement in decision-making (Chapman and Wameyo 2001).

While you can adapt these frameworks or develop a new strategy for your own situation, you will still need to consider the following evaluation basics that are essential for a successful design.

Clarify the Initiative Goals, Objectives, and Activities
As is the case in evaluation of programs and services, the evaluation design stems directly from an initiative's scope and purpose, as well as the specific advocacy strategy and tactics. The stated goals, objectives, and plan of action will provide much of this information, but you cannot assume that these goals and objectives are realistic or will stay the same over the course of the initiative. Characterizing the change aspect of an initiative and its history will help determine whether or not it is likely to follow a predictable course of action.

Understanding the different actors and their interests and information needs over time, such as what constitutes a success, will help determine the outcomes and inform the model and level of stakeholder engagement in the evaluation design. Advocates and their funders (hereafter referred to as stakeholders) may have unachievable, aspirational goals and overlook the incremental gains that are significant wins in their own right. Alternatively, forestalling a significant loss may go unrecognized for the important win that it is. Additionally, stakeholders may diverge on their definition of "success," opting for smaller gains if the opposition proves more formidable than originally anticipated. In all likelihood, the evaluation will provide a reality check and require some flexibility on the part of the evaluator.

Specifying the evaluand and focus of what is being evaluated is critical to the evaluation design. The complexity and maturity of an initiative's strategy, specific advocacy tactics, and levels of engagement (international, national, state, and local) are linked to specific methods and tools of the evaluation design. For example, to help bound the universe of advocacy and policy change initiatives and their impacts, the *IDR framework* uses five dimensions: (1) policy (national, provincial, local, international, other); (2) private sector (national, local, international, multinational, other); (3) civil society (NGOs, popular organizations, community-based organizations, ally organizations, others); (4) democracy or political systems and culture (democratic space, participation of civil society, political legitimacy of civil society, accountability of public institutions, transparency of public institutions, other); and (5) individual wellbeing (material, attitudinal, other) (Chapman and Wameyo 2001). We suggest you refer to the list of advocacy tactics in Chapter 2 in developing an inventory of advocacy tactics in your situation, many of which are from the scholarship on advocacy. It is also important to understand the initiative from the funder and advocate perspective and not assume everyone has the same definition of a particular advocacy tactic or even "advocacy" itself. Having in-depth knowledge of the advocate or advocacy organization and its activities is almost the same as knowing the initiative.

Determine Evaluation Purpose, Strategy, and Questions
Clarifying the purpose of the evaluation follows closely on the heels of developing a detailed understanding of the initiative, be it program improvement, accountability and determining program effectiveness, and/or knowledge generation to advance the field (Rossi, Lipsey, and Freeman 2004; Patton 2012). However, the purpose of the evaluation can vary greatly by initiative type and stakeholder, and taking the time to deter-

mine which learning objectives are important and to whom is time well spent. The conventional focus on assessing program success and whether or not the original objectives were achieved may be less important to program managers who are more interested in the ongoing monitoring of initiative strategy and activities. Also, do advocates really want to know whether or not some advocacy tactics work better than others if they are already savvy advocates and have adopted a variety of strategies? Initially, advocates may be less interested in learning about specific advocacy tactics and strategies, but over time, they may be interested to learn what tactics are most effective with different targets, ranging from policymakers to community representatives. Funder interests may diverge from those of advocates, such as focusing on whether or not an initiative was implemented in the way it was intended and big picture findings that demonstrate that their support contributed to a successful outcome.

Reconciling these diverse interests is doable. It requires brokering partnerships with stakeholders early on and getting consensus about how much of the evaluation will focus on program development, accountability, and knowledge development. APC evaluation tends to be strong in program and knowledge development, such as documenting changes in organizational and network advocacy capacity. While accountability and focusing on achievement of program outcomes, such as increased policymaker support for a particularly policy issue, is a work in progress, increased interest by funders in demonstrating their contribution to prioritized outcomes, as well as whether or not these outcomes contributed to significant systems change are pushing the field in this direction.

Conventional wisdom says that if an organization's advocacy capacity is the key focus of an initiative, then formative evaluation is the appropriate evaluation strategy. This can be a very fruitful area of inquiry. Many advocacy capacity activities and products lend themselves to counting and ongoing monitoring, such as number of contacts by the media, contacts by policymakers, number of times advocates provide testimony, and attendance at policy forums. There are tested tools and metrics that can be used by evaluators and advocates, such as the Alliance for Justice's *Advocacy Capacity Assessment Tool* and the Aspen Institute's *Advocacy Progress Planner*. The formalized tracking of tactics and changes that are characteristic of Monitoring, Evaluation, and Learning (MEL) practice can also be useful. Additionally, utilization-focused evaluation and asking and answering actionable questions, particularly as an initiative evolves can reconcile differences in stakeholder information needs (Patton 2012).

While summative evaluation is difficult in situations where there is a short time horizon and/or lack of measures, funder desire to assess program impacts and determine the overall value of their investment is stimulating new thinking in this regard. Evaluators have multiple options for developing a sound summative evaluation design. Development of a program theory of change and/or logic model can simplify the complexity and surface outcomes that can be measured. Focusing on interim outcomes that are under the control of an initiative, such as changes in policymaker support, can provide useful information about program effectiveness. Approaches well suited for complex environments, such as systems thinking, can reduce the uncertainty and make more transparent the linkages between initiative elements.

The design also depends on program stability and whether an initiative becomes a replicable model or if it continues to transform and adapt to changing circumstances. Advocacy and policy change initiatives typically resemble the latter, such as a campaign to build public will that evolves as the political terrain changes. For those situations where the path forward is not so clear-cut, a developmental evaluation approach and real-time data collection provides evaluators with the means to assess progress and inform strategy. These approaches can accommodate the changing terrain that characterizes an advocacy initiative as well as strengthen the partnership between the evaluator and stakeholders.

The evaluation questions, one of the pillars of an evaluation design, will be shaped by the evaluation purpose, as well as help clarify the purpose of the evaluation. Evaluator Eleanor Chelimsky (2007) reminds us that there are four types of questions: descriptive or how and what questions; normative questions or demonstrating program outcomes as compared to a standard; cause-and-effect questions that focus on attribution; and knowledge-based questions, such as lessons learned. However, stakeholder information needs ultimately decide the evaluation questions. Many funders want to know whether or not an advocacy initiative has been implemented in the way it was intended and the quality of implementation, if an initiative achieved its outcomes, and what role their support played. Depending on the maturity of the initiative, they may also want to learn whether an initiative is applicable elsewhere or if it is adapted elsewhere, what the likely outcome will be. Additionally, the economic gains secured by a community from a policy win may be required by a funder to justify the initiative to its board of directors. Financial analyses speak volumes to funders that want to know how their resources were used and/or leveraged, but they require sound accounting by grantees and well-thought-out models of the financial impacts of a policy. It is wise to clarify the interests of stakeholders here. Do they want a full-blown return on investment (ROI) analysis or an inventory of in-kind resources secured by a grantee?

By contrast, demonstrating cause-and-effect and return on investment may be less valuable to advocates than strategic learning and a detailed description of tactics used to secure policymaker support for a particular piece of legislation or effective tactics in gaining the media's attention. With a mature initiative, advocates may also desire a credible evaluation that demonstrates their actions have resulted in policy action or community empowerment. It speaks to the value of their work while increasing funder and advocate understanding of the mechanisms of causation to the extent that they can be teased out. Stakeholder information needs should flow readily from the discussion about the evaluation's purpose.

Based on our review of advocacy and policy change evaluation designs, the formative evaluation questions being used by APC evaluators include:

- What progress or lack thereof has been made in implementing the initiative and demonstrating achievement of initiative goals and objectives, such as launch of a campaign, testifying at legislative hearings, or building organizational infrastructure to do advocacy?

- How well did the advocate(s) conduct the campaign or activities? What could be improved?

- What are the most significant outcomes to date, such as changes in organizational advocacy capacity, public and/or policymakers reached, or increase in support for the advocate's position?

- What are the facilitating and limiting factors (internal and external) that have been encountered in the implementation and maintenance of the initiative?

- What have been the outputs, such as policy briefs, advocates trained, and increased communications with other sectors or advocacy allies?

- What has been learned from the initiative that can be used to inform advocate strategy and tactics, as well as funder role in supporting advocates? Similarly, typical summative evaluation questions include:

- What strategies and/or tactics were most effective in achieving the desired outcome?

- What was the impact of the initiative strategy/activities on the target audiences, and/or policymakers?

- To what extent were the outcomes of the initiative achieved? Are these outcomes sustainable?

- What role did the advocates and funder play in achieving the outcomes of the initiative? What evidence is there to demonstrate advocate/funder contribution?

- To what extent did the initiative result in individual, organizational, population, and/or system change?

- What contributed to (or impeded) initiative success?

- What can be learned from these successes and failures that can inform funder strategy, such as adaption of the initiative in other settings?

Know the Context: Political Players and the Policy Arena

Identifying and characterizing the universe of individuals and organizations involved and their interests in an advocacy initiative is critical to the success of the evaluation since "who you know" is a fundamental aspect of many APC initiatives. The relationships that are important to advocates and decision-makers may also need to be cultivated by evaluators. An advocacy and policy initiative can be a densely populated and complex milieu. Advocates may partner with multiple allies, including policymakers and the beneficiaries of their advocacy tactics, such as vulnerable populations. Roles may be fluid and difficult to characterize as an initiative evolves. We suggest taking a broad view, beyond the advocate and funder, and include partner organizations that play a pivotal role in an advocacy campaign. Additionally, decision-makers, who may also be advocacy allies, should be given consideration. Don't forget to include the opposition in your map of the political universe, including those who are ambivalent regarding the policy choices, as well as those who are firmly opposed to the proposed changes. Even if the campaign is not conflictual in nature, there are likely to be interests that are ideologically opposed or resistant to change.

For those of you who are already knowledgeable about advocacy and policy change, this is a gentle reminder to familiarize yourself with the particulars of a policy arena. Complexity—multiple key players, competing and conflicting political entities, and an uncertain policymaking process—is the hallmark of many APC initiatives. Do not assume your ability to design and execute a complex APC evaluation design will carry you though. Evaluators need to be sufficiently knowledgeable in the subject matter of the policy or policy arena and the policymaking process, just short of being as skilled in the policy process as the advocates and policymakers themselves. For example, the health policy arena requires different content expertise than transportation policy, and it has an entirely separate cast of players. There are also differences in federal and state policymaking within a policy arena—the bureaucracy, funding, and responsibility for policy implementation. Be realistic about your knowledge of the policy arena and its content, history, and advocates. If you have a shallow understanding of a policy arena, you may need to partner with experts who have content expertise and long-standing experience with a particular policy arena.

Determine Evaluator Role
How the APC evaluation team relates to the initiative can facilitate the successful planning and execution of the evaluation, as well as the appli-

cation of evaluation findings. Assuming the American Evaluation Association's (AEA) five *Guiding Principles for Evaluators* (Systematic Inquiry, Competence, Integrity/Honesty, Respect for People, and Responsibilities for General and Public Welfare) are already incorporated into an evaluation design, we discuss a couple of aspects of the evaluator role that require special consideration: the question of having an external or internal evaluation or both, and the evaluator partnership with stakeholders.

An external enterprise-level evaluation affords opportunities for developing generalizable findings and field building, while also doing some of the heavy lifting that funders and advocates may not be able to do on their own, such as executing a mixed-method design. As APC evaluator Julia Coffman (2009) points out, the potential drawbacks of an enterprise-level evaluation is that it may not focus enough on what advocates find helpful, such as timely information about the results of a specific tactic. The silo approach that characterizes many external evaluations may not take into consideration the embedded forms of oppression that are predictive of initiative outcomes and, at worse, perpetuate the systems that support social injustices. Similarly, an internal evaluation conducted by grantee staff is likely to not have the resources and evaluation expertise to assess longer-term impacts. Nor may there be a level of objectivity or a perspective that provides a pragmatic and candid assessment of initiative progress and achievements.

In practice, the ideal design is an approach whereby the neutral perspective, resources, and strengths of an external evaluation are combined with the insider, ground-level perspective of the advocate. One approach is to include an evaluation technical assistance component that strengthens advocate evaluation expertise in the development and execution of the design as well as increases their understanding of how data is collected and analyzed, and how the results can be used for strategy refinement. Additionally, adopting a "critical friend" perspective can also help establish the external evaluator as an objective insider. Defined as "a trusted person who asks provocative questions, provides data to be examined through another lens, and offers critiques of a person's work as a friend," a critical friend takes the time to fully understand the context of the work presented and the outcomes that the person or group is working toward. The critical friend perspective blends the objectivity that is expected of an evaluator with trustworthiness and sensitivity that are the attributes of a friend (Costa and Kallick 1993, 49).

Compared to other evaluation arenas, the evaluation partnership model can have a profound impact on the design and execution of an APC evaluation. Advocacy and policy change initiatives are typically relationship-based. As Michael Quinn Patton (2012) argues in the latest edition of his classic book, *Essentials of Utilization Focused Evaluation*, evaluation stakeholders should be personally and actively involved in the evaluation with the goal of increasing the use and usefulness of the evaluation. The collaboration with stakeholders is characterized by ongoing negotiation and involvement in the development and execution of an evaluation, including identifying and refining the evaluation questions, conducting a contextual analysis, and developing a program theory of change.

This partnership is at risk if the evaluation team doesn't have the cultural competency to work with diverse stakeholders who may not share their same values and mind-set, particularly in how they regard evaluation. Considered a critical competency for the profession, one of the AEA's *Guiding Principles for Evaluators* is that evaluators should be able to "demonstrate cultural competence and use appropriate evaluation strategies and skills to work with culturally different groups" (AEA 2011). In an advocacy and policy change context, evaluators need to factor into the design the power dynamics and identify whose interests are being served by the evaluation. They need to be sensitive to "inequalities and injustices in everyday social relationships and arrangements" (Freeman, Franca, and Vasconcelos 2010, 7). The evaluation community has identified seven methods for increasing the cultural competency of an evaluation:

1. Consider the community for whom the evaluation plan is created

2. Pre-test survey instruments with different ethnic groups

3. Obtain information about other attributes related to ethnicity beyond self-identification of ethnic group

4. Build a process check into the evaluation by holding ongoing dis-

course with the evaluation team concerning their experiences with participants

5. Use triangulation of multiple information sources

6. Include expert cultural or ethnic consultants on the evaluation team

7. Create research reports that contain full discussions of the sample and sampling methodology used (Dunaway et al. 2013)

Additionally, adopting participatory evaluation approaches and broadening inclusion will help put the evaluation on a more equal footing.

This is an area that has greatly benefited from wisdom within the evaluation field. Michael Quinn Patton's (2009) developmental evaluation model takes stakeholder involvement to the next level with its emphasis on ongoing learning and adaptation. Evaluation is an essential, partnership-based function that is responsive to stakeholder learning and information needs. At the far end of the evaluator/stakeholder partnership continuum is David Fetterman's (2005) empowerment evaluation approach and the ownership of the evaluation by stakeholders or the community. The evaluator is less of an authority figure and more of a facilitator and stakeholders have greater control of the evaluation. Similarly, appreciative inquiry and the proactive examination of positive images of organization-level activities put stakeholders more in the driver's seat. It is particularly well suited for assessing organizational advocacy capacity and can be used to build relationships among stakeholders, strengthen advocate evaluation capacity, and guide the evaluation design and its implementation (Coghlan, Preskill, and Catsambas 2003). We describe the evaluator relationships with advocates, funders, and decision-makers in more detail in Chapter 6.

Effective Communications

Communicating evaluation findings is important to achieving the twin missions of strategic learning and creating and sustaining a legacy for change. Putting some thought to the communications plan during the evaluation planning and implementation stages and creating an information feedback loop will ensure that findings contribute to advocacy strategy and tactics. It is clear that communication begins at the very beginning, as stakeholders are encouraged to provide input into the evaluation questions and into data collection itself, including helping to identify key stakeholders to be interviewed or surveyed. In many regards, they are the end users, so they will also be primed to learn from the evaluation findings.

Developing and disseminating evaluation findings early and often can create a vehicle for change that continues well after the end of the initiative. With stakeholder buy-in, evaluation publications and other products can be used to fine-tune a campaign and its tactics, as well as build organizational capacity to collect and use data. For example, descriptive cases of successful policy gains can educate others, as well as strengthen the case for future support. Unfortunately, there is no one-size-fits-all approach, and different stakeholders require different types of information in different formats. Funder information needs are very different than those of the advocate, such as requiring accessible summary reports that can be submitted to a board of directors. Advocates need practical information that supports advocacy practice, such as descriptive briefs about capacity development and strategy. They also want to let others know about their success, in their voice, though they are often reluctant to share the details of their advocacy tactics lest it reveal too much information to the opposition. Evaluators will want to discuss what formats should be used to disseminate evaluation findings—whether results are best presented through a webinar, a brief, a press release, a power point, a brief summary for a website, and/or other approaches. Given the role of social media and networks, there is higher likelihood that dissemination of findings will occur far more rapidly and often will be picked up through various mechanisms, including tweets and Facebook. Thus, evaluation findings need to be presented in a manner that is also compelling and that is heard above the din. By contrast, at other times, particularly if evaluation results are not in the desired direction, advocates may choose to bury the results, opting not to present them to the external world, but to use findings for internal purposes.

ADDRESSING THE CHALLENGES OF APC EVALUATION DESIGN

Evaluators welcome, if not thrive, on challenge. However, evaluating advocacy and policy change initiatives may be more daunting than other types of programs. Evaluators Steven Teles and Mark Schmitt (2001, 43) sum up the challenges of APC evaluation: "Evaluators must acquire and accurately weigh and synthesize imperfect information, from biased sources with incomplete knowledge, under rapidly changing circumstances where causal links are almost impossible to establish." This is in addition to the usual evaluation problems that confront evaluators, such as resource limitations and starting too late. However, evaluators have some solid options for tackling these challenges, and standard evaluation theory and practice can address many of the design issues that will arise in an APC evaluation. For example, conducting an evaluability assessment to determine whether or not an initiative can be evaluated with available resources and within a specific time frame will surface challenges early on as well as manage the expectations of stakeholders (Bamberger et al. 2012). We suggest that evaluators pay particular attention to the following aspects of the APC initiative when determining the overarching evaluation strategy:

Lack of Transparency of the Advocacy Strategy

The oppositional nature or conflict that characterizes most policymaking creates unique challenges for evaluators, such as the unwillingness by advocates and even funders to disclose the details of their game plan for fear of tipping their hand to the opposition. There may also be an element of risk for advocates who are involved in human rights and other arenas where there is the possibility of retaliation. While discretion is an important element that needs to be factored into any evaluation design, it is even more important in an APC evaluation context. Evaluator Michael Quinn Patton (2008) describes a "First, do no harm" approach to evaluating the impact of a campaign to influence a Supreme Court decision, a stealth campaign designed to avoid attracting strong opposition. The evaluation report was kept confidential, including not producing electronic copies, with distribution to only a select few. Another approach is to have a confidential data collection approach, such as Innovation Network's *Intense Period Debriefs*, which create a safe venue right after an advocacy activity to discuss sensitive questions about success and failures.

Restrictions on Some Forms of Advocacy

It is important for evaluators to understand the definition of "lobbying" or advocacy targeting specific federal, state, and local legislation in its fullest sense. As described by the Alliance for Justice (2015), there are two types of lobbying, direct and grassroots. "Direct lobbying" is a communication with a legislator (federal, state, local) or legislative staff member that refers to specific legislation and expresses a view on that legislation. "Grassroots lobbying" is a communication with the general public that refers to specific legislation, expresses a view on that legislation, and urges the public to contact their legislator(s).

Moreover, the evaluator needs to distinguish legislation, which can include local measures, from other types of decisions. The U.S. Internal Revenue Service defines "legislation" as:

> Legislation includes action by Congress, any state legislature, any local council, or similar governing body, with respect to acts, bills, resolutions, or similar items (such as legislative confirmation of appointive office), or by the public in referendum, ballot initiative, constitutional amendment, or similar procedure. It does not include actions by executive, judicial, or administrative bodies. (U.S. Internal Revenue Service)

In the early 2000s, confusing U.S. federal guidelines that limited nonprofit lobbying resulted in many funders directing resources to less controversial advocacy activities, such as research, education and working with the media.[1] On the one hand, this limits advocates, as they cannot pursue potentially more effective strategies. Nor do they have the tactical advantage that better resourced organizations that engage lobbying enjoy. For evaluators, these restrictions mean ignoring key forms of influence,

---

1. "In general, no organization may qualify for section 501(c)(3) status if a substantial part of its activities is attempting to influence legislation (commonly known as lobbying). A 501(c)(3) organization may engage in some lobbying, but too much lobbying activity risks loss of tax-exempt status" (Internal Revenue Service).

which is a disservice to funders, advocates, and the evaluation field at large. While some of the misunderstanding of the limits on lobbying have been addressed by educating funders about what advocacy is permitted, the U.S. evaluation arena continues to wrestle with the definitional issues and what forms of advocacy are legal. For example, funders may conflate definitions of advocacy and lobbying even though most advocacy tactics are not lobbying.

Addressing Initiative Complexity

Advocacy initiatives like widespread civil society strengthening or a coalition approach to policy change may involve many actors across many sectors and over many years. Additionally, the change mechanism adds another dimension of complexity, and external factors add an element of unpredictability. APC evaluators must wrestle with this complexity without getting flummoxed by it. One strategy is to incorporate a developmental evaluation approach, which characterizes complexity and its properties—nonlinearity, emergence, adaptation, co-evolution, dynamic interactions, and uncertainty—and provides APC evaluators with a strategy and tools to anticipate and learn from a program or initiative that is constantly in a state of flux (Patton 2011).

Systems thinking approaches and looking at an initiative as a web of relationships enables evaluators to understand an APC initiative in a holistic, dynamic way, and not overlook aspects and changes that are not included in a linear model. Using a systems lens has the potential to capture unintended changes as well as surface recommendations for program improvements and identifying levers for change (Foster Fishman, Nowell, and Yang 2007). The potential uses of systems tools for advocacy and policy change evaluation are many and they are compatible with program monitoring strategies and developmental/formative/summative evaluation designs. While this is an area that is still emerging and requires some technical training, particularly characterizing the interactions among system components, the concepts are being translated into guides outside the APC evaluation arena that have applicability, such as Nancy Latham's (2014) *A Practical Guide to Evaluating Systems Change in a Human Services System Context.*

Additionally, new analytical techniques, including contribution analysis, contextual analyses (such as realist evaluation), and social network analysis are making it possible to navigate the complexity and determine what contributes to achievement of interim and long-term outcomes. All of these approaches can be used to connect the attribution dots and provide a more robust understanding of the role of funding, key advocacy tactics, and how a policy change came about, or possibly important lessons learned if a change did not occur. For example, evaluators Todd C. Honeycutt and Debra A. Strong (2012) used social network analysis (SNA) to examine the capacity and functioning of twelve coalitions funded by the Robert Wood Johnson Foundation to advance health insurance coverage expansions. They were able to measure the level of communications among organization members, the level of engagement in advocacy activities, alignment in values, and the overall level of relationships at the coalition level, providing a more robust understanding of coalition dynamics and the opportunities they provide for advancing a policy agenda and sharing of resources.

Last, the wicked problems framework, or intractable problems that do not lend themselves to easy resolution, allows evaluators and stakeholders to view an APC initiative in a fundamentally different way. It acknowledges the underlying complexity of policy issues targeted by funders and advocates, as well as the difficulty in achieving consensus on a particular solution, such as global warming. For example, the framework has been applied retrospectively to two complex policy issues—expanding health insurance for children and strengthening the federal Farm Bill to improve access to healthy food (Sherman and Peterson 2009). The framework forces stakeholders to take a hard look at the problem itself, the effectiveness of the intervention, and stakeholder involvement.

Addressing the Issues of Credibility and Rigor
Policy work is complex and many times nonlinear, and it is characterized by a range of conditions, numerous types of influence, and various points of interventions. Typically, there are multiple actors simultaneously for and against a particular policy or advocacy strategy. There may also be a gap in time between when an advocacy tactic or campaign takes place

and the achievement of a desired policy change, making it difficult to determine cause and effect.

Not surprisingly, the majority of Aspen/UCSF APC Evaluation Survey respondents (84 percent) reported that they used *non-experimental designs* and only 6 percent used *experimental designs*. APC evaluators argue that advocacy efforts by their very nature do not lend themselves to more traditional scientific investigation, and demonstrating a cause-and-effect relationship between tactics and outcomes is a near impossible task. Consequently, the APC evaluation community stands solidly behind the standard of contribution over attribution and collection of evidence that demonstrates that an advocacy initiative played an important role in achieving the desired outcomes (Coffman 2014). By the same token, as Bamberger and others have argued, conditions permitting, evaluators have an obligation to inquire about attribution and what would have happened in the absence of the initiative (White 2013; Bamberger et al. 2004).

Evaluators Steven Teles and Mark Schmitt (2011, 39) eloquently describe the limited options for APC evaluators: "Advocacy evaluation should be seen, therefore, as a form of trained judgment—a craft and tacit knowledge—rather than as a scientific method." However, the issue of conclusively demonstrating that a program works is not unique to APC evaluation, and evaluation can be "as much art as science" in other complex social settings. The evaluation field continues to wrestle with internal validity and providing credible evidence that a program actually did what it was intended to do, as well as producing evaluation findings that are generalizable, or external validity. These issues are more pronounced in APC evaluation. Using experimental designs or randomized control trials (RCTs), the "gold standard," to demonstrate inference are difficult under any circumstances and are even more so in an APC context where the intervention is diffuse and the outcomes are uncertain. Developing generalizable findings may be more informative to stakeholders who want actionable findings, but this can be a difficult line of inquiry since many advocacy initiatives do not lend themselves to random sampling and the identification of a control or even a viable comparison group.

The issue of validity is part of a larger debate and whether or not the Campbellian concept of validity, which was developed for research on teaching and learning, is appropriate for use in program evaluation in general (Chen, Donaldson, and Mark 2011). Is it reasonable or even responsible to push for a rigorous research design in a context where the possibilities for hypothesis testing are limited by the complexity of the situation and difficulties in distinguishing the effects of the intervention from other factors, such as multiple advocacy allies working together to lobby passage of a specific bill? Or, as is the case in many evaluation contexts, there may be budget, time, and data constraints that compromise the quality of an experimental approach and possibly lead to wrong conclusions (Bamberger, Rugh, Church, and Fort 2004). However, if an objective, quantitative approach can be used to discern the effectiveness of a range of advocacy tactics and inform advocate and/or funder strategy, then it should be considered.

We are also venturing into the ongoing debate between the two paradigms that frame social inquiry or logical positivism (one reality, deductive logic, and hypothesis testing) versus constructivism (multiple realities, inductive logic, and the lived experience), preferring the pragmatic vantage point or the appropriate use of both methods of inquiry as determined by the evaluation questions (Christie and Fleischer 2015). APC evaluations tend to tilt toward the latter, emphasizing the importance of the advocate perspective and acknowledging the role of context and many competing realities. Since APC initiatives may include issues of power, control, and social justice, evaluators have a greater obligation to consider the subjective perspective of the stakeholders and explore the synergies in developing a robust methodology (Mertens and Hesse-Biber 2013). Evaluation practice may be a combination of the two paradigms, and evaluators are using a hybrid or pragmatic approach to their designs. Upwards of 24 percent of the respondents of the 2014 Aspen/UCSF APC Evaluation Survey said they used *quasi-experimental designs*.

Happily, there are an increasing number of options for addressing many of these challenges that can result in credible, useful findings. At the design level, adopting a mixed-method approach and triangulating qualitative and quantitative data collection activities will greatly strengthen evaluation findings. For example, combining performance monitoring and real-time evaluation and Rapid Assessment Process (RAP) approaches can inform stakeholders on what works and what does not, as well as provide thick descriptions of advocacy tactics and causal processes and outcomes (Coffman 2014).

The evaluation field has laid out many options for triangulating quantitative and qualitative components, arguing for putting them on equal footing. Evaluator Sharlene Hesse-Biber (2013) recommends that evaluators develop their expertise in weaving both design approaches throughout the course of the evaluation, increasing design credibility and transparency. Similarly, Bamberger et al. (2012) argue for not pitting qualitative and quantitative methodologies against each another and including them based on their strengths. For example, qualitative interview data can assist in the interpretation of quantitative findings, such as identifying the historical antecedents that explain a strong opposition to a particular policy.

Second, if your evaluation context includes a program theory of change and/or logic model, then you are well positioned to monitor progress and achievement of initiative outputs, outcomes, and impacts as well as test the validity of the links between the model components. It is also the means for explaining why program outcomes were or were not achieved and focusing the evaluation on key aspects of the initiative, strengthening the design and implementation of future initiatives (Bamberger et al. 2012). By the same token, in an uncertain and changing initiative, it is important to be flexible and have a nimble theory of change or logic model that can quickly adapt to emergent aspects of an advocacy and policy change initiative, including revisions to the logic model. In a multiyear evaluation, we suggest having an annual review of the evaluation plan by stakeholders to discuss the inclusion of new outcomes if the initiative has gone in a new direction and whether or not to pursue new areas of inquiry that are of high interest but not necessarily covered by the evaluation questions or logic model outcomes. It is also an opportune time to discuss what is not going well or is ineffective. For example, working with the media takes considerable expertise and time, and the pay-off may not be evident for some time or at all (Gardner, Geierstanger, McConnel, and Brindis 2010).

To be sure, an experimental design is not totally out of the question. It depends in large part on the nature of the initiative and whether or not it can be isolated from other influences. For example, an experimental design can be used to assess a targeted media campaign to increase public support for a referendum if there is a comparison group that was not exposed to the campaign. Organizations that receive funding to support a policy director can be compared to similar organizations that do not receive this support. However, advocacy initiatives that target the public more broadly, such as community mobilization, and public-will-building campaigns have diffuse effects, and it is difficult, if not impossible, to distinguish participants from nonparticipants.

Second, there are alternatives to random assignment and identifying a control group, such as constructing a comparison group or using a nonexistent advocacy group against which to compare real advocacy groups to rule out alternative explanation. Referred to as "Survey with Placebo" (SwP), this approach is being used with some success by APC evaluators, including insertion of a placebo advocate organization in a survey of policymaker perceptions of advocacy group influence on a state-level educational policy outcome. The placebo organization had a lower-than-average rating in influence than the actual advocate organizations (Whitehurst and Struit 2014). Another approach to constructing a comparison group is to use propensity score matching and the logistical regression analysis of a sufficiently large sample survey that targets the same geographical population and includes questions of interest to assess change that can be attributed to the initiative (Bamberger et al. 2012).

Moreover, there are a number of ways to increase the rigor of non-experimental designs that lack a control group, such as surveys targeted to just the intervention group. For example, a survey instrument that has high construct validity and measures what it purports to measure, and is completed by a large enough sample of informants to achieve adequate statistical power, may have more robust findings about impact than a poorly designed and executed survey that includes a control group. Other strategies to increase rigor include the following.

Longitudinal designs, such as pretest and posttest comparisons of initiative participants may be less rigorous than several observations over time or a comparison to a control group. Thus, if a robust sample size is achieved and it is combined with qualitative data collection, they may be adequate for answering evaluation questions on program implementation and perceived impacts.

Sampling, while problematic in advocacy initiatives that don't lend themselves to generalization and/or have a small number of participants, policies, or outcomes, affords APC evaluators an opportunity to increase the validity of the findings. Random sampling may not be feasible for many reasons, including cost, small size of the target population, and/or an emphasis on description versus analytical analyses. But it might be applicable in a large-scale media campaign or political event, such as a campaign debate, where a comparison group can be identified. This is an area that continues to evolve as evaluators develop approaches for working with small samples, such as stratified sample designs and cluster sampling. Nonrandom sampling, particularly purposive sampling and the selection of informants who can provide an in-depth understanding of the initiative will prove more informative than a potentially skewed random sample of a small population of informants. Identification of cases that speak to the range of scenarios under an initiative protects against overlooking outliers as well as providing a comprehensive understanding of the initiative (Yin 2014; Bamberger et al. 2012). Similarly, capturing and describing unanticipated results are particularly appropriate since many advocacy and policy change contexts are characterized by uncertainty. Sampling techniques can be applied to other sources of data, such as grantee progress reports, providing evaluators and stakeholders with many options for surfacing useful and valid information.

Collecting baseline data on the political culture, policy landscape, and targets of an APC initiative at the beginning of an advocacy initiative in the form of a Monitoring, Evaluation, and Learning (MEL) system is strongly encouraged. However, resource constraints and the dynamic nature of an initiative may result in overlooking issues that turn out to be of high importance later on. Shifting time frames, strategies, and milestones may render an initial MEL approach obsolete (Laney 2003). However, techniques for reconstructing baseline data using secondary data on so-

cioeconomic factors, commissioned policy analyses, retrospective interviews and surveys of advocates and decision-makers, media coverage
of issues and events, and Geographic Information Systems (GIS) data,
can be used to recreate the conditions at the beginning of an initiative
against which to compare while addressing gaps in data collection activities (Bamberger et al. 2012).

Last, do not underestimate the quality and usefulness of *secondary
data*—policy analyses conducted during the policy formulation stage,
legislative tracking systems and policymaker voting records, project data,
historical data on economic conditions, demographic data on the cultural
context, and media coverage. This information may serve as indicators
as well as reduce the need to collect some types of primary data. It can
be used to reconstruct baseline data when an evaluation starts late in a
project. Last, it can be used in a contribution analysis as part of the proof
that an advocacy tactic contributed to desired change, such as a media
campaign targeted to policymakers who subsequently change their position on a specific policy.

Regardless of type of design and the strategy used to increase rigor, it
is important to identify and consider rival explanations in any evaluation
design. For example, are there other advocates that are not supported by
the initiative but that are instrumental in achieving the program outcomes? To what extent are contextual factors, such as a sudden economic
downturn, responsible for the outcomes of a campaign? On one level,
discussing rival explanations with stakeholders increases the transparency
of the design and its limitations, building evaluation capacity and buy-in.
It also expands the boundaries of the evaluation and consideration of
evaluation questions and methods that might otherwise not be included.

These design and methodological challenges are not unique to APC
evaluation, and considerable thought has been given to addressing these
challenges in other complex, fast-moving evaluation arenas. Michael
Bamberger and his colleagues Jim Rugh and Linda Mabry (2012) developed the seven-step *RealWorld Evaluation* framework to address budget,
time, data constraints, and political influences that challenge evaluations
in developing countries. They describe a number of hard-to-evaluate situations that have parallels with democracy-building initiatives, such as

the impact of a microcredit program on women's empowerment in rural areas. Their seven-step framework stresses clarifying stakeholder use of results, while providing practical strategies for addressing constraints. Of particular importance to APC evaluation are suggestions for reconstructing baseline data, such as focus groups, project records, and secondary data. Bamberger et al. also provide concrete suggestions for understanding and incorporating the political factors, such as key actors and their perspectives, and developing approaches for addressing the political issues that may arise during the course of the evaluation. Last, they provide a variety of design and statistical approaches to increase validity as well as reduce costs and increase efficiencies in data collection.

In sum, the low use of *experimental* and *quasi-experimental* designs by Aspen/UCSF Survey respondents does not necessarily mean that a methodologically rigorous design is not standard APC evaluation practice: there are multiple options for increasing the rigor of your design and instruments and producing validated findings. Moreover, stakeholders are not always seeking "gold standard" evidence of program effectiveness. They are hoping to document concrete evidence to help guide advocacy strategy, confirm funder contribution, and inform funder strategic planning for future endeavors. APC evaluators have many options for addressing these information needs and producing credible and useful findings. However, they need to be knowledgeable about advocacy initiatives and which type or which aspects of an initiative lend themselves to an experimental design, determining the appropriateness of the method to the evaluation question. Additionally, they need to effectively communicate the threats to validity of all aspects of the evaluation.

Timing of the Evaluation

The timing of an APC evaluation makes a huge difference to the technical quality of the design and usefulness of the findings. While conducting a midpoint prospective or retrospective program evaluation is standard practice for programs that have relatively straightforward sequence of inputs, activities, outputs, and outcomes, it can greatly undermine the utility of an evaluation in the situation of a fast-paced APC initiative. If possible, try to launch the evaluation before the kick-off of an advocacy initiative and set up a reporting system that reports findings in real time. Rapid Evaluation (RE) methods, such as Participatory Action Research (PAR), Rapid Assessment Process (RAP), and Rapid Assessment, Research, and Evaluation (RARE), which are effective in developing countries and where resources and time are limited, are highly applicable in this quickly evolving context. Using a team-based, fieldwork strategy, these approaches can be used to answer developmental, formative, and summative evaluation questions, providing an insider's perspective and identifying emerging or unexpected problems (I-TECH 2008).

The second reason for getting in on the ground floor is to be able to apply evaluation findings to advocacy practice throughout the initiative or campaign. Monitoring ensures ongoing alignment of funder goals and advocacy strategy while providing guidance on strategy. One evaluation scenario is combining a prospective approach that documents benchmarks and measures the progress of a project at the beginning of an advocacy effort, with a retrospective evaluation that focuses on outcomes (Guthrie, Louie, David, and Foster 2005). The learning here could be significant, including an understanding of what worked and what did not. Plus, you have a tactical advantage in that collecting information from political actors and advocates will be easier since you will have developed a relationship with them.

Another challenge is not having a long enough evaluation time frame and the opportunity to examine longer-term impacts of an initiative. However, it is not always clear when an initiative actually comes to an end. The optimal end-point may be when sustainability has been achieved and grantees are able to maintain advocacy tactics and partnerships after an initiative is over (Carden 2004). Anticipating an uncertain project end-point and collecting data throughout the initiative will at least provide a solid foundation for a rigorous retrospective evaluation later on.

Evaluator as Advocate

APC evaluation practice by nature is not neutral or apolitical. It can take place in a charged, high-risk arena where the opposition can be fierce and the stakes can be high. The evaluator cannot consider him- or herself to be an entirely objective observer without any interest or stake in the initiative. While not tasked with influencing policy formulation, passage, and implementation, it is near impossible to separate APC evaluation from the politics and the interactions among political actors. There is consensus in the APC evaluation community that evaluation should inform grantee and advocate strategy and tactics, both in the planning and execution stages. However, this service orientation comes with significant responsibilities on the part of the evaluator to preserve the integrity of their work, as well as navigate these political waters with discretion and sensitivity to stakeholder needs. Evaluators need to adhere to high standards of evaluation practice, such as using a quality assurance process and keeping records that demonstrate that proper evaluation methods were used, while acknowledging their potential role as advocate even if it is very tangential. They also need to maximize evaluator responsiveness to the political actors and their context, including protecting confidentiality of certain information and providing a balanced, clearly written report (Mohan and Sullivan 2006). The AEA's *Guiding Principles for Evaluators*, particularly the need to pay special attention to rules of ethical behavior, are helpful here:

> Evaluators should abide by current professional ethics, standards, and regulations regarding risks, harms, and burdens that might befall those participating in the evaluation; regarding informed consent for participation in evaluation; and regarding informing participants and clients about the scope and limits of confidentiality. (AEA 2011)

We do not want to minimize the two other perennial challenges to APC evaluation practice: limited or no grantee evaluation capacity, and resource constraints. However, advocacy and policy change evaluation has evolved, providing new approaches to minimize or circumvent these challenges. For example, adoption of a theory of change approach to detailing an advocacy strategy is helping to reshape funder strategy and expectations. Organizational capacity assessment tools and developmental evaluation approaches provide the means for bolstering advocate evaluation capacity. These topics are discussed more fully in Chapter 6.

The APC evaluation field continues to wrestle with many of these challenges to developing a nimble, rigorous evaluation design that anticipates the unanticipated and meets the sometimes divergent needs of advocates and funders. There are solid strategies and resources to address many of these challenges, but for many evaluators it is the sharing of real-life strategies and models that is "grist for the mill." In the next section, we focus on evaluation practice and discuss the findings from the Aspen/ UCSF APC Evaluation Survey on evaluation design approaches used, followed by an examination and comparison of two evaluation cases, Let Girls Lead and the Initiative to Support Sustainable and Equitable Transportation.

EVALUATION PRACTICE: DESIGN APPROACHES
USED BY APC EVALUATORS

The findings from the Aspen/UCSF APC Evaluation Survey indicate that on average APC evaluators typically use four or more of the approaches in their APC evaluation practice, though not necessarily all at the same time. When we take a closer look at the evaluation approaches that are "used" more frequently by APC evaluators than others, we see that they use approaches that support ongoing learning at the advocate and sponsor levels, corroborating the observation that stakeholders want useful information and they want it often, or *performance monitoring* (64 percent), *participatory evaluation* (62 percent), and *process tracking* (55 percent). As described in Table 3.1, evaluation approaches that work in complex, fast-moving, and fluid environments are used frequently, such as *systems thinking* (61 percent), *developmental evaluation* (61 percent), and *real-time evaluation and rapid assessment approaches* (46 percent).

The midlevel ranking of *contribution analysis* (37 percent) suggests that evaluators are starting to take a hard look at causal relations and validating the program strategy and determining what works and what does not.

We can only speculate on the two lesser-used approaches or *appreciative inquiry* and *empowerment-based evaluation*, 29 percent and 22 percent, respectively. They are aligned with the ideals of policy and advocacy policy change initiatives, but they seem to have had limited traction so far. The low or no use of *general elimination method* may reflect the lack of expertise in using this approach or limited opportunities for using it.

We feel the results are fairly representative of the state of current APC evaluation practice. APC evaluators are early adopters, using approaches that address the challenges of complexity, such as a systems-thinking perspective. Working with stakeholders is a high priority, ranging from developing working partnerships to empowering stakeholders to play a partner role in the evaluation. Last, the differences in approaches used by survey respondents may speak to approaches that may be less applicable to APC evaluation and/or possible areas of growth. Notwithstanding this ambiguous finding, we can say with some confidence that APC evaluators have sound options from which to choose and they are using them. Through comparison of two similar evaluation designs, we explore how these survey findings play out in evaluation practice and whether or not there is good alignment in what evaluators say they do and what they actually do.

EVALUATION PRACTICE:
TWO EVALUATION CASES

While not a recipe for a successful evaluation design, it is helpful to see how evaluators of advocacy and policy change initiatives mix and match different design components, partner with stakeholders, and address limitations in resources and time. For this chapter, we compare the evaluation designs of two very different advocacy and policy change initiatives: the evaluation of the Let Girls Lead program, a capacity-building program for adult leaders advocating for adolescent girls' rights in Liberia, Guatemala, Honduras, and Malawi; and the evaluation of the Initiative to Support Sustainable and Equitable Transportation (hereafter referred to as the Transportation Initiative). Both initiatives aim to strengthen civil society capacity but use a different mechanism of change: the Let Girls Lead model built a global network of advocates who receive training to advocate for specific policy wins at the national or local level; the Transportation Initiative targeted the federal Surface Transportation Reauthorization Bill while supporting state-level policy work and creating a ripple effect and advancing the dialogue on transportation in the United States.

Conducted in 2013, toward the end of the first five years of the Let

Table 3.1. Most Frequently Used Evaluation Approaches by Aspen/ UCSF APC Survey Respondents

*Evaluation Approaches (*not mutually exclusive)*	*Percent of Respondents that said they used the approach*
Performance monitoring – Tracking an advocacy effort's performance on its outputs and outcomes, including identifying benchmarks or indicators of progress and tracking these at regular intervals.	64%
Participatory evaluation – Partnering with multiple stakeholders— such as advocates, service providers and service end users—in developing the evaluation (such as objectives and design) and in all phases of its implementation.	62%
Systems thinking – Using elements of systems theory to evaluate how an advocacy initiative intervenes in a social system. A system is defined as a configuration of interacting, interdependent parts that are connected through a web of relationships, forming a whole that is greater than the sum of its parts.	61%
Developmental evaluation – Coined by Michael Quinn Patton, this approach features long-term partner-like relationships between evaluators and those implementing the strategies under evaluation, including the frequent use of feedback loops for the continuous development of the advocacy initiative.	61%
Process tracking – Tracing the causal process and examining the role of interim outcomes and intervening variables in the causal sequence.	55%
Real-time evaluation and rapid assessment – Systematically collecting data, typically using mixed-methods, as an advocacy effort intensifies. This data is usually relayed back to advocates for adjustments to advocacy strategy and tactics.	46%
Contribution analysis – Determining whether or not a credible case can be made that an advocacy effort contributed to its policy-related outcomes or impacts.	37%

Table 3.1. Most Frequently Used Evaluation Approaches by Aspen/UCSF APC Survey Respondents (continued)

*Evaluation Approaches (*not mutually exclusive)*	*Percent of Respondents that said they used the approach*
Appreciative inquiry – A process that delves into, identifies and further develops the best of what is in an organization in order to create a better future, which typically includes a collective design with relevant stakeholders of what a desired future state looks like.	29%
Empowerment-based evaluation – Using evaluation concepts, techniques and findings to foster improvement and self-determination among key target audiences, which may take the form of increasing their capacity to plan, implement and evaluate their own advocacy.	22%
General elimination method – Gathering evidence to eliminate alternative or rival explanations for effects until the most compelling explanation remains, which may or may not be tied to the advocacy initiative under evaluation.	0%

Source: Aspen Planning and Evaluation Program, The Aspen Institute.

Girls Lead initiative, the external evaluation team was tasked with assessing the program's effectiveness, capturing part of the Let Girls Lead story, and providing guidance to other groups. Evaluators developed a four-country, mixed-methods evaluation with four summative evaluation questions: (1) What evidence is there to demonstrate Let Girls Lead's contribution to key advocacy and policy results aimed at improving adolescent girls' health, education, livelihoods, and human rights? (2) What differences have Let Girls Lead made in the lives of adolescent girls who have been involved in the initiative? (3) What evidence is there to demonstrate Let Girls Lead's contribution to advocacy capacity building for Fellows, their organizations, and the Let Girls Lead supported networks? and (4) Has the Let Girls Lead model catalyzed advocacy efforts and policy change? If so, how has this been achieved?

The evaluation of the Transportation Initiative had three aims: (1)

learning and improvement throughout the life of the initiative to support achievement of initiative outcomes; (2) accountability for funds invested in the initiative; and (3) contribution to knowledge in transportation policy, advocacy, and philanthropy and the field of evaluation as a public good. The evaluation was conducted between 2011 and 2013 and was implemented in two phases. The first phase included a retrospective summative evaluation of the federal policy reform initiative. For the second phase, evaluators conducted a formative evaluation design for the state-level work since it was more in its infancy, including a monitoring component to inform foundation strategy decisions.

The two cases illustrate many of the evaluation design principles and challenges discussed above, particularly the need to be pragmatic and tap into conventional evaluation principles and approaches. Evaluation teams in both contexts took measures to understand and be sensitive to the advocacy and policy change context. The Let Girls Lead evaluators worked with national evaluators who had greater familiarity with the context, language facility, and better access to policymakers, as well as ability to travel to remote places to interview village leaders, adolescent girls, and other stakeholders. National evaluators focused on documenting evidence of Let Girls Lead's contribution to advocacy and policy results, as well as its contribution to capacity building for Fellows and their organizations and networks. The evaluators of the Transportation Initiative partnered with a transportation expert and organized an evaluation reference group to provide assistance with federal transportation policy. Last, evaluators in both contexts worked with the funders to vet the evaluation design and inform client strategy going forward, providing recommendations to increase program success as well as fine-tuning aspects of the programs to improve their effectiveness.

At the design level, both evaluation teams included a theory of change and evaluators developed a logic model linked to the evaluation questions, though the evaluators of the Transportation Initiative included activities to examine the causal relationships. Evaluators of the Transportation Initiative also developed individual logic models for each state-level grant, aggregating the strategies and outcomes to ascertain how the state component was going to achieve its outcomes.

There are some similarities in the methods used. Both evaluation designs used interviews and a survey instrument, though they were used for different aims. The Transportation Initiative interview instrument focused on perceptions of the role of the grant, achievement of outcomes, capacity, and benefits. Evaluators surveyed grantees and collected quantitative data about progress, coalition and organization capacity, and perceived future needs. The Let Girls Lead evaluation team surveyed Let Girls Lead Fellows on their perceptions of the contribution and effectiveness of the program in achieving a policy change, facilitating factors, and challenges. They also interviewed key stakeholders, including Fellows, staff, trainers, and representatives of the UN Foundation, on perceived benefits and effectiveness of specific program activities. The two evaluation teams included a document review, including program documentation though for different purposes. The Let Girls Lead evaluators included a document review in its contribution analysis and verification of the program's contributions to one or two advocacy and policy results per country. The evaluators of the Transportation Initiative reviewed and coded internal program documentation and reviewed secondary data, such as media coverage and bill language and status, to validate findings and claims of impact.

The two evaluation cases also speak to evaluator flexibility and willingness to mix and match conventional approaches while including emerging approaches. The Let Girls Lead evaluation team used contribution analysis, specifically interviews, a document review, and the Most Significant Change (MSC) technique to assess the role of the program in achieving key advocacy and policy results aimed at improving adolescent girls' health, education, livelihoods, and human rights and advocacy capacity building for Fellows. The evaluators of the Transportation Initiative used an appreciative inquiry approach, relying on perceptions of most significant changes to evaluate the communications grants, which had less defined outcomes than the other two components.

The two evaluations wrestled with similar challenges or launching the evaluation late in the initiative and having a short time frame during which to carry out multiple data collection activities. The Let Girls Lead evaluation was conducted in year five of the program and took six months to plan, collect data, and develop a draft report. The two phases of the Transportation Initiative each took about six months, with some overlap in the federal, state, and local components. While evaluators of both initiatives collected data on a range of formative and summative evaluation questions, both wrestled with the limits of a point-in-time model, such as conducting the evaluation in an unpredictable political environment. For example, the reauthorization of the federal Surface Transportation Bill did not occur by the time the federal evaluation component was conducted.

There were also challenges to validity in both contexts. The complexity and scope of the transportation policy arena and the issue itself precluded comprehensive data collection, as well as access to policymakers. The Let Girls Lead evaluation team had to contend with limitations in data with which to triangulate the findings, as well as language differences that limited the distribution of the findings more widely, though it increased the team's access to stakeholders. Despite these limitations, the learning from these two evaluations were broader than just program effectiveness, including documenting the contribution of the Let Girls Lead initiative and model to specific policy outcomes and assessment of the role of the federal reform component of the Transportation Initiative and its relation to state-level portfolio of advocacy capacity and policy change grants. (Please see Appendix A for descriptions of the two evaluation cases.)

In sum, these are two very different advocacy and policy change initiatives, but their evaluations had similarities in their designs, methods, and an emphasis on client learning. The evaluations shared similar limitations, namely, challenges to validity and time constraints. While these initiatives and their evaluations do not account for the range of scenarios that an evaluator may encounter, they reflect in large part the findings on approaches used by a majority of Aspen/UCSF Survey respondents in Table 3.1 above, including use of a participatory evaluation design that focuses on performance and funder and program contribution. However, there were some fundamental differences in the two initiatives, precluding a one-size-fits-all approach to evaluation design. Evaluators mixed and matched a similar slate of evaluation approaches and methods to suit their particular contexts, which is more than the norm.

CONCLUSION

The foundation has been laid whereby there are many established and some emerging approaches to evaluation design that can be combined in a variety of ways. While traditional evaluation design principles and strategies will address many of the challenges posed by APC initiatives, we suggest being open to adapting new and possibly untested approaches and frameworks. For the most part, APC designs are nonexperimental or quasi-experimental, and they rely on triangulation and use of conventional and emerging approaches, particularly performance monitoring and use of contribution analysis to validate findings. Balancing rigor and reflection is difficult under any situation and your evaluation partnership model will determine in large part on how this tension is resolved. In most cases, the evaluation design hinges on stakeholder information needs and the ability to adjust the evaluation to a changing environment. As illustrated by our two evaluation cases, advocacy and policy change evaluation design has come a long way from focusing primarily on short-term, process outcomes, to incorporating different approaches to determining program effectiveness and program contribution to specific policy gains.

In Chapter 4, we examine the details of the evaluation design and review the many methods, outcomes, and measures that are being used by APC evaluators with good success.

OUTCOMES AND METHODS IN ADVOCACY
AND POLICY CHANGE EVALUATION

INTRODUCTION

Guided by the Aspen/UCSF 2014 APC Evaluation Survey findings on methods most frequently used by advocacy and policy change (APC) evaluators and the methods used in the six evaluation cases, we review a plethora of evaluation methods, outcomes, and measures that are being used by APC evaluators under a variety of situations. Useful conventional and emerging evaluation methods are emphasized, such as case studies, as well as unique methods and tools that have been specifically developed for evaluating advocacy and policy change initiatives and that are being used by the field. Many of these instruments and measures have been organized into user-friendly toolkits, which have been widely distributed and are available to advocates, evaluators, and funders. (Please see Appendix B for a list of these tools and toolkits.)

Since the selection of methods many times stems from a theory of change or logic model, we discuss the pros and cons of developing and working with a program theory of change and/or logic model. Although it is sometimes a contentious issue, there are advantages to developing a shared understanding of how an initiative works and/or using a sequential set of outcomes to guide the evaluation design in the context of an advocacy and policy change initiative. We also discuss strategies to address the limitations of a theory of change/logic model approach, such as the nonlinearity of an APC initiative.

Since identifying measures to monitor progress and assess program effectiveness are inherent in the discussion of methods, we provide a quick overview for selecting or developing meaningful and appropriate measures. APC evaluators have identified a robust body of measures (also referred to as indicators) targeted to specific outcomes. The challenge is to choose the ones that are feasible, correspond to the outcomes targeted by an initiative, and are informative to stakeholders.

To organize these methods, instruments, and measures, we use a logic model framework, starting with inputs or required resources, followed by outputs and outcomes that result from these inputs, and finishing with evaluating the impacts of an advocacy and policy change initiative on systems, individual lives, social norms, and expanding democratic space.

Last, we describe the Aspen/UCSF survey findings on methods used and not used, and we continue our examination of APC evaluation practice, comparing the design and methods of two advocacy and policy change evaluations: the *International Land Conservation Campaign* and the *Oxfam GROW Campaign*. Both evaluations focus on land-use issues, specifically forest conservation and agricultural land use, and both have an international focus. In particular, we are interested in the methods used by evaluators in a midpoint evaluation design when initiative outcomes are still being pursued and strategic learning is a high priority.

DEVELOPING A PROGRAM THEORY OF CHANGE
AND/OR LOGIC MODEL

Currently, there is good consensus among APC evaluators on developing and using a program theory of change, and/or logic model as part of an advocacy and policy change evaluation design. For example, a majority of the Aspen/UCSF APC Evaluation Survey respondents indicated they had used *theories of change* (98 percent) and *logic models or logframes* (96 percent) in their APC evaluation practice and considered them highly useful. Proponents argue that a program theory about how an advocacy and policy initiative achieves its results is essential to developing a design with appropriate outcomes and indicators. There are others who say that advocacy initiatives and the policy change process are too unpredictable to lend themselves to one fixed explanation about how a program works as well as a sequential ordering of inputs, activities, and outcomes. Fast-moving advocacy initiatives that are developmental in nature and continue to evolve may never reach a steady state during the period of assessment, such as a coalition strategy to support federal policy reform that never materializes. This may be true, and forcing an outcomes chain that has little or no basis in reality or grossly understates the complexity of an initiative is not advised. However, the logic of the "logic model" may help to elucidate the types of resources being tapped and at least some of the strategies being developed to reach desired outcomes.

The question for APC evaluators is whether focusing on causal mechanisms or the linkages between inputs, activities, outputs, and outcomes is feasible and/or desirable. Is a theory of change important to determining the effectiveness of a program? Are the conditions conducive to developing a theory of change? If the answer to both of these questions is "yes," then there are many resources that can be used to help you along your path. The policy change theories described in Chapter 2 should be revisited. They provide an informed starting point on which to build a theory of change. Some digging into the political science and public policy research literature will help provide guidance into the types of evidence that can be used to demonstrate the hypothesized causal linkages. Additionally, the *Advocacy Strategy Framework*, developed by Julia Coffman, is a helpful first step in developing a theory of change. As described in more detail in Chapter 5 on unique methods, the framework maps specific advocacy tactics according to their desired changes and target audiences (Coffman and Beer 2015).

The evaluation field has also made significant advances in developing theory-based evaluation approaches, such as realist evaluation and the collection of information on the relationships among context, mechanism, and outcomes. Tools like process mapping and development of workflow diagrams that provide detailed information on the "who, what, when, how, and where" of the inputs, outputs, and outcomes can be used to develop visual representation of these elements. Additionally, there are methods to strengthen the causal analysis, such as network theory and developing a diagram depicting the relationships among people, organizations, and coalitions. Systems dynamics and causal-loop diagrams provide a more nuanced understanding of a complex initiative's components and their relationships, offering more flexibility than a linear, sequential rendering of outcomes (Funnel and Rogers 2011).

It is important to anticipate a range of conditions under which a theory of change may be developed. Many funders are proactive in developing their own theory of change, what evaluators Huey Chen and Nanette Turner (2012) and others call a "stakeholder theory" based on observations and experience that can be used to develop an evaluation logic model. However, we advise caution here since the evidence to support the stakeholder theory may be weaker and be based primarily on perceptions. Still, it can serve as a good stepping-stone since it reflects funder familiarity with the program and its antecedents. Alternatively, there may be limited interest or resources to construct a model of the initiative, and evaluators will have to consider developing their own theory of change and/or logic model for identifying methods and sources of data, as well as getting better acquainted with the initiative and its political context.

Five of the six evaluation cases illustrate the multiple ways that a theory of change can be incorporated into an APC evaluation. For example, as we described in Chapter 3, the evaluations of the Let Girls Lead program and The Initiative to Support Sustainable and Equitable Transportation included a theory of change and evaluators developed a logic model, which was linked to the evaluation questions. The evaluators of the Transportation Initiative included activities to examine the causal relationships, while the evaluators of Let Girls Lead did not. Evaluators of the Transportation Initiative also developed individual logic models for each state-level grant, aggregating the strategies and outcomes to ascertain how the overall state component was going to achieve its desired outcomes. Only the International Land Conservation Program did not include a theory of change and/or logic model because of the fluid, quick-moving nature of the initiatives. Whether it is a top-level theory of change that plays a guiding or behind-the-scenes role or a tested theory of change with tightly connected outcomes and indicators, evaluators need to determine the appropriate role and integration of a theory of change given their circumstances. (Please see Appendix A for a description of the use of a theory of change and/or logic model in the five evaluation designs.)

If developing a theory of change is not a priority or is not feasible, we recommend developing a flexible logic model or outcomes chain to focus the evaluation design on what is under the control of the initiative. While the distinction between a theory of change and a logic model can be a little murky, Michael Quinn Patton (2012, 235) provides a simple rule of thumb: "Specifying the causal mechanism transforms a logic model into a theory of change." There are many good resources for developing and working with logic models within the advocacy and policy change evaluation arena, as well as in the evaluation field more broadly, including the Aspen Institute's *Advocacy Progress Planner* and the Harvard Family Research Project's *Advocacy and Policy Change Composite Logic Model,* which were developed to support advocates in developing their own logic models and in the planning, execution, monitoring, and evaluation of their advocacy initiatives. By "flexible," we mean the evaluator should revisit the logic model regularly and adjust the outcomes to reflect changes in the campaign. If there is no logic model, the evaluation questions will drive the selection of outcomes and/or methods.

INPUTS, OUTPUTS, OUTCOMES, METHODS, AND MEASURES

A key aim of this chapter is to lay out the many outcomes and methods that evaluators can include in their evaluation design to systematically assess progress and/or initiative accomplishments (or lack thereof). Before turning to our review of the many inputs, outcomes, and impacts, we discuss the selection of measures and instruments and the challenges posed by APC initiatives, as well as some of the creative ways that APC evaluators have circumvented these challenges.

Meaningful Measures

APC evaluation questions and outcomes also determine in large part the selection of measures (sometimes referred to as "indicators") or ways to determine in precise terms initiative progress and achievement of initiative outcomes. The trick is to pick indicators that are feasible and meaningful. Marc Holley, Cheri Recchia, and Valarie Bocksette (2016) identify five grant performance measurement traps that can be used as guidelines for selecting measures or: (1) the "micromanagement trap" or over measuring; (2) the "hedge trap" and use of readily achievable measures that overstate grantee success; (3) the "at-least-it's measurable trap" and not using measures that are more tightly aligned with the outcomes, but are more difficult to implement; (4) the "full-control trap," or not using measures that relate to larger and more difficult to control outcomes; and (5) the "complexity-cannot-be-measured-objectively trap," which is what it sounds like, or avoiding measurement in complex situations just because of the complexity. Additionally, just because you can measure something does not mean you should measure it although what is meaningful to one stakeholder may not be meaningful to another.

We suggest using the following criteria for identifying meaningful and appropriate measures: validity and the degree to which the measure corresponds to the phenomenon in question; feasibility and available resources, such as time, grantee and evaluator capacity and/or funding; and utility and the extent to which the measure is informative and to whom.

Some advocacy and policy change outcomes are more measure-rich than others and can be easily measured, such as votes, signatures, and participants. Advocacy tactics may have more than one measure per tactic. For example, to document policymaker education activities, one can look at the number of meetings or briefings held with decision-makers, as well as both the number and type of policymakers reached. Many of these measures can be tracked by advocates themselves, including media, coalition building and grassroots organizing, voter education, research and education, targeting decision-makers and the public, litigation, and lobbying.

Notwithstanding the many measures available to evaluators, there are still some hurdles that are unique to APC initiatives in identifying and working with measures. Some aspects of APC initiatives don't readily lend themselves to measurement, such as "influence," and are better if they are described. Or, something may be measurable, but the numbers may not demonstrate that a desired change has occurred due to the intervention, such as the development of policy briefs that can be tracked, but is only one of many tactics used in a campaign. There is also the issue of resources and having the capacity at the grantee and/or evaluator level to collect this information. Process measures, such as the number of published letters to the editor are easy to collect, even retrospectively; however, conducting a content analysis of the letters may be less feasible. Last, some measures require significant evaluation expertise and resources, particularly measures of system-level impact, such as changes in civil society.

APC evaluators have developed some practical and sound approaches to overcoming many of these hurdles. Because an advocacy campaign can change course or aspire for outcomes that are beyond the time-frame of an evaluation, the APC evaluation community has focused on process or interim outcome measures and the identification of benchmark indicators at specific points in time that are part way toward the goal. They provide immediate feedback on progress and introduce an element of flexibility into the execution of an initiative (Stachowiak, Reisman, and Boardman 2013). Also, one measure does not necessarily take into account the multiple facets of a program, and experienced APC evaluators suggest considering a range of measures to determine whether or not an advocacy tactic or campaign has been successful, such as using qualitative approaches to describe advocacy tactics or actions. Multiple measures safeguard against overlooking an important program effect, as well as corroborate or strengthen the findings from other measures. For example, a policymaker rating survey can be combined with other forms of data collection to provide information about broader contextual factors. Using a mixed-methods approach provides the opportunity to ascertain whether or not there are consistencies in findings across different data collection approaches, as well as providing further contextual information for the quantitative data gathered. Last, the correspondence of an indicator to the advocacy strategy or tactic may be weak, and an indicator, like number of attendees at a policy forum, may only be a proxy for achievement, hence the suggestion to have more indicators than less. For example, collecting longitudinal data on program progress and using methods to identify and eliminate alternative explanations can strengthen evaluators' claims that the results are truly the result of a set of strategies that were incorporated by advocates (Henry et al. 2013; Rog 2012).

To select meaningful measures, we recommend using a participatory approach and working with stakeholders during the design stage to identify measures, as well as to explain the technical aspects of individual measures, such as their correspondence to the outcomes and how they work alone and in tandem to demonstrate program progress or effectiveness. This will manage stakeholder expectations and reduce the possibility of measure "shock" later on if the results are contrary to what was expected, as well as increase buy-in and use of the findings to strengthen the program.

Selecting Instruments

During the methods selection process, evaluators should also make transparent and communicate the strengths and limitations of using a particular data collection tool, such as face validity and whether or not an instrument actually measures what it is supposed to measure. For example, if you develop an interview guide de novo, be sure to pilot it with stakeholders to increase the fit with the context, such as using the name of an advocacy tactic that is used in a particular context, or even the name that advocates call themselves, who sometimes refer to themselves as "activists." Second, there should be a discussion on how instruments can work together to strengthen validity of the findings. While quotes and anecdotal accounts may win the day in some contexts, such as with policymakers who may be persuaded by the personal accounts of individual constituents, the evaluator should explain the benefits of pairing this type of information with other qualitative and/or quantitative data. This increases the likelihood that there will be buy-in and understanding of the findings. It is also an opportunity to play a technical assistance role and increase stakeholder knowledge of the many evaluation instruments—interview questionnaires, focus groups, surveys, observations, content analysis, grantee reports, budgets, case studies, tracking forms, and mapping tools—that can be used in an APC evaluation.

In the next sections on inputs, outputs, outcomes, and impacts, we refer to specific methods, providing examples of their role and under what circumstances they are applicable. In Table 4.1, we pair these inputs/outputs/outcomes/incomes/methods to measures of progress and achievement of outcomes. While there are many good options, the challenge is to identify meaningful methods and measures that produce information that is informative, provide further insights, including unanticipated consequences, and has utility for the next phases of the effort, for example, future campaigns.

Characterizing Inputs: Advocacy Capacity, Context, and Resources
In the 2000s, foundations worldwide realized building advocacy capacity was a necessary first step to achieving longer-term policy change objectives. It was regarded as an important short-term outcome, and foundations were committed to understanding their portfolios of advocacy investments. While not always tied to policy, advocacy capacity development has proven to be a well-defined area to support, with clear organizational and individual strengths that could be cultivated. The information gathered is equally useful to funders and advocates, and it can be used to identify priority areas for capacity building as well as helping organizations leverage the skills they do have to effectively engage in advocacy work. Consequently, substantial support was directed to organizations unaccustomed to doing advocacy as a means to increase participation in the policy arena. Nonprofits, health and human service organizations, and educational institutions, many of which had no or limited capacity (such as dedicated staff, skills, and a mandate to advocacy) were asked to up their game. However, advocacy is not a simple task for newcomers. It requires relationships, a presence, a special skill set, and a strong familiarity with the policy arena. Moreover, gaining entry and successfully navigating a policy arena requires maintenance of effort and resources to ensure ongoing participation and having a seat at the table.

Investing in advocacy capacity has not been limited to first-time advocates; organizations well-versed in advocacy periodically need to retool in order to undertake new types of advocacy, or they may need to acquire additional capacity in order to carry out a new type of advocacy initiative, such as working with the media or incorporating social media. Keep in mind that advocacy capacity is an evolving skill set. Increasingly, research (also referred to as "education advocacy") is being conducted by advocates, and they are developing research and policy reports targeted to decision-makers, establishing themselves as credible voices in a policy arena (Boaz, Fitzpatrick, and Shaw 2008). Additionally, advocates are being encouraged to work in coalitions and to develop additional relationships with other advocacy partners. At times, partners may take turns leading a particular advocacy effort. Yet, together, they work in common purpose to advance a more just environment for issues that are deemed controversial, such as reproductive health.

At the evaluation design level, assessing advocacy capacity provides formative information about the resources and skills in areas important to supporting advocacy. It also looks at all levels of an organization, including leadership, staff, membership, and the board of directors. The information from interviews, focus groups, process data, and capacity assessment tools can be used to assess readiness to engage in effective advocacy and key areas for strengthening, and to check the alignment of funder and advocate goals with the available resources and skills. Document analysis can be used to establish a baseline against which to compare to see if an intervention was successful in addressing gaps in capacity (such as increased knowledge about advocacy, improved media skills, and dedicated advocacy resources). Last, if sustainability is important, there can be ongoing monitoring of organizational capacity, such as the ability to respond to changing conditions and opportunities as they arise.

There are many options in this area, including off-the-shelf tailored advocacy capacity assessment tools and capacity assessment tools that have been developed and validated through the course of an evaluation. These instruments overlap, so it is really a matter of choosing the instrument that corresponds to the purpose of the evaluation, as well as the cultural and organizational context. For example, do you need to assess capacity broadly defined or capacity in a specific area? Do you need an instrument that speaks to a specific policy arena? For the international arena, you may want to include a human rights perspective, such as the involvement of women and citizen empowerment. Strengthening organizational ability more broadly—nongovernmental organizations (NGOs), businesses, community groups—to strengthen civil society and create the conditions for greater citizen involvement in the policy arena is an important precursor to successful advocacy later on (Chapman and Wameyo 2001). (Please see Chapter 5 for more information on these tailored instruments.)

Additionally, spider diagrams can be used by organizations to visually compare and contrast advocacy competencies, as well as track advocacy work over time. Organizations can rate their level of competency and develop a web that characterizes its strengths and weaknesses in a range of areas, such as working with the media or evaluation (Riesman, Gienapp, and Stachowiak 2007).

While the self-administration of a capacity assessment tool can greatly boost organizational learning and strategy, there may not be a sufficiently large enough sample of respondents to generate robust findings in an evaluation context. It is important to get feedback from the advocacy organization, the funding organization, the board of directors and membership, as well as a sympathetic ally or partner organization as to whether or not the group has the necessary skills to mount an advocacy campaign. An external evaluator can play a key role in synthesizing information garnered from all stakeholders and offer insights regarding potential implications of the data for an organization's next steps. This external assessment may also enable respondents, assured of full confidentiality, to disclose even greater information than might be the case if they feel that their responses are being directly attributable to themselves.

Focusing on organizational advocacy capacity is only part of the picture. Evaluators will want to broaden their gaze to include other inputs, particularly the larger context and the opportunities it affords advocates as well as challenges. For example, advocates and evaluators can describe the initial features of an advocacy and policy change context using systems theory. There are a few ways to apply systems theory concepts to a complex APC evaluation context. System elements in an APC initiative can be identified and categorized, such as government institutions, levels of government, advocates, funders, individuals, or populations, bounding an APC initiative during the evaluation planning stage and creating a baseline. Second, there are different system archetypes that can help characterize the overall initiative. Systems can be unorganized and chaotic, they can be organized and be simple with linear relationships, or they can be organized and complex, such as systems within systems and indirect relationships among system components. Third, a variety of tools can be used to map and describe the relationships among components of an APC initiative, such as systems dynamics causal loop diagrams, which depict the interactions among program parts either as amplifying (reinforcing) or neutralizing (balancing), or can be used to identify high-leverage points of intervention, such as reversing a current state. There are a few systems mapping tools, but for the most part they aim to identify key system elements and show a relationship between these elements using connecting lines and arrows to indicate directionality, cause and effect, or a time-delay (Stroh 2009). Conventional methods, such as Rapid Evaluation (RE) approaches, which include interviews, focus groups, social mapping, and direct observation, can also be used to quickly characterize the initial conditions and establish a baseline against which future data can be compared (I-TECH 2008).

There is also the perennial interest in documenting the influence that political actors, organizations, and collection of organizations have, including: the level of influence or whether a tactic or advocate organization(s) achieves longer-term outcomes over which they have increasingly limited influence (ODI 2014); the pathways of influence or who is being influenced and how (Chapman and Wameyo 2001; ODI 2004); role of policy influencers (ODI 2004); and the sphere of influence and assessing the amount of sway that an advocate has over policymakers, other advocates, and the public. Advocate influence on political actors, stakeholders, and community entities can be characterized by the type of control an advocate has, such as no control, less control, or more control, and indirect control or direct control. There is also a host of power mapping software products that detail the universe of actors and their relationships to another and type of influence. However, the definition of "influence" varies by instrument and user, and it requires due diligence on the part of evaluators to be clear on the definition, whether the aim is to describe who is trying to influence whom or who has more influence.

Additionally, documenting the resources important to launching and/or sustaining an initiative, such as funding to support a dedicated policy director or staff training in framing media messages, will have bearing later on if financial analyses are undertaken or others want to learn about what were important ingredients contributing to success or failure.

A resource-rich area, there are many toolkits targeted to advocates that include easy-to-use approaches to characterizing the political context, networks, and power dynamics within and between groups. (Please see Appendix B for a listing of toolkits.)

Assessing Outputs: Performance and Implementation

The primary focus of APC evaluation at this stage is whether or not an organization successfully planned, developed, and executed a strategy, and the findings are enormously useful to advocates, funders, and evaluators. Adopting a Monitoring, Evaluation and Learning (MEL) approach and setting up a data collection system to monitor the implementation and results of an advocacy initiative on an ongoing basis allows the evaluator and the advocate to evaluate progress, determine what works and what does not and why, and demonstrate early results to stakeholders. Additionally, self-assessment questionnaires with scoring rubrics can be used to query advocates to rate how well they planned and implemented an activity.

A second area of examination is on the implementation of the advocacy activities themselves, be it a multifaceted campaign or a discrete tactic, like increased media coverage. As we describe in Table 4.1, there are many types of advocacy activities, for which there are many methods and measures, including: strengthened alliances and partnerships; influencing policymaker understanding and support, cultivating champion; public will building and engagement; engaging the media; and research and policy analysis. This is a very robust area of evaluation practice, and there are many approaches to monitoring and assessing implementation of activities prospectively and retrospectively, including grantee monitoring reports, interviews right after an event, document review, observations of an event, real-time data collection, such as Rapid Assessment Process (RAP), and focus groups. Another approach is to generate a visual representation of the initiative and the status of its components. In addition to assessing advocacy capacity, spider diagrams can be used to display changes in advocacy tactic effectiveness over time in a visual format. The logical framework, also referred to as a "logframe," is a planning tool that can be used by evaluators to determine how well an advocacy initiative has been implemented (Organizational Development Institute 2014). It is a table that describes the initiative goal, outputs, indicators of success, the means for monitoring whether or not the changes have taken place, and assumptions or conditions that are necessary for achieving the goal.

Additionally, there is an examination of the results of the strategy or the tactics with the intention of adjusting them to increase effectiveness, such as having the right skill set, and identifying facilitating factors and barriers. You can use conventional methods, such as a survey instrument or interview questionnaire, to provide basic information about execution and perceived effectiveness of a set of itemized advocacy tactics. The findings can be used to bound the evaluation and narrow the focus to just what is under the purview of the initiative. However, the "cover the waterfront" strategy has its limitations. First, it does not reflect the synergy between activities. Second, it is a shallow approach to understanding a set of tactics. Last, depending on how quickly an instrument can be administered and analyzed, there can be issues with informant recall and separating multiple tactics from one another.

In all likelihood, stakeholders and you will want to know more about key aspects of specific strategies and tactics (such as a media campaign, in-person meetings with decision-makers), including why a particular tactic was chosen and whether it was implemented on time, the target(s) of the activity, and whether it was perceived to be effective. There are a few options for examining specific tactics, including conventional approaches, such as interviews with media representatives and unique or tailored methods, such as policymaker rating surveys. You can also combine methods. To assess the execution of multiple media activities, we used a mixed-method approach that combined interviews with media representatives, advocacy perceptions of their media advocacy activities, as well as content analysis of newspaper clippings (Gardner, Geierstanger, Brindis, and McConnel 2010).

Qualitative data, such as structured observations, semistructured interviews, and progress reports, can provide useful insights about how and why a tactic was executed, the role played by an organization and partners, facilitating factors and challenges, and how a tactic might be implemented differently. Evaluators also can work with advocates to develop a tracking system (such as a media contacts tracking form that is easy to maintain) to provide information about the number of contacts, quality of their activities, as well as problems that emerged while carrying out these activities and how these were addressed. Descriptive grantee project reports are a useful means for collecting information about how a tactic was deployed, its status, and possible impact. Interviews and focus groups can be used to gather information about policymaker awareness of an advocate, such as an advocate's position on global warming, as well as to probe specific types of tactics and/or facilitating factors and challenges. Last, questions about tactics can be woven into story collection and journals that are completed by participants. All of these approaches are opportunities for evaluators to increase their understanding of a particular advocacy initiative and its context while documenting the initiative and stakeholder perceptions of changes, facilitating factors, and barriers.

Another aim at this stage is to document the tangible products generated by advocates—research briefs, policy forums, responses to requests for information, advocacy technical assistance materials, data collection systems, blog postings—that are used to educate the public and policymakers, as well as establishing advocate credibility. An emerging area that is gaining traction, and what is referred to as "education advocacy" or "policy research," resources developed by the Methods Lab and others are helpful in developing a design to assess the influence of these activities (Pasanen and Shaxson 2016).

Based on our experience in evaluating advocacy tactics, we have identified four challenges to evaluation in this area that evaluators need to be aware of. First, many tactics may be bundled together in a strategy, making it difficult to assess the effectiveness of any one tactic. It may be the combination of tactics that has the greatest impact. Second, using a real-time approach and informing advocacy practice may be stymied by the time it takes to collect this data, as well as the fast-moving nature of a campaign or policy process. Rapid Assessment Process (RAP) data collection can be done in a minimum of four days, but it requires a team for the data collection and analyses (I-TECH 2008). Third, success in executing a tactic may not translate into success in achieving a desired outcome, particularly if there are unexpected events. Finally, it can be difficult to provide evidence that a specific tactic or set of tactics results in a short-term outcome like changes in policymaker understanding of a policy issue. It is important not to conflate the successful execution of an advocacy tactic with the achievement of short-term or intermediate outcomes and undervalue the important gains made by an advocate. Despite these challenges, there is great value in clarifying and defining tactics and having a dialogue with advocates and funders about which funded activity is the intervention and how it will be included in an evaluation theory of change and/or logic model. Also, some of this information can be readily collected by advocates themselves and used in real time to inform strategy and funding, such as the extent to which activities were carried out as planned and identifying barriers that impeded implementation.

Evaluating Outcomes

The same issues that challenge development of a plausible logic model also stymie the identification and assessment of APC outcomes or initiative complexity, unpredictability, and uncertainty. These attributes also make it difficult to identify measures that are sensitive to change and/or measure what they are intended to measure. APC evaluators have prevailed and there are a few frameworks for identifying APC outcomes and corresponding methods and metrics. For example, Jim Coe and Juliette Majot (2013) of the Overseas Development Institute take an international perspective and identify three general categories: (1) internal outcomes that speak to changes in organizational advocacy capacity; (2) advocacy context outcomes such as changes in power relations; and (3) policy and practice changes, such as changes in the broader policy debate.

There is also the issue that outcomes may change over the course of the initiative, requiring nimbleness on the part of the evaluator and flexibility by the funder. Focusing on multiple outcomes using multiple methods—qualitative and quantitative, monitoring, and performance—ensures that evaluators do not overlook unforeseen changes, while simultaneously increasing funder and advocate ability to navigate these sometimes chaotic circumstances. Outcome Mapping (OM) can be used to monitor program progress in achieving outcomes. A retrospective contribution analysis can be used to document the trajectory of the initiative after the fact so that unanticipated outcomes are not overlooked, as well as documenting causal relationships that can be replicated elsewhere. Similarly, Outcome Harvesting is an emerging approach that is being used in the international arena to evaluate networks, nonprofits, and others, and can be used retrospectively to document the role played by the initiative in influencing a set of outcomes. Using verifiable data from multiple sources, outcomes are identified postinitiative with users, primarily funders, and outcome descriptions are developed that include information on "who changed what, when, and where" as well as the initiative's contribution (Wilson-Grau and Britt 2013).

Until recently, identifying measures or evidence of achievement for each outcome has been challenged by a lack of metrics, sources of data, as well as limited capacity to collect this information. Perhaps the bigger challenge has been gaining consensus with stakeholders about the type of evidence that will demonstrate achievement of program outcomes. One strategy to overcome these traditional barriers is to use a combination of quantitative and qualitative methods. For example, counting the number of policies passed does not describe what was achieved. A better strategy is to combine the number of policies passed with case studies that document the advocacy tactics, the policy change process, and the short- and longer-term impacts achieved.

We have organized conventional and unique evaluation methods by logic model outcomes that reflect the generic policy stage model described in Chapter 1, including the outcomes of advocacy activities that may not necessarily focus on policy change, such as strengthened alliances and partnerships and public will building and engagement. We have also organized these outcomes by when they are likely to occur during the policymaking process. There are some differences in where evaluators draw the line between short, intermediate, and long-term outcomes, although most evaluators characterize a policy change or passage of a law, particularly at the national and international levels, as a long-term outcome. We acknowledge that this linear, sequential ordering of outcomes may not be true for your situation and you may find that your outcomes branch out, are bidirectional, or include a feedback loop. For example, achieving passage of a bill may have a positive impact on organizational advocacy capacity, further reinforcing and building additional confidence among the advocates. We have opted to be as inclusive as possible in our list of outcomes, methods, and measures, drawing on the APC evaluation literature, frameworks, and evaluation designs.

Short-term, Interim Outcomes (0–2 years)

A unique feature of APC evaluation is the emphasis on short-term or interim outcomes. "Interim" has two meanings here. In evaluation parlance, these are process measures in a formative evaluation framework that are the immediate results of advocacy activities. They are indicators of progress and whether or not advocacy tactics are on track to achieve their desired goals. In the APC evaluation community, "interim" also refers to a temporary or a stopgap approach to evaluating longer-term outcomes that until recently were difficult to identify and assess. It is the point when the focus of the evaluation may shift from formative to summative evaluation and judging the effectiveness of an initiative that could be slow to fully "blossom" compared to other types of programs. Consequently, many APC evaluations have tended to focus more on strategic learning and gauging whether a strategy and/or its tactics are effective and then making recommendations for midcourse corrections.

APC evaluator Julia Coffman (2009) recommends focusing on a range of interim outcomes so as not to overlook areas where advocacy tactics have been successful (or unsuccessful). Drawing on evaluation design resources in this area, we have identified six categories of short-term, interim outcomes that are typical of advocacy initiatives and from which evaluators may want to select one or more outcomes: terms of the debate; strengthened partnerships, networks, and coalitions; influencing policymaker understanding and support; cultivating champions; public will building and engagement; and engaging the media. We have also identified evaluation approaches, measures, and tailored tools that have been used by the field in each of these areas.

Terms of the Debate

For many advocates the end goal is not a policy change, and an initiative may end well before policy proposals are formulated or occur well after a policy has been implemented, such as launching a public education campaign on the impact of economic disparities on the broader community. Aligned with the *Agenda Setting* stage in our policy stage model, changing the terms of the debate and influencing the discourse on an issue can be accomplished by working with the media to reframe an issue to increase saliency with the public and producing educational briefs and reports, increasing the visibility of an issue so it is higher up on the political agenda. These are potent, if not essential, advocacy tactics that lend themselves to assessment, including public opinion polls, media content analysis, document review, and interviews with influential policymakers and bellwethers.

Strengthened Partnerships, Networks, and Coalitions

Because relationships can be critical in determining the outcome of a policy change process, advocates, particularly new advocates, have received significant support to expand their networks and partnerships. There is no one partnership model and partnerships may change as the situation demands. Moreover, some partnerships take longer to cultivate than others, such as partnerships with decision-makers that require a certain degree of tenure and credibility. Regardless, collaboration across organizations or multiple sectors is a rich area of inquiry, fueled by funder interest in building or strengthening networks to undertake collective action, achieving outcomes that individual organizations could not achieve on their own (Network Impact and Center for Evaluation Innovation 2014). There are a few instruments and approaches to characterizing progress in creating new partnerships under a variety of circumstances.

Collaboration/Coalition/Network/Partnership Assessment Surveys. There are several approaches that focus on the capacity of an organization or network of organizations to form high-functioning partnerships. Examples include *The Amherst Wilder Collaboration Factors Inventory* that can be completed online. More recently, this has evolved into a discussion of network "health" and how to assess whether or not a network is achieving its objectives and how can networks be supported to achieve social change goals (ORS Impact 2010).

Social Network Analysis. This approach characterizes how close or tightknit the relationships are between individuals or organizations, as well as identifies which individuals or organizations are more tightly connected than others. One drawback is that it requires expertise in network software and mapping. Fortunately, other network evaluation methods are emerging, such as analyzing network documents, interviews, and focus groups with members to capture this information (Network Impact and Center Evaluation Innovation 2014).

Intensity of Collaboration Scales. These scales describe the level of collaboration on a scale ranging from "infrequent information sharing" to "joint funding and execution of projects among organizations." They can also be used to assess changes in particular partnerships over time.

Constituent Tracking. Spark Policy Institute has developed a *Constituent Tracking System* that includes a scale to assess advocate success in transforming their constituents into advocates going from "demonstrating interest" to "leading advocacy efforts" (Spark Policy Institute 2011).

Spider Diagrams. Spider diagrams are versatile and can be used to assess community support from various sectors, such as business, media, public agencies, and decision-makers. Stakeholders rate the level of support on a scale of 0 to 5 where 5 = "very high" support. Thus, a web that has equally high support among all sectors will be round. The web can be created pre- and postinitiative to assess change in support or other relationships among sectors, such as collaboration (Feinstein and O'Kane 2005).

There are discrete measures of collaboration and partnerships that assess the number (such as new partners), type (such as unlikely partners), and alignment among partnerships (such as position on a particular policy issue). To strengthen the findings, this information can be collected longitudinally on a pre/post basis to demonstrate positive change over time. However, we have seen some partnerships wax and wane or even become polarized as the policy environment changes, pitting allies, such as labor unions and nonprofit health care providers against one another.

Additionally, evaluators are starting to look across a group or field of advocates and assess the recent efforts of funders to build field advocacy skills and resources, increase connectivity among participants, and diversify and broaden field participation. Evaluator Jewlya Lynn (2014) and others from the APC evaluation community have developed a framework to assess advocacy fields and the efforts by funders to build and/or strengthen them, using methods to identify the "field frame," which is important in determining policy goals (such as Q-methodology to measure values).

Influencing Policymaker Understanding and Support

In many advocacy initiatives, policymakers are the primary target of an advocacy campaign or tactic, such as educating U.S. members of Congress about the challenges in developing countries. We suggest examining the impact of these activities on policymaker understanding and support as early as possible to inform advocacy strategy. Decision-makers are also part of an advocate's network of partners and how close or tightknit this relationship is can determine how much influence an advocate will have. For example, advocates that are perceived to be credible resources are likely to be consulted on an ad hoc basis by decision-makers for their opinions and the evidence for those opinions about a particular issue.

However, having access to and collecting data from decision-makers is challenging for a variety of reasons. Their busy schedules make getting a timely response near impossible. They work on multiple policy issues at once while fundraising for reelection, limiting informant recall. Last, even though what elected officials say is a matter of public record, they may be less than willing to disclose particular details about their position on a policy. Given this, there are a couple of strategies that evaluators can use. They can broaden the target population to include legislative staffers who have behind-the-scenes knowledge as well as content expertise about a particular policy issue. They can also maximize convenience and discretion.

A key focus of political scientists, traditional approaches to gauge policymaker support include counting the number of bills introduced on an issue, number of bill cosponsors or cosigners, number of votes for or against a bill, and a policymaker's voting record. Conventional evaluation approaches, such as surveys, informant interviews, and focus groups, can be used to assess policymaker knowledge, attitudes, and if an issue is important to them. Last, as we describe in Chapter 5, there are a few tailored instruments in this arena, such as policymaker rating instruments that can be used to assess policymaker level of support, policymaker level of influence, and willingness of policymakers to act in support of a specific policy proposal. These findings are enormously helpful for informing advocate strategy, particularly a policymaker's attitude about an issue or policy proposal and a policymaker's perception of the role and effectiveness of an advocate or advocacy tactic.

Cultivating Champions

Similar to educating and partnering with policymakers to support an issue are efforts by advocates to secure support by high-profile individuals or champions who are willing to publically advocate for an issue or bill (Beer and Coffman 2015). In addition to collecting data from grantee reports on their efforts to cultivate champions, the Aspen Institute's *Champion Scorecard* tracks advocate progress in cultivating champions who can take steps to advance an advocate's policy objectives, such as sponsoring legislation. There are also tools for advocates to support and assess their efforts to identify and engage champions broadly defined, not just policymakers. Evaluators Sarah Roma and Carlisle Levine (2016) developed the Champions Toolkit to support advocates of the Save the Children's Saving Newborn Lives (SNL) program and that includes a combination of advocacy resources and approaches for monitoring and evaluating champion work.

Political Will

A term that has been characterized as "the slipperiest concept in the policy lexicon," increased policymaker political will is a desired outcome since it is perceived to result in political action (Hammergren [1998] cited by Post, Raile, and Raile 2010). However, there is no one agreed-upon definition of "political will." There are narrow definitions that focus on demonstrated willingness to take action, but these definitions don't account for the collective nature political will. There are broader, multidimensional definitions that are intended to guide assessment. Lori Post, Amber Raile, and Eric Raile (2010) break political will into four components that can be operationalized: (1) a sufficient set of decision-makers support a particular policy; (2) a common understanding of a particular problem; (3) decision-makers committed to supporting policy; and (4) a commonly perceived potentially effective policy solution. Alternatively, pollster and political scientist Craig Charney (2009) defines "political will" as the combination of having an opinion on an issue, intensity or how strongly held these opinions are, and saliency or how important an issue is. These dimensions can be translated into measures and incorporated into existing instruments. For example, ORS Impact adapted the Harvard Family Research Project's Policymaker Ratings method, specifically the policymaker level of support questions, to assess political will in diverse policy contexts (Stachiwiak, Afflerback, and Howlett 2016).

Public Will Building and Engagement

Interim outcomes that signal a change in public willingness to act are the end goal of many advocacy initiatives. APC evaluators Jane Reisman, Annie Gienapp, and Sarah Stachowiak (2007) argue that general public support is a "major structural condition for supporting changes in policies." There are many ways to increase public engagement, including grassroots mobilization, social movements, community organizing, and increased voter registration, and evaluators have a variety of options for assessing involvement of the public and change in public will. Be forewarned, the public can be large, comprised of many different subpopulations, and geographically spread out over a large area. Evaluation of levels and/or changes in public knowledge and support can be difficult and costly to ascertain.

Conventional evaluation approaches (such as focus groups, public polling, interviews, meeting observations, and surveys) provide information about changes in public awareness and knowledge of a specific issue, as well as its salience. Organizational capacity instruments can be used to assess changes in advocate ability to mobilize a grassroots campaign. Measures of increased public engagement and activism are straightforward and can be tracked by advocates, such as the number of people who attend a political event, voter turnout, and membership.

Documenting changes in public opinion about a particular issue or policy can be an effective means for evaluating a multifaceted public-will-building campaign or a targeted media event. Experimental and quasi-experimental designs are an option for assessing changes in knowledge, attitudes, and behaviors of an individual, such as the likelihood to vote in support of or against a particular policy. Since media campaigns are limited in time and geography, it is a little easier to identify a comparison group, specifically, communities where funding for a media campaign precludes its implementation, as well as conduct a survey that compares public knowledge, attitudes, and behaviors before and after the campaign within the targeted geography.

Evaluators rarely administer public opinion polls, but they are another source of data for assessing changes in voter intentions due to a particular tactic. Traditionally, these are collected over a period of time and comparisons can be made, for example, when specific strategies were introduced and whether or not there were changes in public opinion on evolving issues, such as immigration reform.

Evaluation of communications campaigns directed at the public is experiencing significant growth as the number of channels of communication proliferate—blog posts and traffic, video, Twitter—and as advocates develop expertise in doing electronic advocacy, such as conducting online petitions, submitting letters to the editors of online publications, and fundraising. These online activities lend themselves to monitoring and measurement, and there are research organizations that have developed the analytical expertise to assess online advocacy by sector and policy issue, such as the monitoring of online performance by nonprofits (Wolfson et al. 2012). An area not to be overlooked due to lack of analytical expertise, the use of technology in advocacy will only continue to grow in use and importance.

Last, as we will discuss in Chapter 5, funder support for community organizing and empowering communities to make desired changes, or a "grassroots versus treetops" strategy, has fueled the development of unique evaluation frameworks and instruments (Foster and Louie 2010).

Engaging the Media

Research on the role of the media indicates that it shapes how the public and policymakers perceive an issue, and advocates need to know whether or not their media efforts are working to their advantage. However, not all problems and issues lend themselves to media coverage, such as changes in complex funding allocation methodologies. Additionally, media coverage can bring unwanted attention or may not be culturally appropriate. Working with the media is context dependent and can be very unpredictable, such as an unanticipated current event that overshadows other issues the advocate had been working on.

During the 2000s, developing organizational capacity to work with the media was a focus of many foundations. Consequently, there are many opportunities and approaches for evaluating the immediate outcomes of expanded media advocacy capacity. Some efforts to secure coverage, such as printed letters to the editor and paid media or radio advertisements, have a short time horizon and can be readily tracked. There are several good tactical reasons for focusing on the partnership aspect of engaging the media and not just securing coverage. We have found that cultivating and maintaining relationships with individual media representatives can greatly benefit an advocate even if it does not result in actual coverage. Media representatives need information to do their jobs and being the expert in a particular policy arena increases the visibility of an organization or an individual as well as educates media representatives about the issue itself (Gardner, Geierstanger, Brindis, and McConnell 2010).

Conventional evaluation approaches are useful, but with some caveats. While media representatives can be surveyed, the difficulties with access are similar to those of policymakers. There are issues with informant recall and turnover in the media sector is high. If there is ongoing coverage, content analysis techniques can be used to track changes in article length, placement, key words used, and how the issue was framed. Last, new media, such as Twitter and other social media, are becoming the norm, and advocates cannot rely on only one form of media. With the expanded role of social media, measuring the type of presence on the Web and its contents, such as the number of hits or downloads of support materials, can also be used as measures of public awareness.

Evaluators also need to be familiar with multiple types of media, including daily newspapers, neighborhood newsletters, and radio, along with the Internet. It is exceedingly difficult to assess the impact of a specific type of media on public and/or policymaker awareness, understanding, and support for an issue or policy. The field of media research is helpful and experimental designs can be used to investigate the effects of a specific media campaign, but they require significant resources and evaluation expertise.

Since media advocacy takes several different forms, there are a few good measures to choose from, including: paid media, such as amount spent on advertisements, number, and type of distribution outlets; earned media, such as press releases distributed, outreach to reporters, length and placement of articles in large and small print newspapers, radio coverage; electronic media, such as a new website, social media; media partnerships, such as number, beat covered, and frequency of contact; and change in salience of an issue, such as frequency of coverage in the media and contacts by media. Multiple measures can be combined into one data collection instrument. Tracking forms and logs are fairly common and can be developed and used by advocates themselves to track the date of publication, type of media, placement, and whether it was paid or earned. Being contacted by the media can be readily tracked by advocates and be used to inform subsequent strategy. Resulting coverage, based upon those contacts, and the way that the issue is depicted also help inform whether or not the type of messaging strategy being used is the most effective.

Intermediate Outcomes (2–4 years)

Intermediate outcomes are the longer-term results of advocacy tactics, including the identification and shepherding of policies prepassage (such as sustained working relationships with policymakers). They signal the transition to summative evaluation and assessing what worked. Strategic learning continues to be an important focus of an evaluation design, but it is important to show that an organization has achieved changes in the target of its advocacy be it the policy arena, public opinion, or the advocacy environment.

Developing outcomes has been challenging for a number of reasons, such as determining attribution and defining success. However, APC evaluators have defined some concrete outcome areas and corresponding indicators, particularly changes in policy and creating a constituency for policy change.

There is also the issue of classifying an outcome as a short-term or an intermediate outcome. Depending on the starting point of an advocacy initiative, some of the short-term outcomes listed in Table 4.1 may actually be intermediate outcomes and vice-versa. Evaluators need to be sensitive to the timing and maturity of an APC initiative and develop a timeline and ordering of outcomes that works for their initiative. In this section, we describe two broad categories of intermediate outcomes: setting the stage for a policy change, and creating a constituency for policy change.

Setting the Stage for Policy Change

Laying the groundwork for achieving a policy change, such as changes in bill language or securing policymaker support for a specific policy, are significant accomplishments and are policy wins in their own right. Developing case studies and characterizing the entire history of a piece of legislation using interviews with policymakers and other influentials and document review is helpful for understanding how a policy has changed over time. The number, content and progress of bills, resolutions, and regulations, as well as identification of their sponsors and supporters, can be used to determine whether desired policy goals are likely to be achieved. In the United States, policy proposals can be monitored using federal and state online legislative websites, such as thomas.loc.gov.

This is also the stage when government agencies, universities, and think tanks develop policy analyses. While the focus is on the financial impacts and the strengths of a specific policy proposal, these analyses typically provide detailed information about the nature of the problem being addressed, the historical antecedents, as well as recommendations that are being incorporated into the legislation. While not typically considered part of an evaluation toolkit, policy analysis is a method that can be readily adapted to an evaluation design that has multiple policy options.

Creating a Constituency for Policy Change

Having a broad base of support explains in part why a policy does or does not move forward, or why some policies have greater salience and are higher up on the policy agenda than others. Documenting the context, including the political culture, media interest, and public support, provides information on the extent to which an advocacy initiative has succeeded in persuading its targets more broadly—the public, the media, and policymakers—in supporting a policy change. Similarly, ratings of policymaker awareness and understanding and the Bellwether Methodology can be used to assess policymaker support or stance on a particular policy. The Most Significant Change (MSC) technique can be used to identify and document changes in support and critical events. Other methods that take the pulse of the media and public, such as public polling and interviews with the media, can be used to document the reach of an initiative, if that was its intention. (These unique methods are described in more detail in Chapter 5.)

Long-term Outcomes (5+ years)

Long-term outcomes, specifically policy adoption (or defeat), are the actions resulting from the intermediate outcomes and fall squarely in the summative evaluation arena, although they may not be the final outcome if funders are pressing for information about impacts. Until recently, long-term outcomes were considered aspirational and beyond the reach of an APC evaluation design. This is less and less the case as outcomes are better defined, conventional evaluation approaches are adapted, and new instruments are developed to document a range of outcomes. Conventional evaluation methods (particularly case studies) have proven to be very useful for describing the link between short, intermediate, and long-term outcomes, and for addressing the issue of attribution. Case studies unpack the range of factors and conditions and make transparent the contextual factors that influence an advocacy initiative, such as the political culture and social context. The combination of document review, interviews, and vetting by stakeholders can be used to establish the links between strategies, tactics, influence and policy change, and intervention effectiveness.

We describe three types of long-term outcomes and suggested evaluation methods and measures: policy adoption or defeat; policy implementation; and the advocacy context.

Policy Adoption or Defeat

Passing a law or bill is no easy feat, not even for experienced policymakers for whom this is a primary focus. Many things can go wrong at many points in the process. A bill can pass in both houses of the state legislature with strong bipartisan support, but then be vetoed by the governor. In states with a referendum process, laws can be repealed. Still, there is an unambiguous point in time when a bill is chaptered and considered passed. A blocked bill at any of the decision-making stages does not necessarily mean total failure and is an indication of its support and potential for success later on if it is resurrected during the next legislative cycle.

Evaluators have some solid options for evaluating the *policy adoption* stage. First and foremost, it is helpful to have a working knowledge of the decision-making process and the progress of a bill as it winds its way through the committee process, the floor of the House and Senate, and if all goes well, to the desk of the governor or president. Legislative databases can be used to document legislative action at specific points in the process and whether a policy is adopted and signed into law, or if it was blocked and why. Policies can be readily counted and coded, such as the status of a bill (pending, passed, failed, vetoed) and a bill's elements (amount of funding, policy arena, target population). The voting record for a specific policy provides information about a change in policymaker support or opposition, which can inform advocacy strategy, as well as provide evidence that a campaign targeting decision-makers is effective or not. For example, increased bipartisan support for a policy issue bodes well for passage later on. Last, using case studies to describe a policy and the antecedents to its passage using a policy change model is enormously helpful to advocates and funders for assessing a bill's reach or whether it will be broad or narrow in impact, as well as identifying opportunities for further advocate action as the policy moves to the *policy implementation* stage.

Arguably, the adoption or blockage of a policy can be a long and many times impossible achievement, making it a poor measure of success in many situations. Qualitative methods, particularly stakeholder interviews and case studies, are useful for characterizing why a policy is or is not adopted and the contextual factors that contributed to its success (or failure). For example, Michael Quinn Patton (2008) used the General Elimination Method (GEM) case study method, which eliminates rival explanations, to develop detailed retrospective cases that concluded that a campaign did significantly contribute to a U.S. Supreme Court decision. Additionally, documentation, such as media coverage, committee testimony transcripts, and the wording of the policies, provides important sources of information and lends themselves to content analysis approaches. They can be used to assess whether or not advocates succeeded in informing the debate and influencing the wording of the policy solution. Because the environment is a little less complex, surveys can be administered before and after passage to assess fidelity in implementation, effectiveness, and satisfaction with a particular policy (Reisman, Gienapp, and Stachowiak 2007).

Policy Implementation

The policy implementation stage can be parsed out into multiple important decision points that are opportunities for advocates to intervene. Deal making along the way can undermine the original intent of a policy and result in a bill that has no teeth later on or a bill that is co-opted. After being signed into law, a bill typically goes through a process of being drafted into rules and regulations. While public agencies oversee the process, interested individuals, organizations, and groups can weigh in. For example, a trade association may be invited to serve on an agency advisory committee to help develop a funding methodology. Since many policies are about funding, this is a key time for advocates to muster policymaker and constituent support as well as legal and financial expertise. This stage tends to be a little more behind-the-scenes, though some controversial or high-impact issues may remain in the media light. Case studies detailing stakeholder involvement, advocacy tactics, and the financial impacts and perceived benefits are frequently used to provide a robust understanding of a policy change and its impacts. Advocacy capacity and maintenance of effort through this stage can be assessed using the capacity assessment tools listed above.

Alternatively, a public policy can be contested in the courts and advocacy acumen in litigation and legal advocacy may be the focus of an evaluation. Less of a focus than other types of advocacy, this is an important arena nonetheless. Opposing a policy is just as potent a vehicle for policy change as garnering support for adoption of a policy. It helps to have an understanding of the legal process and alternative policy scenarios depending on what the courts decide.

In many cases, a policy win can result in the allocation of new resources and is an opportunity to demonstrate a positive return on investment on grant funding to advocates and their beneficiaries. From a funder perspective, there is a desire to understand which models or tactics should be scaled up and expanded. Usually advocacy is one of many areas in the portfolio of a foundation and its costs have to be justified.

This is an area of assessment that does not have widespread support from APC evaluators and for good reason. Most cost analyses are difficult to do and require expertise in developing financial models and attaching a dollar value to an advocacy effort. The question of attribution and the link between individual advocacy tactics and funding secured through passage of a bill or measure is tenuous at best. If there is no financial gain does this necessarily mean an advocacy initiative has failed? There is also the issue of limited resources and whether or not a financial analysis should be done at the expense of other potentially more informative assessments. Despite these limitations, there are some cost-related analyses that can be included in an APC evaluation design. For example, advocates and evaluators can conduct a simple "value for money" analysis and track the resources they have used for specific advocacy tactics and compare these expenditures to the results of these tactics and determine whether this was money well spent (Hilt 2014).

While difficult to do, the information from Return on Investment (ROI) analysis or total monetary gain from policy wins divided by funding invested in advocacy to determine the financial return on every dollar invested can greatly inform advocate and funder organizational strategic planning, such as whether resources are being used efficiently. For example, Lisa Rangeli (2008) and the National Committee for Responsible Philanthropy were able to demonstrate that for every dollar invested in New Mexico advocates, there was $157 in benefits to New Mexico communities, and the total benefits amounted to more than $2.6 billion. We used a similar approach to demonstrate a positive return on investment of a multiyear, multigrantee initiative. However, we learned that focusing on funding secured tends to provide an incomplete picture of the results of a policy win (Gardner, Geierstanger, Nascimento, and Brindis 2011). Characterizing the qualitative aspects of a policy, be it new funding secured or preservation of funding, provides insights into successful advocacy tactics, such as advising on an allocation formula. Documenting the larger financial factors that influence these gains, such as budget and economic pressures, can be predictive of future gains. Documenting the partnerships, opposition, political culture, and prior efforts to secure funding provides a more complete understanding of the nonmonetary factors that contribute to a policy win. While most policy is about the money, the money may only be part of the policy story.

The ROI analysis is informative, but it has its limitations. It is difficult to document every input that may have contributed to a policy win, particularly the ones that fall outside of a grant. Additionally, not all wins are quantifiable, such as a moratorium on freeway development, which means that a ROI analysis may not capture all the economic gains.

Depending on the time horizon and accuracy in accounting of funds, it may be possible to conduct a cost-benefit or a cost-effectiveness analysis and track the dollars to the ultimate beneficiaries and conduct more sophisticated analyses on impacts. Both approaches examine the relationship between program costs and outcomes with the goal of producing the greatest impact. Cost-benefit analyses focus on monetary outcomes, such as the federal resources directed to states due to a policy to expand program services. A cost-effectiveness analysis of the impacts of this policy would focus on the costs of expanding state programs to administer a significantly larger program.

Funders are also interested in seeing how their support gets leveraged into other financial wins, be it financial, political, or in-kind donations. For advocacy and policy change grantees, this can translate into policies that shape changes in their communities (such as land development policy) and policies that increase or maintain funding for desired programs. The funding linked to specific bills or measures is relatively easy to collect and track and can be a good proxy indicator of longer-term impacts on the beneficiaries. In addition, financial information can be collected and analyzed longitudinally for one or multiple policies as an indicator of maintained effort. The challenge is attributing some or all of the changes to a particular grant or advocacy strategy, particularly if the funder wants to understand the gains from its investment.

The policy monitoring and evaluation activities of the policy implementation stage focus on questions of fidelity: Is the law being implemented in the way in which it was intended, resulting in the programs or services that are in the language of the law? For example, a state-level policy may delegate responsibility to the counties to allocate funding, increasing the likelihood of differences in implementation and program impacts. Evaluators can draw on the policy evaluation arena, the implementation sciences, as well as a long tradition of political science scholarship about policy implementation, to conduct these follow-up studies.

Advocacy Context

For many advocates, improved policies are not the only end goal and there is the intent to build stable and influential alliances, partnerships, and networks that support permanent structural changes in a policy arena or issue. There is a shift from advocacy silos to advocacy allies and increased public and individual engagement. Informed by social movement and advocacy coalition network theories, this is an area that is gaining traction in the evaluation community. The evaluation focus can be quite broad, focusing on changes in individuals, types of constituent groups, organizations, and institutions.

Conventional evaluation approaches can be used to examine changes in political relations and stakeholder involvement. Longtime decision-makers and bellwethers can be interviewed about perceptible changes in the policy dialogue and political context, such as a broadening and/or deepening of awareness, ideological shifts, and emergence of new, potent voices. Social network analysis can be used to determine if strong, stable networks and advocacy alliances are sustained, ensuring continued support (or opposition) for a specific policy or issue.

Assessing Advocacy and Policy Change Impacts

APC evaluators and the rest of the evaluation arena continue to wrestle with the difficulties in evaluating the impact of a specific advocacy campaign or policy on its targets, be it individuals, the environment, the economy, or civil society. On the one hand, it can be difficult if not impossible to demonstrate a cause-and-effect relationship between an advocacy strategy, such as community organizing, and changes in civil society. It is also difficult to isolate a particular policy from other contributing factors, such as a change in the economy. Some argue that focusing on impacts is a distraction from focusing on the key features of an initiative or the contribution of an advocacy initiative and how it achieved its results (Carden 2004). Last, impacts may not be within the advocate's purview or range of influence and may not reveal themselves until years after an advocacy initiative.

The APC field's response has been to focus more on contribution versus attribution, focusing on the roles played by advocates within a larger context and developing a rich account of the relationship between advocacy, policy change, and impacts. This is an examination well worth undertaking for a number of reasons, including: demonstrating the value of expanded advocacy capacity; enhancing program performance and accountability; increasing support for a policy issue; and providing direction for future advocacy and policy. While accountability is stressed (particularly by funders), there is still much to learn about successful advocacy practice at this late stage.

APC evaluators are using qualitative methods—process tracking, systems analysis, progress journals, and General Elimination Method (GEM)—to explore the causal mechanisms and relative contribution of different advocacy tactics to a policy change. They are also using John Mayne's (2012) six-step process to verify a theory of change with some success. The six steps are:

1. Define the attribution problem

2. Develop a theory of change

3. Gather evidence

4. Assemble and assess contribution theory

5. Seek out additional evidence

6. Revise and strengthen the contribution story

A plausible contribution story is developed when there is high stake-holder agreement. This story is used to assess the factors that are pur-ported to have significant or minor contribution, such as financial incentives and penalties.

There are other approaches to conducting a contribution analysis, but they share similar features, particularly the marshaling of evidence to confirm or refute contribution. For example, APC evaluators Tanya Beer and Julia Coffman (2015) describe three tools, in addition to contribution analysis, that funders can use to assess grantee contribution to advocacy efforts: (1) a question bank or asking grantees about the role being played by advocacy allies and interim outcomes they expect to achieve; (2) struc-tured grantee reporting of their unique role and contribution; and (3) an external partner interview guide to collect information on grantee contri-bution as they perceive the organization to function. Careful reconstruc-tion of the path from outcomes to impacts can be done with document review and triangulation with stakeholder interviews representing differ-ent perspectives.

Additionally, case studies can be built into an evaluation during the formative stage to monitor an initiative and assess its impacts, such as the Most Significant Change (MSC) technique, which is an inductive case study method. Referred to as "monitoring without indicators," the tech-nique embodies democratic principles of stakeholder participation while providing formative and summative evaluation information. It is an alter-native to quantitative indicators and provides information about the most significant changes that took place for participants in the program during a reporting period. Participants describe the mechanisms and pathways of change, providing in-depth information about who was involved, what happened, where it happened, and why. Second, participants must explain what makes a particular change significant or what impact it had on people's lives. It can be a positive or negative change. These descriptions are reviewed by stakeholders at multiple levels and can be used to assess program performance. This detailed summative information can be linked to logic model outcomes as evidence of success, while laying the groundwork for a contribution analysis (Dart 2000).

We describe four types of impacts and corresponding methods and measures: systems change; changing lives; social norms; and expanding democracy.

Systems Change

A driving force behind many APC initiatives is the desire to achieve lasting, systems-level change, ranging from strengthening the institutions that shape our daily lives (such as public schools) to addressing the conditions that contribute to poor health (such as poverty and gender inequality). Improved policies are the vehicle for establishing rights and launching the programs and services that can bring about changes across a community, a population, a state, or a nation. While undoubtedly the strongest evidence of APC success, systems-level outcomes can be the most difficult to assess, since they may happen well after passage of a policy. Or the effects may be so diffused through a large population that they require significant resources and expertise in sampling and large-scale survey administration.

There are also differences in the types of systems change that require different evaluation frameworks and metrics, such as large-scale land use policies that can be documented using GIS mapping. Tailored frameworks for evaluating these complex arenas are starting to emerge. For example, Grantmakers for Effective Organizations (GEO) developed a place-based evaluation framework that includes indicators of the political, economic, and cultural context and outcomes such as change in leadership and community engagement and collective action (Community Science 2014). Additionally, systems change evaluation frameworks are being developed that can help with the development of a theory of change that reflects a more complicated understanding of "system" and identification of appropriate outcome statements. For example, the *Im-*

pact, Influence, Leverage, and Learning I2L2 Outcomes Framework developed by Organizational Research Services (ORS) expands the focus of an evaluation to include population-level outcomes, as well as influence, leverage, and learning outcomes, not just individual-level outcomes (Reisman, Gienapp, and Kelly 2015). Systems-thinking tools, such as causal loop diagramming and systems mapping, can be used to diagram the initiative and its impact. For example, APC Evaluators Julia Coffman and Tanya Beer are using systems mapping, specifically causal loop diagramming, as part of a developmental evaluation of the Hewlett Foundation's Madison Initiative, an effort to create the conditions under which the U.S. Congress can deliberate policy issues. Social network analysis can be used to map the stakeholders and their relationships while identifying the nodes or influencers.

However, as pointed out by evaluators Hallie Preskill and Srik Gopal (2015), many quantitative and qualitative evaluation methods, such as interviews, social network analysis, rapid evaluation (RE) methods, contribution analysis, and case studies, can be used in a systems change evaluation with good results.

Changing Lives

Policy change is about improving the well-being of people and increasingly other living species and the planet as a whole. As a result of the outcomes movement in the early 2000s and the shift to assessing the impact of programs on their intended beneficiaries, APC advocates are being held accountable for the impacts of policy change on its target population or the broader community. APC evaluation practice is less challenged by assessing the impacts of social programs and services that result from a policy change, and it can readily apply conventional program evaluation approaches, such as experimental and quasi-experimental designs to this priority. An experimental design can be used to evaluate whether a new program is more effective than an existing program, or no program at all. However, it is a stretch to connect the advocacy push to fundamental changes in individual lives, and APC evaluators are resorting to using the Most Significant Change (MSC) technique to "connect the dots" and demonstrate initiative contribution.

On the other hand, evaluating changes in the rights of individuals, populations, and more recently, the rights of animals, is less straightforward. The type of rights and the state's role in respecting, protecting, or fulfilling these rights depends on the context and the issue itself. Fueled by the many humanitarian crises that are increasingly common, tackling human rights abuse cases, such as protecting civilians from armed conflict, is gaining policymaker recognition. Evaluator Rhonda Schlangen (2014) summarizes the challenges to evaluating human rights advocacy or the moral and legal dimensions that undergird this arena and the misperceptions of evaluation as an activity that focuses on measures and accountability. She provides a persuasive argument for building evaluation culture and teaching advocates how to work with a Monitoring and Evaluation (ME) process.

Social Norms

An outcome category that has its origins in the APC evaluation community, social norms are defined as "the knowledge, attitudes, values and behaviors that compose the normative structure of culture and society" (Reisman, Gienapp, and Stachowiak 2007). Posited as a prerequisite to, and an outcome of, policy change, assessing changes in social values (such as women's rights) typically entails a pre/post examination of societal knowledge, attitudes, and behaviors. Referred to as the "social norms marketing approach," evaluation approaches include analyzing media coverage and how issues are presented, public polls, focus groups, and interviews with policymakers (Mansfield 2010). Another approach is what is called "social justice advocacy," such as advocacy that targets social disparities, gender inequities, or marriage equality. To orient evaluators, Barbara Klugman (2010) identifies three values that are woven through many social justice advocacy campaigns that can be used to focus an evaluation design and selection of outcome or equitable distribution of resources, equal human rights, and equal representation.

Expanding Democracy

While not always a primary objective of an advocacy and policy change initiative, expanding civic engagement and the number and types of voices in the political arena is a result of many APC initiatives. In open or pluralistic societies, the goal may be to increase the partnerships between advocates and policymakers, as well as expand the range of policy options that include the voices and engagement of the most marginalized, which are often underrepresented unless advocacy is effective. In societies that are early in their democracy-building projects or have a civil society that has limited advocacy capacity, the focus is more on empowerment and building a base of support, such as increasing the opportunities to educate decision-makers. Under either scenario, the intention is to expand the overlap between civil society and the policy arena so that there is sustained participation in the future (Mansfield 2010). Similar to the evaluation approaches for social norms, stakeholders can be queried about changes in the political culture over time, such as who can participate and who cannot, as well as changes in vehicles of communication, such as decision-makers reaching out to advocates.

In sum, our intention is to provide a compendium of inputs, outputs, outcomes, and impacts and corresponding methods and measures that apply to a wide range of advocacy and policy change initiatives and can inform the evaluation design. Similar to Chapter 3, we turn to the findings from the Aspen/UCSF APC Evaluation Survey on the usefulness and use of many of the methods mentioned above and the comparison of the design and methods of two evaluation cases to take the "pulse" of the field.

EVALUATION PRACTICE: METHOD USEFULNESS, METHODS USED

The results of the Aspen/UCSF APC Evaluation Survey suggest that advocacy and policy change evaluators are resourceful and will consider inclusion of many conventional methods (such as *interviews, focus groups,* and *document review*) and unique APC methods (such as *advocacy capacity assessments* and *intense period debriefs*). Table 4.2 lists useful and used methods, as well as methods that may not be used much now but which have the potential to advance evaluation practice. Not surprisingly, the approaches that are rated more highly in "usefulness" are nearly the same ones that were reported as most "used" by respondents or *document review*

Table 4.1. Advocacy and Policy Change Inputs/Outputs/Outcomes/Impacts, Indicators, and Data Collection Methods

Inputs, Outputs, Outcomes, Impacts	Indicators	Data Collection Method
Inputs (required resources)		
Organizational infrastructure: * Advocacy tactics, e.g., media advocacy, lobbying, public will building campaign, messaging * Leadership development * Networking * Strategic adaptability * Research and policy analyses * Community organizing * Coalition building, partnering * Resources, e.g., staff time, financial * Planning and evaluation	Organizational advocacy ability to undertake advocacy tactics Organizational member advocacy knowledge and skills Communications with other groups in coalitions Ability to plan advocacy strategy Ability to retrieve and use Ability to collaborate with other sectors, advocates	Capacity assessment instruments (advocate, coalition) Document review: internal tracking documents, policy analyses Interviews with advocates, observers Rapid Evaluation (RE) approaches
Base of support * Power dynamics * Stakeholder analysis	Number of affiliated groups Size of membership Trained local leaders Citizen organizations	Social network analysis Influence mapping Surveys of coalition members Systems thinking techniques Rapid Evaluation (RE) approaches
Outputs (what is produced by project)		
Advocate performance	Progress in developing and executing strategy Determine which activities work were implemented and which were not	Capacity assessment instruments Monitoring, Evaluation and Learning (MEL) Rapid Evaluation (RE) approaches Surveys on advocacy tactics Initiative case studies Document review: grantee/ advocate progress reports and budgets Focus groups Log frames Spider diagrams

Table 4.1. Advocacy and Policy Change Inputs/Outputs/Outcomes/Impacts, Indicators, and Data Collection Methods (continued)

Inputs, Outputs, Outcomes, Impacts	Indicators	Data Collection Method
Strengthened alliances and partnerships	# and type of communications among members and sharing of information # and type of member organizations Agreements to collaborate (e.g., MOUs)	Survey of network/coalition members Social Network Analysis Interviews
Influencing policymaker understanding and support	# of meetings with decision-makers # of committee presentations # of requests for information, meetings by decision-makers and their staff	Policymaker interviews Policymaker Rating Survey
Cultivating champions	# and type of champions cultivated # of meetings with champions # and type of communications with champions # and type of public presentations by champions	Champion Scorecard
Public will building and engagement	Events held # and type of participants, members Meetings with decision-makers Message framing and salience	Membership tracking Attendance tracking Community organizing capacity assessment tools

Table 4.1. Advocacy and Policy Change Inputs/Outputs/Outcomes/Impacts, Indicators, and Data Collection Methods (continued)

Inputs, Outputs, Outcomes, Impacts	Indicators	Data Collection Method
Engaging the media	# of media contacts and requests Amount and type of media coverage earned (e.g., print, radio, internet) # of Op-eds, letters to the editor # of advocate citations in the media # of articles with preferred framing of issue # of advocate trained spokespersons Use of social media (e.g., # of tweets) Participation in talk shows	Media tracking system Clipping service
Research and policy analysis	# and type of policy proposals # and type of policy briefs # and type of policy forums Dissemination: public, policymakers Mode distributed: media coverage, peer-review literature, blogs, website Reach: downloads, website visits, citations, hand-outs Expand knowledge base	Policymaker and other influential interviews Forum session surveys

Table 4.1. Advocacy and Policy Change Inputs/Outputs/Outcomes/Impacts, Indicators, and Data Collection Methods (continued)

Inputs, Outputs, Outcomes, Impacts	Indicators	Data Collection Method
Outcomes (what change occurred)		
Short-term, Interim Outcomes		
Terms of the debate	Nature of the discourse on the issue Public opinion Profile of the issue and its place on the public/political agenda Reach – coverage, visibility	Public opinion polls Content analysis – media Document analysis
Strengthened alliances and partnerships	# and type of partnerships among network/coalition members Alignment among partners, collaborators # and type of collaborative actions taken Funding secured Sustainability of activities New sectors represented Peer support Advocacy field alignment, values	Collaboration/partnerships assessment surveys Alignment Index Social Network Analysis Document review Intensity of collaboration scales Interviews with coalition members Q-methodology
Influencing policymaker understanding and support. Changing political will	Policymaker knowledge, support of a policy # of issue mentions in policymaker speeches or debates Policymaker perceptions of advocate effectiveness, credibility Quality of advocate/policymaker relationship, e.g., maintained engagement # and type of bills introduced # of bill co-sponsors or co-signers # of votes against a bill Policymakers voting record	Surveys of decision-makers and their staff Focus groups Interviews with advocate, policymakers Bellwether Methodology Champion Scorecard Policymaker Rating Survey Intense-Period Debrief Protocol

Inputs, Outputs, Outcomes, Impacts	Indicators	Data Collection Method
Public will building and engagement	Awareness, knowledge, and attitudes toward a policy issue # of citizens who advocate Change in willingness to take action on a specific issue Participation at political events Voter turn-out	Focus groups Public opinion polls Document review Interviews Meeting, event observations Surveys
Engaging the media	Nature of relationships with media, e.g., ongoing, credible source Framing, e.g., placement of story, message in print media Public, policymaker knowledge and support Social media reach, e.g., # of podcast downloads, Twitter followers	Media tracking system (contacts, coverage) Interviews with media representatives Content analysis Policymaker Rating Survey

Intermediate Outcomes (summative evaluation)

Inputs, Outputs, Outcomes, Impacts	Indicators	Data Collection Method
Policy Change – prepassage	#, content, sponsors, and progress of bill, resolutions, regulations Policy reflects advocate priorities	Policy analyses Legislative tracking system Document review Monitoring committees Interviews with influentials, policymakers, champions Intense-Period Debrief Protocol
Creating a constituency for policy change	Policymaker support for policy, decreased support for opposition Media coverage in support for policy Public participation in events, e.g., town halls, testifying, meeting with decision-makers	Policymaker interviews Policymaker Rating Survey Media interviews Media content analysis Public opinion polling Most Significant Change technique Bellwether Methodology Champion Scorecard Intense-Period Debrief Protocol

Table 4.1. Advocacy and Policy Change Inputs/Outputs/Outcomes/Impacts, Indicators, and Data Collection Methods (continued)

Inputs, Outputs, Outcomes, Impacts	Indicators	Data Collection Method
Long-term Outcomes		
Policy adoption or defeat	Status of policy (passed, defeated, vetoed, repealed) Target population Policymaker support (bipartisan, levels) Contribution of advocacy initiative Breadth of policy reform Policy type (incremental, new, radical) Link of policy to other policy arenas	Legislative tracking system Case studies Policymaker voting record Intense Period Debriefs Contribution analysis General Elimination Method Intense-Period Debrief Protocol
Policy implementation	Advocate participation in drafting of rules and regulations Funding secured Legal challenges Fidelity of implementation to the intent of the policy	Case studies Financial analyses, e.g., ROI, cost-benefit, cost-effectiveness Analysis of court ruling Implementation sciences methods
Advocacy context	Political context Democratic space Increased leadership Strong, stable networks	Interviews with policymakers, influentials, champions Social Network Analysis Surveys of coalition members Focus groups Power analysis Most Significant Change technique

Table 4.1. Advocacy and Policy Change Inputs/Outputs/Outcomes/Impacts, Indicators, and Data Collection Methods (continued)

Inputs, Outputs, Outcomes, Impacts	Indicators	Data Collection Method
Impacts (change in beneficiaries of policy, civil society)		
Systems change	Change in economic conditions, physical environment, crime and safety	Case studies
		Contribution analysis
		General Elimination Method
		Advocacy Assessment
	Increased access to health care, education, social services	Framework
		RAPID Outcome Assessmen
		Systems thinking methods
	Change in institutions, e.g., accountability, transparency	Social Network Analysis
		Rapid Evaluation (RE) approaches
	Change in political will	GIS and documentation of conservation
	Sustainable resources	
	System performance	
	Community awareness of initiative	
	Change in policies, e.g., "health in all" policymaking	
Changing lives	Strengthened human rights, such as food, education, health	Most Significant Change technique
		Experimental, quasi-experimental design, e.g., high school graduation rates, decrease in obesity
	Improved health and welfare (people, animal rights, environment)	
		Case studies
		Rapid Evaluation (RE) approaches
Social norms	Change in values, attitudes and behaviors	Framing of issues in media
		Public polls
		Focus groups
		Interviews with policymakers stakeholders

Table 4.1. Advocacy and Policy Change Inputs/Outputs/Outcomes/Impacts,
Indicators, and Data Collection Methods (continued)

Inputs, Outputs, Outcomes, Impacts	Indicators	Data Collection Method
Expanding democratic space	Increased civic engagement and collaboration Improved power relations Increased civic voice in policymaking arena Increased effectiveness of civil society work	Interviews Focus groups

Sources: Innovation Network, Inc.; Guthrie et al. 2005; Guthrie, Louie, and Foster 2006; Foster and Louie 2010; Chapman and Wameyo 2001; Laney 2003; Coe and Majot 2013; Coffman and Beer 2015; Evaluating Community Change 2014; TCC Group 2012.

(99 percent), *interviews* (98 percent), and *feedback forms, questionnaires, and surveys* (98 percent). Despite the complexity and/or unpredictability of APC initiatives, nearly all respondents (98 percent) said they used a *theory of change* in their evaluation practice, rating it high in usefulness (3.6 out of 4, where 4 = "very useful").

Methods that were rated highly in usefulness (3.0 and above) but lower in use (below 60 percent "used") may speak to methods that are useful in specific situations or methods that are gaining traction in use. These include: *intense period debriefs* (57 percent); *systems mapping* (55 percent); *financial analyses* (53 percent); *outcome mapping* (49 percent); *public opinion polling* (48 percent); *story collection and journals* (45 percent); *policymaker ratings* (39 percent); and *most significant change technique* (28 percent). In all likelihood, this gradual expansion of the APC evaluation toolkit characterizes the state of APC growth in the near future.

Alternatively, the evaluation methods that were rated lower than 3.0 in usefulness may be methods that are losing traction in the APC evaluation community, such as *benchmarking* (75 percent), or have yet to prove their usefulness, such as *structured observation* (58 percent), *policymaker surveys* (49 percent), and *social network analysis* (51 percent). Alternatively, these methods may be less useful due to feasibility issues, such as the time and expertise required to conduct a *social network analysis,* access issues, such as the *policymaker surveys,* or limited applicability, such as *social media analysis.* Or in the case of *benchmarking,* it has proven less useful than other methods.

Similar to Chapter 3, we look to two of our evaluation cases to see which methods are used and under what circumstances, and to what extent the cases mirrors the Survey findings.

EVALUATION PRACTICE:
TWO EVALUATION CASES

For this chapter, we compare two midpoint evaluation designs of two very different advocacy and policy change initiatives: an evaluation of the *Oxfam GROW Campaign,* a multinational campaign to tackle food injustice, including a six-month campaign targeting World Bank land use policy; and an evaluation of the Pew Charitable Trust's *International Land Conservation Campaign* to conserve old-growth forests and extend wilderness areas in Canada and Australia. Both initiatives sought specific policy wins using a similar set of tactics activities including lobbying, direct advocacy to decision-makers, public engagement, media coverage, and research and policy analysis. While limited to a short time frame, evaluators worked with the funders to develop the evaluation design and inform client strategy going forward, providing recommendations to increase program success, as well as fine-tuning aspects of the programs to improve their effectiveness.

At the macro level, we see there were some differences in the evaluation designs that reflect differences in the two initiatives and stakeholder information needs. The evaluators of the Land Conservation Program conducted a retrospective assessment of the two campaigns and a prospective analysis of how the overall strategy might be refined going forward. The GROW Campaign evaluators conducted a retrospective assessment of the twenty-one-month period and was broad in scope, focusing on the overarching strategy as well as "deep dives" into specific national and team campaigns and projects. The GROW Campaign included a theory

Table 4.2. Usefulness and Use of Evaluation Methods by Aspen/
UCSF APC Survey Respondents

Evaluation methods	Average usefulness (1 = not useful and 4 = very useful)	Percent of survey respondents that indicated they had used method
Interviews: in-person, telephone, open and closed-ended questionnaires that are used to document stakeholder perceptions of an initiative's activities, outcomes and effectiveness.	3.8	98%
Theories of change: use of program theory of change, outcome chains, logic models in the evaluation design	3.6	98%
Feedback forms, questionnaires, and surveys: print, online, telephone data collection.	3.6	99%
Document reviews: can include internal program documentation, secondary data, and policy analyses and be used for contribution analyses, baseline data and case studies.	3.6	99%
Outcome mapping: identifying and monitoring program progress in achieving desired outcomes.	3.6	49%
Focus groups: facilitated discussions with advocates, coalition members, and other stakeholders to elicit their perceptions of program effectiveness.	3.5	84%
Single-case or multiple-case studies: qualitative descriptions of advocacy strategy, tactics or policy change.	3.5	84%
Systems mapping: creation of a visual depiction of the parts of a system and their relationships that are expected to change.	3.4	55%
Tracking policy change using program or public data: use of legislative tracking systems to track a bill's progress.	3.3	76%
Intensive period debriefs/after action reviews: elicit policymaker and other influentials on advocacy effectiveness.	3.3	57%
Logic models/log frames: use of outcomes chains in evaluation design.	3.2	96%

Table 4.2. Usefulness and Use of Evaluation Methods by Aspen/UCSF APC Survey Respondents (continued)

Evaluation methods	Average usefulness (1 = not useful and 4 = very useful)	Percent of survey respondents that indicated they had used method
Advocacy capacity assessments: online or paper organizational capacity assessment instrument.	3.1	65%
Policymaker ratings: rating of policymakers' support for and influence on, the issue.	3.1	39%
Most significant change technique: participants describe the mechanisms and pathways of change and what makes a specific change 'significant.'	3.1	28%
Content analysis of media coverage: counting specific aspects of media coverage, such as word count, placement of articles, key themes.	3.0	67%
Financial analyses, such as cost-benefit: determination of funding allocated and secured and what can be attributed to the grant.	3.0	53%
Public opinion polling; telephone interviews with random sample of the public to document their knowledge, attitudes and behaviors.	3.0	48%
Story collection and journals.	3.0	45%
Benchmarking: use standards to measure the progress of an initiative.	2.9	75%
Structured observation: such as protests, policy forums.	2.9	58%
Social media analysis: monitoring and analyzing data from social media, such as blogs, image sharing sites, and online forums.	2.8	51%
Social network analysis: map and measure how close the relationships are between individuals or organizations, blogs.	2.8	51%
Policymaker surveys: survey of policymaker perceptions of advocacy tactics, media coverage, etc.	2.8	49%

Sources: Aspen Planning and Evaluation Program, The Aspen Institute; Coffman and Reed 2009; Guthrie et al. 2005.

of change and a logic model, which was linked to the evaluation outcomes and indicators. A logic model was not deemed appropriate for the Land Conservation Program, though outcomes and indicators were used to identify progress toward program goals.

While qualitative methods played a prominent role in the designs, both evaluations were able to identify measures to assess progress in achieving campaign objectives. Petition signatures and analysis of social media data provided information on the progress of the GROW Campaign in global mobilization and constructing strong networks. The analysis of the GIS data on land conservation and development was pivotal to demonstrating the positive impact of the Land Conservation Campaign in achieving the goal of preserving 500 million acres by 2022.

There were also some similarities in the two evaluation designs and their focus. Both evaluations were conducted toward the end of specific advocacy and policy change tactics and used a mixed-methods approach, which included formative and summative data collection to support program improvement and assess program effectiveness to-date. Both evaluations focused on multiple levels, with the GROW Campaign being broader in scope. The evaluators of the Land Conservation Program focused on local and national tactics and the GROW Campaign evaluation team focused on international, national, local, and institutional advocacy and policy.

Evaluators also took measures to understand and be sensitive to the advocacy and policy change context. The evaluation teams of both initiatives worked with experts who were familiar with the contexts and working with indigenous peoples, who had language skills, as well as the ability to travel to remote places to conduct interviews.

There are similarities in the methods used in the two evaluations, mirroring the other four cases—the use of internal and external interviews, the development of case studies of the campaigns at different levels, and a document review, which was a key component of a contribution analysis. As part of the six-month World Bank Land Freeze Campaign, the GROW Campaign evaluation team interviewed a variety of informants: Oxfam staff, World Bank staff, and NGOs working on land use issues. The evaluators of the Land Conservation Program conducted in-depth interviews with partners and stakeholders involved in the campaign, as well as knowledgeable observers. They also spoke to representatives of groups that were politically opposed to campaign's objectives.

The case studies served a similar purpose in the two evaluations: to inform the overall strategy while assessing the effectiveness of individual campaign components. Evaluators of the GROW Campaign produced five case studies, the World Bank Land Freeze Campaign and four country-level cases (Burkina Faso, Bangladesh, Guatemala, and the Netherlands) and documented achievements, facilitating factors, and challenges. The evaluators of the Land Conservation Campaign documented the tactics, policy gains, and role of indigenous communities in achieving these gains and their role in land conservation management. Last, the two evaluation teams included a document review as part of a contribution analysis. The evaluators of the GROW Campaign had sufficient documentation for the World Bank Campaign that they could pinpoint the change in bank policy language. The evaluation team of the Land Conservation Campaign used documents, media coverage, and interviews to piece together the sequence of events that led to the outcomes of the program.

The two evaluations differed by a couple of methods. The GROW Campaign evaluation team included a media analysis of social media activities and the reach of GROW Campaign components, including the World Bank Land Freeze Campaign, which included a performance by the internationally known band, Coldplay. A broader initiative than the Land Conservation Program, the evaluators conducted a cross-campaign survey of Oxfam staff and a policy analysis of the World Bank Campaign, which focused on whether the policy change happened, and the influence of Oxfam on the change seen. The evaluators of the Land Conservation Program conducted a quantitative GIS analysis of the amount and type of conserved and protected land.

Last, the two evaluations wrestled with similar challenges including the broad scope of the initiative and a relatively short time frame (six months) during which to carry out data collection activities. While evaluators of both initiatives collected data on a range of formative and summative evaluation questions, both wrestled with the limits of a point-in-time model.

In the GROW Campaign, the complexity and scope of the campaign itself precluded comprehensive data collection. Both evaluation teams included external informants and people who were not involved in the campaigns to offset the potential for bias. The evaluators of the Land Conservation Campaign had to tailor the analyses to the ecological differences in the two countries, which precluded ready adoption of the 50/50 land development framework in Australia. There were also geographic challenges with some sites being in remote areas of Australia and evaluators partnered with experts in Canada and Australia to lead the country-level components, as well as an expert in working with Indigenous peoples.

In sum, though these are two different advocacy and policy change initiatives, there are similarities in their purpose, foci, designs, methods, and challenges to data collection and validity. There are some parallels with Real Evaluation (RE) designs, which are quick (four weeks to six months), use a team approach, and use a battery of methods, most of which are qualitative in nature (I-TECH 2008). Perhaps what is more telling is the ability of the two evaluation teams to assess progress while evaluating achievement of short-to-midterm outcomes using a handful of methods in a short time period. Some tactics and policy changes, such as the World Bank Land Freeze Campaign, took place in a relatively short time frame (six months) and could be used to document achievement of medium-term outcomes or policy adoption and improved standards or regulations.

These midpoint evaluations corroborate the Aspen/UCSF survey findings on high use and usefulness of conventional methods, such as interviews, document review, and surveys, but with a few caveats. The truth of how methods are combined is more nuanced, speaking to how methods are used in tandem to strengthen the findings as well as create efficiencies. More methods do not necessarily translate into a stronger design; a rigorous midpoint evaluation may not require an exhaustive data collection enterprise to assess formative and summative outcomes. Having a core set of methods that are broad in focus, such as surveys that include qualitative and quantitative questions, plus methods specific to a particular advocacy or policy change tactic, such as tracking social media, may be sufficient in many APC situations where time and resources are limited and perhaps when they are not.

CONCLUSION

Stepping back, we see that there are an almost overwhelming number of outcomes, methods, and measures from which to assemble an advocacy and policy change evaluation. While adopting a theory of change and/or logic model is increasingly common, it is heavily context-dependent and can play multiple roles, be it to increase evaluator understanding of an APC initiative, develop a shared understanding of the program theory of change among stakeholders, and/or identify the outcomes that will shape the evaluation.

Our logic model approach for organizing the outcomes methods, measures, and instruments is intended to help you identify the ones that are appropriate for your evaluation context. However, the essential elements for selecting the appropriate evaluation methods and instruments are an understanding of the purpose of the evaluation and stakeholder information needs and policy acumen.

In short, evaluators need to maintain a level of nimbleness and have a number of approaches in their "back pockets" to respond to a very dynamic environment in which advocacy efforts are launched and implemented. The reality is that most APC evaluations are greatly constrained by time and resources and may include only a handful of methods. But this may adequately address advocate and/or funder information needs. Interviews are versatile and can be used to collect qualitative and quantitative information on a range of outcomes and the impacts of a policy change initiative, such as improved services. Case studies can describe an initiative from the planning stage to its conclusion, including operations, program contribution, and impacts. Document review can be used to triangulate and validate findings, such as corroborating statements made by decision-makers or a change in policy, as well as recreate baseline data.

On the whole, the news is good: evaluators have a number of conventional and emerging evaluation methods that are appropriate for advocacy and policy change evaluations from which to choose or on which they can build. Moreover, as we will discuss in Chapter 5, they can use tailored, unique methods, expanding their focus on activities and outcomes that distinguish APC evaluation from other evaluation arenas.

UNIQUE INSTRUMENTS
FOR ADVOCACY AND POLICY CHANGE

INTRODUCTION

As the advocacy and policy change (APC) evaluation field was developing, one of the biggest challenges was the paucity of evaluation instruments and metrics that could reliably assess advocacy and policy change initiatives and their impacts. To address this deficit, APC evaluators and funders have been very proactive in developing evaluation frameworks and toolkits targeted to evaluators, which we list in Appendix B. Evaluators and funders have also developed instruments and measures to address some of the barriers to data collection, such as access to policymakers, as well as a focus on key attributes of an advocacy and policy change initiative context that have not been measured before, such as the level of "champion-ness." Though constrained by limited time, resources, and expertise, as well as a complex and evolving context in which to conduct their research, evaluators now have some tailored instruments from which to choose.

In this chapter, we describe unique APC evaluation measures and instruments that are being used by the field with some degree of success, as indicated by the results of the Aspen/UCSF APC Evaluation Survey and a review of APC evaluation literature. Some of them are off-the-shelf tools that can be used by advocates themselves, while others entail significant evaluation expertise in their administration and analysis. Please note that inclusion of an instrument is not an endorsement of that instrument. Many of these tools are highly context-dependent, and what works in one setting may not work in another. Moreover, most APC evaluation instruments have not been psychometrically tested and validated though they can be rigorously administered, such as inclusion of a comparison group. Therefore, we are fairly inclusive in what we present, preferring to give evaluators the option of weighing the strengths and weaknesses of each tool and deciding which one is most effective. We hope that enterprising evaluators will continue to improve upon these tools and share them with others in the field. (Please see Appendix B for a list of these tools.)

Similar to Chapter 4, we organize these tools by logic model stages— inputs, outputs, outcomes, and impacts. Additionally, we draw on the Aspen/UCSF APC Evaluation Survey findings and the six evaluation cases and describe inclusion of these methods in current evaluation practice. To illustrate their use, we compare two multiyear evaluations that commenced during the early stages of the two initiatives—the *Tribal Tobacco Education and Policy Initiative* and *Project Health Colorado*—which included a robust cachet of methods to assess formative and summative outcomes, a best-case scenario for APC evaluation practice. The two initiatives include situations that will speak to a broad swath of evaluators or a grassroots advocacy to educate the community on tobacco use and create smoke-free environments and a public-will-building campaign to expand access to health care.

INPUTS

There has been substantial effort to assess and document the earliest stages of advocacy and policy change initiatives, many of which were focused on expanding organizational capacity and mobilizing communities. Consequently, there are a number of methods and instruments from which to choose, some of which have been used for over a decade and with good success. In this section, we focus on three types of inputs: organizational advocacy capacity; coalition, network advocacy capacity; and contextual factors, specifically power relations. We provide thumbnail descriptions of specific tools—their domains, how they are administered, and type of data collected.

Organizational Advocacy Capacity

An area that has received a lot of attention and has many solid tools from which to choose, instruments that assess advocacy capacity can be administered and analyzed by organizations themselves, strengthening organizational evaluation capacity and facilitating an internal conversation about advocacy goals and readiness. Evaluators can support use of these instruments as well as include them in the evaluation design and track changes in capacity over time. Funders can use these tools to identify specific areas of technical assistance for increased advocacy capacity. There are modest differences in the categories of capacity, but for the most part, these instruments focus on organizational infrastructure, such as the ability to raise funds or the ability to communicate successes, as well as the ability to plan and undertake specific advocacy tactics.

The Alliance for Justice's *Advocacy Capacity Tool for Organizational Assessment* has been used by foundations and grantees since 2005 to assess organizational readiness to engage in four areas of advocacy: (1) advocacy goals and strategies; (2) conducting advocacy; (3) advocacy avenues or targets of influence; and (4) organizational operations to sustain advocacy. Each area includes specific measures that describe capacity, such as whether an organization relies on partners to undertake a tactic. Respondents use a five-point scale to describe the organization's strengths. The questionnaire can be completed electronically by funders and grantees and can be used to target resources as well as identify gaps and strengths that contribute to organizational advocacy effectiveness.

There are also tailored tools for the international arena. Recently, the Alliance for Justice developed the *International Advocacy Capacity Tool*, which can be used by groups around the world to measure their readiness to engage in advocacy. Similar to the U.S. version of the tool, the international instrument also includes advocacy targeted to corporate and private sector entities, use of strategies and tactics from other countries, and some fine-tuning of language to reflect an international audience. Individuals answer questions about their organization's skills, knowledge, practices, and resources for developing and implementing issue campaigns, influencing legislation, or other forms of advocacy. Another instrument that has been used internationally is USAID's *Advocacy Index*, which is comprised of eleven dimensions that together form a framework for engaging in and measuring capacity for advocacy. It can be used as a self-assessment tool as well as completed by an independent panel as part of an external reporting system.

Alternatively, questions about advocacy capacity are included in instruments that assess organizational capacity more broadly. For example, the TCC Group's *Advocacy Core Capacity Assessment Tool* (CCAT) provides a snapshot of an organization's effectiveness in four core capacities: (1) leadership; (2) adaptability; (3) management; and (4) technical capacities. The responses to the 146-item online survey are compared to TCC's database of more than one thousand nonprofits. It is different from the Alliance for Justice's *Advocacy Capacity Tool* in that it focuses primarily on whether an organization can meet the demands within its internal and external environment. (Note: TCC recently developed an addendum tool for the *Advocacy CCAT,* which includes key measures of organizational effectiveness that are important for policy and advocacy organizations.)

Coalition, Network Advocacy Capacity

Successful advocacy relies heavily on partnerships and may require many players for an issue to gain traction, such as using a coalition approach to influence federal policymaking. Advocacy capacity instruments for multi-organization alliances have been developed and used by the field to assess the functioning and influence of these collections of organizations. For example, Innovation Network's *Coalition Assessment Tool* assesses coalition advocacy capacity in seven areas: (1) basic functioning and structure; (2) ability to cultivate and develop champions; (3) coalition leadership; (4) ability to develop allies and partnership; (5) reputation and visibility; (6) ability to learn and improve; and (7) sustainability. The organization or coalition members rate their level of agreement on seventy-four criteria (within the seven areas) using a four-point scale. Since coalitions are assessed relative to their goals, the instrument needs to be adapted to a coalition's unique situation.

Mathematica Policy Institute's *Advocacy Coalition Capacity Baseline Assessment* focuses on core capacities of a coalition's leadership team. Part one is a forty-three-item questionnaire that focuses on overall capacity and six to seven specific capacities in the following areas: (1) building and maintaining strategic alliances; (2) ability to build a grassroots base of support; (3) developing and analyzing winnable policy solutions; (4) developing and implementing health policy campaigns; (5) developing and implementing media and communications strategies; and (6) generating resources from diverse sources to sustain efforts. It includes social network measures to describe the relationships among individual organizations. Part two (called the Follow Up Leadership Team Survey) is used to collect information about an organization's experience on the leadership team, including the policy issues addressed by the team. Both instruments are configured for the Consumer Voices for Coverage Initiative and would need to be adjusted for other policy contexts and coalitions.

ORS Impact and the Bill & Melinda Gates Foundation Education Pathways team developed a cross-sector *Alignment Index* that measures five dimensions of alignment among organizations working toward a common goal. The dimensions include: (1) common language (such as using the same language across a variety of communication materials); (2) common frameworks and clear understanding of roles; (3) data sharing and consistency in measuring progress; (4) changes in culture and mutual respect; and (5) shifts in practice, such as increased collaboration and sharing of resources. The thirty-nine-item instrument has been piloted and statistically analyzed for validity and reliability.

Last, funders are increasingly interested in building fields of advocates and using many of the same coalition and network building techniques but targeted to advocates who are engaged in policy work. Evaluator Jewlya Lynn and others have assembled a toolkit of conventional, unique, and emerging evaluation methods, such as Q-methodology, to map the values of the field and qualitative social network analysis that looks at the what and how of relationships in a network (Lynn 2015).

Unlike other areas of advocacy and policy change evaluation, there are many advocacy capacity instruments and measures from which to choose. However, we urge caution here. At first glance, there appears to be significant overlap in the organizational skills and competencies being assessed, but there are some significant differences in the model of capacity building that underlies each instrument, such as whether or not advocacy goals need to be identified beforehand. It is important to have stakeholder agreement about the conceptual model of advocacy capacity and competencies being assessed while ensuring that an instrument can help document actionable findings. Alternatively, you may decide to develop your own instrument as a way to address a unique advocacy context, such as having stakeholders rate a well-defined set of skills on a simple rating scale from low to high. These instruments can be used both before and after capacity training occur and over time, when individuals have greater opportunities to test their expanded capacity.

Contextual Factors—Power Relations
Increasingly, APC evaluators are taking a closer look at the political and cultural contexts to better understand the factors that contribute to initiative success or failure, as well as provide the foundation for constructing a robust theory of change. While not necessarily unique methods in the strictest sense in that they can come from outside the APC evaluation arena, tools that analyze power relations and the base of support can provide baseline information, as well as inform advocates and funders on progress and what is possible.

There are a couple of ways that a power analysis can be done to describe the power dynamics and advocate capacity to navigate the political culture. Some of the capacity assessment tools include different dimensions of cultivating power and/or relating to the political system. For example, the Alliance for Justice has included a "Power Analysis" section in its *Powercheck: Community Organizing Capacity Assessment Tool* to assess the key elements of building institutional power. Another approach is to work with tools specifically designed to analyze and understand power relationships. The power cube developed by John Gaventa (2006) provides a three-dimensional representation of three aspects of power: levels (global, national, local, and closed); spaces (closed, invited, claimed/created); and forms (invisible, hidden, visible). (See Figure 5.1.) The sides of the cube can be rotated, like a Rubik's cube, providing a framework for analyzing the interrelationships among the dimensions. The cube can used to characterize the political space in which an advocate participates, the types of power that challenge advo-

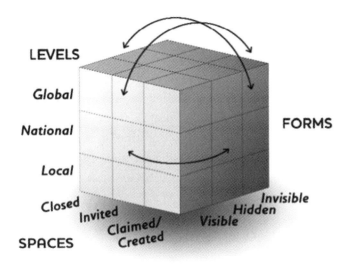

Figure 5.1. The Power Cube: The Levels, Spaces, and Forms of Power. Source: Gaventa 2006. Reprinted with permission.

cates, as well as facilitate a discussion on how their strategies and tactics may influence these dimensions.

OUTPUTS: ADVOCACY TACTICS

Another area that has received considerable attention by APC evaluators is the monitoring of advocacy tactics—the heart of an advocacy and policy change initiative. A focus of political science scholarship, there are instruments that use a cover the waterfront approach whereby multiple advocacy tactics are assessed simultaneously using one instrument. The APC evaluation community has made progress in developing unique methods that take a real-time, systems approach to understanding the implementation and effectiveness of a range of advocacy activities. For example, the *Advocacy Strategy Framework* consists of a visual three-by-three table that maps advocacy strategies across initiative outcomes (awareness, will, and action) and audiences (public, influencers, and decision-makers) (Coffman and Beer 2015). (See Figure 5.2 below.) Information about advocacy strategies can be graphically displayed as bubble maps, providing a snapshot of advocate targets and tactics that can be matched to specific data collection tools. The maps can be used to assess changes in advocacy strategy before and during an initiative, and they can determine whether or not the tactics achieved the desired change, as well as assess the alignment in funder goals and actual advocate activities (Campbell and Coffman 2009). The framework allows for substitution of outcomes, audiences and advocacy activities, and it is also a useful tool for thinking through and characterizing the relationships between these three dimensions of an advocacy initiative and developing a theory of change (Coffman and Beer 2015).

Alternatively, point-in-time data collection can provide a wealth of information on tactics deployed and their effectiveness, such as Innovation Network's *Intense-Period Debrief Protocol*, which is used to collect in-depth and real-time qualitative information shortly after an intense activity period occurs. A focus group of key players from an organization—leadership, staff, and consultants—is convened to discuss an organization's response (such as roles and communications), what worked and what could be improved, the outcomes of the activities, and insights gained from the experience. The advantage of this approach is that the multiple players can be queried at one time and their responses will be less prone to recall issues. There are some challenges in administering this approach, such as timing and having access to stakeholders shortly after an incident. Given the sensitivity of the information, participants may not be willing to divulge the specifics of their activities.

Assessing advocacy tactics is an area that continues to attract attention and new evaluation tools and frameworks are in the pipeline. Dalberg Global Development Advisors is working with the William and Flora Hewlett Foundation to pilot its framework for assessing organizational effectiveness that focuses on three dimensions: strategic positioning (whether or not an organization is well positioned to achieve a desired policy change); selection of tactics (how an organization chooses the specific tactics it uses); and tactical effectiveness (how effective they are at using those tactics).

Figure 5.2. Advocacy Strategy Framework. Source: Coffman (2008). *Foundations and Public Policy Grantmaking.* Paper prepared for The James Irvine Foundation.

OUTCOMES

Compared to efforts that evaluate advocacy capacity and implementation of tactics, the development of instruments and measures to assess the success of these tactics has proceeded slowly. Conventional approaches— surveys, interviews, case studies, document analysis, and focus groups— are being used by APC evaluators with good success. Qualitative approaches have been strongly endorsed by practitioners since they capture the complexity and the interrelated aspects of an advocacy initiative. They also readily lend themselves to adaptation and use in diverse settings. We describe unique methods in three areas of inquiry: terms of the debate; changes in policymaker awareness and support; and strengthened community action.

Terms of the Debate

An outcome that is more common in communications campaigns and public and/or policymaker-will-building campaigns, there are some techniques that have a long track of use within and outside the evaluation arena or *public opinion polling* and *content analysis of media coverage*. Because they are adequately addressed elsewhere, we will refrain from providing a detailed description of their use.

Influencing Policymaker Understanding and Support

Assessing whether or not advocates are successful in moving an issue onto a short list on the policy agenda that are likely to be addressed by decision-makers is no small feat since an advocate's issue is competing with a host of other pressing issues and policy proposals. Moreover, a decision-maker's priorities may be driven by larger political forces as well as reluctance to take an unpopular or not well-supported position. The Harvard Family Research Project's *Bellwether Methodology* is used to assess advocacy strategies to increase policymaker awareness and support. Bellwethers are knowledgeable, politically savvy insiders from the public and private sectors whose opinions carry substantial weight. They are advocates, business representatives, policymakers, media, and academics. The sampling approach distinguishes this approach from other interviews. At least half of the informants should not be involved directly with the policy issue or policy of interest. The Bellwether Methodology Protocol is comprised of questions that elicit information about a policy arena and its dynamics as well as where an issue stands on the policy agenda. Using structured interviews, the protocol intentionally avoids providing details about the policy of interest prior to the interview. Additionally, informants are asked to predict whether or not a policy will advance or be adopted in the next five years, providing information about how likely policymakers are to act on it. The analysis of the interviews provides formative data about strengths and shortcomings of a recent strategy. It does not speak to the success of a specific tactic, like the use of media to advance a policy agenda, but it does provide a multisource reality check about whether or not an initiative is moving the needle in advancing visibility and prioritization of a policy issue. Results from this analysis can be used to adjust the original strategy pursued.

Focusing on policymakers and gauging political will is a perennial evaluation approach, but access issues to key stakeholders and informant recall can be significant barriers. Mathematica Policy Institute's *Baseline and Follow-up Policymaker Interview* questionnaires can be used to gather policymaker views about the involvement and influence of advocates in shaping a policy issue, the role of a group in the nature or outcome of a policy issue, and the effectiveness of their advocacy. The interviews can be conducted by phone and are targeted to high-level policymakers. You will want to tailor it to your policy issue and the strategies adopted by the advocates.

Additionally, advocates can use the Harvard Family Research Program's *Policymaker Ratings Scale* to rate policymakers as a group or independently on three scales: (1) policymaker level of support for a policy issue based on his/her behaviors or actions; (2) policymaker level of influence, such as seniority; and (3) rater level of confidence in the accuracy of the first two scales. It can be administered longitudinally to advocates to assess change in policymaker support or at a point in time to assess progress toward achieving a policy change. ORS Impact (2016) describes its experience working with the policymaker ratings in three settings, including changes in the focus of the ratings scales, sampling, and administrating the instrument. Their experiences provide insights into the challenges in rating policymaker support, such as advocate unwillingness to negatively rate individual policymaker and the fluidity of a policymaker's position. Though the original rating scales are robust, the evaluators suggest modifying the rating scales to deepen the inquiry as well as tailor it to a specific policy context. They also suggest bringing to bear descriptive data, such as policymaker party affiliation and geography in reporting the findings.

Last, you can collect information about aspects of policymaker support indirectly from knowledgeable insiders and advocates with whom decision-makers partner. The Aspen Institute's *Champion Scorecard* tracks advocate progress in cultivating champions or decision-makers who can take steps to advance an advocate's policy objectives, such as sponsoring legislation. Aspen has translated this champion-ness behavior into observable traits that can be measured and ranked in terms of level of engagement. These traits fall under three broad categories of behavior: (1) demonstrates awareness; (2) promotes awareness and understanding; and (3) advocates for improved policy and practice. The instrument can be adapted to different levels of government and different behaviors, and it can be used to track change over time in champion behavior, as well as the impact of an intervention, such as education activities targeting decision-makers. Advocates and funders can complete the scorecard (Devlin-Foltz and Molinaro 2010). The scorecard has been used by CARE USA to evaluate change in one hundred members of Congress' activism after CARE-sponsored learning tours. The primary limitation is that it requires ongoing monitoring and quantification of decision-maker actions, such as public appearances and congressional hearing transcripts. Similarly, Spark Policy Institute has developed a *Policymaker Champion Tracking* tool to monitor policymaker actions besides their voting record to determine if they are champions for a particular issue. Last, the Saving New Lives *Champions Toolkit,* includes a section on monitoring and evaluating champion influence, engagement, and effectiveness. Targeted to advocates, the toolkit is comprised of the Champion Framework and Mapping Tool and the Champion Tracking Sheet: Champion Activities and Interim Outcomes, which can be used by advocates to document their work with champions broadly defined, as well as suggestions for working with evaluators and using existing APC evaluation methods. These include: periodic reviews, after-action reviews, intense period debriefs, impact stories, outcome harvesting, contribution analysis, and process tracking (Roma and Levine 2016).

Strengthened Community Action

There are many types of community-level engagement—grassroots mobilization, social movements, community organizing, and increased voter registration—and evaluators have a variety of options for assessing their involvement and influence, such as the use of surveys and focus groups.

The challenge is to navigate the complicated universe of multiple groups with amorphous boundaries and shifting alliances. The Alliance for Justice's *Power Check: Community Organizing Capacity Assessment Tool* anticipates this complexity while focusing on the bottom-up model of advocacy that characterizes community organizing. While not exclusively focused on advocacy capacity, the online instrument questions focus on an organization's ability to strengthen its position, use empowerment tactics, devise a campaign strategy, activate stakeholders, and influence decision-makers. Organizations or groups rate and reflect on their strengths in several skill areas, some of which are optional, and receive an immediate tabulation of their summary scores in six areas.

IMPACTS

Evaluating the impacts of an advocacy campaign or policy change initiative on individuals, organizations, communities, or society as a whole is challenging and informative. There are few off-the-shelf tools that focus exclusively on impacts. As such, many evaluation approaches use a combination of document review, interviews, focus groups, and surveys. Some of the instruments that are used to assess advocacy capacity can also be used to collect data about impacts, such as perceived benefits to a target population, changes in power relations and influence, and laying the groundwork for further policy change.

Evaluation frameworks and recommended outcomes are being developed that can be used to design a systems-level evaluation, such as the *Impact, Influence, Leverage and Learning (I2L2) Outcomes Framework* that provides sample outcome areas and statements at the systems-level, such as change in regulations and changes in public funds (Reisman, Gienapp, and Kelly 2015). To help evaluators consider the range of influential factors supporting and opposing a policy change, the Western Energy Project (WEP) and several other organizations created the *Advocacy Assessment Framework* to evaluate an advocacy campaign's chance of success. At the core of the framework are nine conditions thought to be essential to a successful policy campaign, such as conducive contextual factors, advocacy capacity, policymaker support, and commitment to implementing the policy. These nine conditions can be used as a checklist to monitor progress and assess results (Barkhorn, Huttner, and Blau 2013). Last, the Overseas Development Institute's *RAPID Outcome Assessment* examines the links between the advocacy initiative, political actors, and the context to identify which factors led to a change. It uses a group process to create a map of observed changes and the links to actors and contextual elements that are thought to have contributed to a change. It does not depend on having a theory of change and can be used to develop one.

We close this discussion of instruments with a suggestion to also review the evaluation toolkits that have been developed for advocates by foundations and APC evaluators in the United States and international arena, some of which are based on actual evaluations. While they may or may not include unique methods per our definition, they include simple, easy-to-use tracking templates, sample questions, and instructions for developing an evaluation design, identifying outcomes and indicators, and collecting and analyzing data. The Aspen Institute's *Advocacy Progress Planner* and the Harvard Family Research Project's *Advocacy and Policy Change Composite Logic Model* have been used by foundations and advocates to plan and evaluate advocacy initiatives and, as such, have been more thoroughly vetted. And toolkits continue to be developed. For example, the Spark Policy Institute recently assembled the *Advocate's Evaluation Toolkit*, which can be found online and provides definitions and instructions for use.

These and other advocacy evaluation toolkits can be found in Appendix B. By the time this book is published, there will probably be more unique methods and toolkits to use or adapt to your evaluation situation. Staying vigilant and monitoring the Center for Evaluation Innovation and Innovation Network's Point K websites, the AEA Annual Meeting Advocacy and Policy Change Topical Interest Group sessions and aea365 online discussions, and the Aspen Institute's weekly blog, *So What? Your Weekly Guide to Advocacy Impact*, will help you stay up-to-date.

EVALUATION PRACTICE: USEFUL
AND USED UNIQUE METHODS

The Aspen/UCSF APC Evaluation Survey findings on unique methods indicate that evaluators are including unique methods in their evaluation designs to a limited extent though they are finding them to be very useful. As described in Table 5.1, *intensive period debriefs* were rated highly in usefulness (3.3, where 4.0 is "very useful") and were more likely to be "used" than other unique methods (57 percent), suggesting that quick, well-timed instruments are highly applicable in advocacy and policy change initiatives. The finding that *advocacy capacity assessments* are rated highly in use (3.1) and used more by survey respondents (65 percent) is not surprising. As we discussed earlier in this chapter, the APC evaluation community has produced a treasure trove of instruments that have been widely disseminated and used. The high usefulness (3.1) and moderate use (49 percent) of *policymaker ratings* suggests that gathering information from policymakers is highly informative, but access to decision-makers is difficult or many APC evaluators may not focus on the policymaking process. The relatively high usefulness and use of two traditional unique methods—*content analysis* and *public opinion polling*—speaks to the importance of tried and true methods, as well as continued focus of APC evaluators on conventional advocacy tactics or media advocacy and advocacy targeting the public. Last, the low usefulness (2.8) and moderate use (49 percent) of *policymaker surveys* may be an indicator of the difficulties in securing policymaker participation in conventional data collection activities, such as access, informant recall, and time constraints. (For a comparison of these methods to conventional methods, see Table 4.2 in Chapter 4.)

In sum, unique methods are being used by the field with good success, generating useful information on inputs, outcomes, and impacts that heretofore had been difficult to evaluate. However, as we discuss in the comparison of two comprehensive evaluations below, the reality is that unique methods are less likely to be the core of an evaluation design. Context and stakeholder information needs will drive use of unique methods, and they may not be applicable in every situation. Second, conventional methods are versatile. Questions on advocate capacity and impact can be included in a survey, an interview instrument, and can be developed into a case study or presented as a stand-alone finding.

Table 5.1. Usefulness and Use of Unique Methods by Aspen/UCSF Survey Respondents

Evaluation methods	Average useful- ness (1 = not use- ful and 4 = very useful)	Per- cent of respon- dents that indicated they had used method
Intensive period debriefs/after action reviews: elicit policymaker and other influentials on advocacy effectiveness.	3.3	57%
Advocacy capacity assessments: online or paper organizational capacity assessment instrument.	3.1	65%
Policymaker ratings: rating of policymakers' support for and influence on, the issue.	3.1	49%
Content analysis of media coverage: counting specific aspects of media coverage, such as word count, placement of articles, key themes.	3.0	67%
Public opinion polling: telephone interviews with random sample of the public to document their knowledge, attitudes, and behaviors.	3.0	48%
Policymaker surveys: survey of policymaker perceptions of advocacy tactics, media coverage, etc.	2.8	49%

Source: Aspen Planning and Evaluation Program, The Aspen Institute.

EVALUATION PRACTICE:

TWO EVALUATION CASES

For our last comparison of two evaluation designs and methods, we have chosen the two longer-term evaluations that were executed early in the initiative and that deployed a variety of instruments to assess formative and summative achievements, as well as longer-term im-pacts, such as systems change: the Tribal Tobacco Education and Policy (TTEP) Initiative, and Project Health Colorado. These evaluations also represent the range of advocacy and policy change scenarios that evalu-ators might encounter, with both initiatives including multiple advocacy tactics. *The Tribal Tobacco Education and Policy (TTEP) Initiative* focused on local-level advocacy capacity, community education, and creation of smoke-free policies. *Project Health Colorado* did not target a specific policy and focused on statewide public will building about improving access to health care using a communications plan, social media tactics, neighborhood mobilization, a messaging framework, canvassing, and educating decision-makers. The contexts were similar in that they required evaluation expertise in social norms and values. The TTEP Initiative emphasized the values of respecting the history of trauma and survival, sovereignty, and choosing a path to change, as well as restoring traditional tobacco use. Project Health Colorado aimed to achieve access to health care for all Coloradans—a social rights issue—using a social movement strategy.

At the design level, the two evaluations provide some insights into approaches that anticipate and work with the complexity of an initiative, as well as the developmental nature of some campaigns. Project Health Colorado evaluators had a complex evaluation context with many partners and interactions among the multiple interventions and included a developmental phase. They drew on adaptive systems evaluation concepts, including a retrospective abductive analysis and fieldwork to understand the stakeholder insider experience and to identify emergent outcomes. The TTEP evaluation team adopted a utilization-focused framework and incorporated empowerment strategies to build capacity and identify areas for revising and strengthening.

Additionally, both evaluations used a participatory approach to their design and used findings to facilitate strategic learning, including real-time reporting of findings to grantees and the funders. The TTEP Initiative evaluators worked with stakeholders early on to revisit the core elements, eliminating one of them and adding an additional evaluation question on how mobilization works in Native American communities. Evaluators worked closely with TTEP coordinators at the five tribes and convened regular meetings of grantees, called Sharing Sessions. Throughout the evaluation, there was an emphasis on describing the initiative and advocacy tactics from the vantage point of tribes. A key aim of the Project Health Colorado evaluation was to support ongoing strategic learning by grantees and the funder, resulting in the creation of a formal technical assistance structure, which was later evaluated by an external evaluator. Grantees worked with strategic learning coaches to develop learning plans and strengthen their capacity to undertake systematic data collection, collective interpretation of the findings from the data, and identification of actionable changes.

Since both evaluations commenced early in the initiative and continued long enough to assess a mature program, both evaluations had evaluation questions that focused on process and outcomes and on context. Project Health Colorado worked with a theory of change that was developed by the Colorado Trust and had five outcomes that focused primarily on strengthened health advocacy and improved media coverage. Individual grantees also had theories of change focusing on messenger development and organizational partnerships. Additionally, the evaluators worked with the Metropolitan Group's five-point framework for social movements. Evaluators developed a framework showing the correspondence between the theory of change outcomes, evaluation questions, and social movement framework stages. Indicators were identified for each evaluation question. The TTEP logic model was developed by ClearWay Minnesota, one of the main funders, early in the program. The model was later modified by the evaluators, who also worked with the funder to develop the evaluation questions and corresponding indicators, including a systems change outcome to reduce commercial use of tobacco and health system changes that supported quitting. Both evaluations assumed their evaluation plans would be dynamic and experience change in methods as the initiatives matured.

The two evaluations used a mixed-method, cover the waterfront approach, evaluating nearly all of the components of the two initiatives, collecting data from multiple sources, and using triangulation to strengthen the findings. Evaluators of both initiatives developed or adapted survey instruments to assess training activities and target audience perceptions and organizational partnerships. For example, the TTEP Initiative evaluators used a Spider Support diagram to describe the level of support by community members. Additionally, TTEP Initiative activities and some outcomes lent themselves to observation, and evaluators were able to observe changes in signage to restrict tobacco use and use of tobacco in the community, including powwows and casinos, a data collection activity that could also be done by TTEP coordinators.

The evaluators of the two initiatives included different unique methods that were integral to documenting initiative progress and effectiveness. The TTEP evaluators developed Community Change Stories, a structured storytelling method that is similar to the Most Significant Change (MSC) technique in that it results in a narrative of the change process from the community point of view. They documented the five tribes and their respective strategies and tactics, working closely with the tribal TTEP coordinator to collect data, reporting findings in real time, and to facilitate reflection to inform planning. The evaluation team also worked with the Aspen Institute's Advocacy Policy Planner to develop a Policy Mapping approach and used the tactics section of the tool, dropping and adding some tactics, such as advocacy to restore traditional use of tobacco. The evaluators of Project Health Colorado examined aspects of the messaging campaign using a survey of individual messengers, analysis of message use by grantees and their audiences in their written, audio and video materials, analysis of communications campaign tracking data, a GIS analysis of messenger distribution combined with field work in intensity areas, and Choice Modeling, a marketing research technique that focused on surfacing which combination of messages will reach the highest percentage of audience members. They also used a storytelling technique and the development of six stories from the initiative that were then included in a survey that was administered to an online intervention group and control group to assess the impact of the stories in persuading people to take action.

While equipped with a robust battery of methods, evaluators of the two initiatives had to contend with some significant challenges, some methodological and some contextual. To strengthen the validity of the findings, the TTEP Initiative evaluation team relied heavily on triangulation and methods were not used in isolation. They also used a rigorous approach to collecting and coding qualitative data and conducting the media analysis, engaging two evaluators and using interrater reliability assessment techniques to check for agreement in coding and of the instrument. Where possible, they collected baseline data. The Project Health Colorado evaluation team took measures to strengthen the validity of individual instruments, including a robust participation rate in its surveys, interviews, and targeted methods to determine the reach of the strategy as a whole and by component, such as paid media, website visits, and electronic communication. Evaluators also analyzed this information by zip code and developed Reach Maps.

The evaluation teams also had to contend with contextual challenges though both teams had anticipated changes in their designs early on, including dropping and adding instruments as the initiatives matured. The Project Health Colorado team added Choice Modeling, the marketing research technique. The TTEP Initiative evaluation team used the Tobacco Experience Inventory survey for two years, but they dropped it after they had collected enough information about capacity. They also dropped the Support Spider diagram, which was helpful for learning about support early on and instead focused on assessing support for specific policies in the grantee work plan objectives. Later, the TTEP evaluators added the Policy Mapping instrument. This nimbleness was particularly useful in the Project Health Colorado initiative, where the funder changed its strategy and included a field-building assessment. Similarly, the TTEP Initiative evaluation design had to take into consideration the different strategies being adopted by the five tribes. (Please see Appendix A for descriptions of the two evaluations.)

CONCLUSION

The good news is that there is a growing body of APC instruments and measures that evaluators can choose from. These unique approaches are gaining traction, providing more options as well as filling in gaps in data collection that heretofore were beyond the gaze of even the most resourceful evaluator. The not-so-good news is that the development and use of these tools cluster at the advocacy capacity and short-term outcomes end of the logic model, leaving evaluators the option of drawing on emerging methods from other evaluation arenas, such as systems-thinking approaches, and inclusion of multiple sources of data to assess longer-term outcomes and impacts, most notably the Most Significant

Change (MSC) technique. However, this may be methodologically the most rigorous and informative evaluation approach as evidenced by our six evaluation cases and growing body of evaluation frameworks.

Additionally, ready-made instruments provide a leg-up, but users have to be careful to make sure they align with the initiative and stakeholder information needs. A validated instrument developed in one context may be ill suited in another setting. The grow your own approach to instrument development may be better aligned with initiative objectives and goals, but it requires expertise in developing, validating, piloting, and administration. As demonstrated by some of our evaluation cases, evaluators are adapting these instruments to their own contexts.

The findings from the Aspen/UCSF survey speak to the high usefulness and moderate use overall of unique methods, with some methods rating lower in use than others, such as the *policymaker ratings, public opinion polling,* and *policymaker surveys.* Differences in use may be context dependent and/or an indication of slow uptake by the APC evaluation community, which may change as the field continues to broaden its focus.

The comparison of the two evaluation cases speak to the APC evaluation design in its broadest and deepest sense or when evaluators are brought in early and are able to collect multisource data across a range of initiative activities and in settings that mirror advocacy and policy change initiatives worldwide. While they still fall short of the gold standard in evaluation design or lack of an experimental design or even a quasi-experimental design, they demonstrate proactive use of triangulation, sensitivity to the cultural and political context, and ability to increase the validity of individual data collection activities.

In short, APC evaluators have a robust toolkit of conventional, emerging, and unique methods and instruments with which to evaluate advocacy and policy change initiatives, and they are willing and ready to use many of them. The benefit is that it expands the areas in which evaluators can focus their gaze with a higher degree of certainty that they will produce credible, actionable findings. The downside is that many of these methods are still relatively new and as of yet have not been psychometrically assessed or widely adopted. Being transparent in the limitations of these, as well as conventional methods, is the time-honored approach.

While developing a comprehensive toolkit of evaluation designs, out-comes, methods, and measures is a key aim of this book, the actual design depends in large part on identifying stakeholder information needs, be it an impact evaluation that focuses on changes in target beneficiaries or validating the funder contribution to program success. It is a dialogue and partnership that serves as the foundation for evaluation practice and not the other way around. In Chapter 6, we explore the perspectives of the end-users, advocates, funders, and decision-makers, and we discuss the opportunities for strengthened partnerships and use of the evaluation process and findings.

Part 3

Leveraging Wisdom from the Field

EVALUATOR ROLES AND RELATIONSHIPS
WITH STAKEHOLDERS

INTRODUCTION

The evaluator's relationship with advocates, funders, and other stake-holders will ultimately determine whether or not an advocacy and policy change (APC) evaluation is successful. These relationships can take many forms. Because APC initiatives include multiple stakeholders with diverse and sometimes conflicting information needs, evaluators of these initiatives will find themselves playing multiple roles as researcher, educator, strategist, and influencer. On the one hand, they are responsible for informing advocates and their private and public sponsors about program effectiveness and strategy. On the other hand, evaluators have an opportunity to educate decision-makers and provide information that influences a policy outcome. For example, a case study that describes a grassroots advocacy campaign to educate the public on the negative economic impact of low literacy rates may carry considerable weight with decision-makers, possibly moving the issue further up the agenda.

In addition to figuring out who needs to know what and when, evaluators must navigate a fluid environment with shifting alliances and complicated political and institutional environments. Changes in leadership, organizational mission, and cultural values, as well as external political circumstances and public opinion, can challenge the implementation of the best-designed evaluation plan as well as the use of evaluation findings later on. It may also be difficult to document what worked and what did not, unanticipated consequences, and lessons learned for future APC endeavors. Traditionally, private funders have recognized the importance of the systematic collection of evaluation findings to help inform the next wave of advocacy efforts, yet, persistently, it may be challenging to be funded to conduct these studies in real time.

In this chapter, we explore the roles and relationships that an APC evaluator may cultivate with three evaluation end-users: advocates/grantees, their funders, and policymakers. We tap into the literature about evaluation more broadly, such as Evaluation Capacity Building (ECB), utilization-focused evaluation, and participatory evaluation. We describe different ways that APC evaluators may collaborate with these users and create positive evaluator-stakeholder relationships.

We also reflect on the results of the Aspen/UCSF APC Evaluation Survey on use of evaluation findings and the experiences of the six evaluation cases, and we provide suggestions for working with diverse stakeholders to surface different perspectives and create a shared understanding of stakeholder goals and the objectives. For example, evaluators can craft an information feedback loop to apply evaluation findings to APC initiatives and advance organizational learning. They can discuss findings in-person and not just produce reports that are at risk of going unread. These strategies will increase evaluator responsiveness as well as cultivate an informed insider perspective that can aid decision-making.

EXPANDING ADVOCATE EVALUATION CAPACITY AND KNOWLEDGE

Increasingly rigorous U.S. government and funder-reporting requirements mean organizations of all types are under pressure to evaluate their activities and show evidence of achievement. This has been accelerated in the United States by devolution of federal programs to the state level and the shifting of responsibility for publicly funded programs to the private sector. However, the data about internal evaluation practices in organizations that conduct advocacy suggests that there is uneven organizational capacity to meet these demands.

That many advocates do not evaluate their APC work 100 percent of the time is no surprise. Significant gaps exist in internal organizational evaluation capacity, including working with external evaluators and marshaling evaluation findings to inform advocacy practice and achievements. In 2008, the top three challenges to conducting evaluations identified by nonprofit advocates were a combination of a lack of resources (time and/or money), lack of evaluation knowledge, and technical challenges in evaluating advocacy work (such as lack of measures and limited data collection and analysis capacity) (Innovation Network 2008). This gap is slowly closing as grantees expand their capacity to evaluate their activities more broadly. In 2012, upwards of 90 percent of nonprofit organizations (N = 535) surveyed by Innovation Network reported evaluating their work, up from 85 percent of organizations in 2010 (Innovation Network 2012).

Efforts to expand evaluation capacity more broadly increase the likelihood that internal APC evaluation will expand as well, and there are many types of evaluation assistance that APC evaluators can provide. For example, they can engage in Evaluation Capacity Building (ECB) and educate organizations on how to develop logic models and data collection systems. An area that has grown exponentially and has produced numerous frameworks and models, ECB practitioners still have to wrestle with the limited attention span of foundation and nonprofit staff, limited organizational and leader evaluative capacity, and sustaining evaluation knowledge and skills (Preskill 2013).

A strong case can be made for making evaluation technical assistance and strengthening advocate internal evaluation capacity standard APC evaluation practice, particularly for nonprofits that primarily provide services. Internal evaluators can play multiple influential roles if they have the wherewithal and resources:

- Change agent, or using evaluation to inform organizational learning and improve program performance;

- Educator, or increasing advocate understanding of the value and use of evaluation, such as training advocates about successful monitoring practices;

- Decision-making supporter, or working with leadership to integrate evaluation with decision-making;

- Researcher/technician, or bringing to bear evaluation methods to solve organizational problems;
- Advocate, or championing for using evaluation to help programs succeed; and
- Organizational-learning supporter, or advancing organizational learning by increasing the utility of internal evaluation information (Volkov 2011).

The evaluation field has also focused on the spread of evaluation capacity within an organization, including greater staff and leadership involvement in evaluation activities, beyond reflecting on the findings, or what Michael Quinn Patton calls "process use," which he defines as:

> Process use refers to and is indicated by individual changes in thinking and behavior, and program or organizational changes in procedures and culture that occur among those involved in evaluation as a result of the learning that occurs during the evaluation process. Evidence of process use is represented by statements such as this one after an evaluation: The impact on our program came not just from the findings but also from going through the thinking process that the evaluation required. (Patton cited by Amo and Cousins 2007)

Vetting an evaluation plan, developing data collection systems, and integrating findings into communications and decision-making—all of these are opportunities for APC evaluators to support sustainable internal evaluation practices and ongoing organizational learning. And since most organizations have limited resources for external evaluators, increasing evaluation capacity in its broadest sense will continue to help groups when they must conduct their own evaluations.

The evaluation field, funders, and advocate field builders have also been proactive and have developed a number of checklists and tools to build internal nonprofit evaluation capacity, such as the *Institutionalizing Evaluation Checklist* (Baron 2011) and the Alliance for Justice's *12 Tips for Nonprofits Doing Their Own Evaluation* (Alliance for Justice 2016). Evaluators are doing a major service by sharing these resources with advocates regardless of their involvement in the design and implementation of an evaluation.

Additionally, evaluators need to be mindful of the organizational context and recognize that a nonprofit service provider that devotes some resources to advocacy will have different organizational structure and priorities than a professional or consumer association that has a membership on behalf of which it advocates on a full-time basis. Nonprofits may have lower levels of commitment to the evaluation, as well as limited abilities or resources to take on additional responsibilities. They may also be concerned about being transparent about evaluation findings if the evaluation results are not as as positive as they would like them to be. While internal evaluation lends itself to organizational self-improvement, formal results may dishearten the "troops" if not presented in the way that is constructive and encouraging about identifying alternative strategies.

Though the trend is toward strengthened internal evaluation, the benefits of expanding organizational evaluation capacity are not always well understood by advocates and their organizations. In many situations, evaluation is viewed with suspicion, particularly if imposed on advocates by funders as a requirement for continued funding. Embracing openness to quality improvement requires a commitment on the part of leadership, particularly if a funder is carefully monitoring their accomplishments. Monitoring and evaluating advocacy has to be credible and demonstrate value added to the advocate or provide real-time information that informs strategy and next steps, something that is not always easy to do.

Moreover, the savvy advocate who believes he or she knows how well a campaign is progressing and when and how to change course may not see the value of adding evaluation activities to his or her workload. This may be true, and APC evaluators need to know how to support and leverage—not burden—this expertise. They must also see themselves as partners, not leaders, in facilitating the process of thinking through an evaluation and supporting organizational learning. In this regard, collecting lessons or "lessons learned data" may be helpful to the organization as it regroups and considers what future directions it needs to pursue.

But for many advocates this is not the case, and evaluation can inform advocacy practice. In its 2015 analysis of the advocacy capacity of 280 nonprofits, the Alliance for Justice found that organizations rated themselves highly in *developing advocacy partnerships* and *legislative and administrative advocacy* and low in their *capacity to fund advocacy* and do *media relations, electoral activities, litigation,* and *ballot measures.* However, nonprofits also reported relying on partner organizations in areas where they are weak. Interestingly, there were no differences by organizational size or budget, with these organizations rating their advocacy capacities similarly (McClure and Renderos 2015).

APC evaluators can also conduct external evaluation activities that advocates themselves are unable to do, such as administering a community-wide public opinion survey. The challenge is to balance internal and external evaluation perspectives. A compelling argument can be made for increased inclusion of external evaluation from a funder perspective. This allows for credible, unfiltered feedback that can improve practice while sharing learnings more broadly (Moralu and Brennan 2009). There are also efficiencies to be gained from integrating external and internal data collection activities, such as leveraging internal evaluation capacity for an enterprise-level external evaluation. Traditional grantee reports to funders can be used to collect formative and summative data. These and other strategies can be used to devise a multilevel evaluation plan that addresses different information needs. For example, we found that conducting a Return on Investment (ROI) analysis provided new information about impacts that grantees themselves could not have learned from their own data collection activities. It also provided evidence to funders that advocacy provided a reasonable ROI (Gardner, Geierstanger, Nascimento, and Brindis 2011). Last, this approach resulted in an easy-to-use accounting system that grantees could utilize to demonstrate financial gains from their policy work. Funders, in some cases, may need to wait several years due to the nature of advocacy to receive an ROI analysis, but it can be well worth the wait and the initial resource investment.

In sum, there are many opportunities for APC evaluators to work with advocates to address gaps in evaluation capacity of all types while supporting organizational learning, such as partnering with advocates to interpret and apply evaluation findings to advocacy practice at quarterly briefings and providing accessible written documentation. Last, they can serve as a liaison between the funder and advocate, such as communicating findings and supporting a partnership-based approach to evaluation.

However, these opportunities are shaped by larger forces, namely, funder requirements to evaluate the success of advocacy initiatives and advocate interest in learning from evaluation findings. While the former is necessary for many APC evaluations, there is not always alignment between the information needs of the funder and those of the advocate, creating less than ideal conditions for conducting an evaluation. Moreover, funders may not be willing to underwrite evaluation activities that do not directly inform their strategic thinking. Funders may need to be sold on the value of collecting process data and informing advocate strategic learning, while advocates may need to see the value of explaining how specific incremental progress can lead to longer-term outcomes. Both require discussions about the role of the evaluation and potentially divergent stakeholder interests early on.

INFORMING FUNDER GRANT-MAKING
AND STRATEGY

Knowing the depth and breadth of the funder role in supporting advocacy and targeting policy issues is important for addressing their information needs and determining how to engage them in the evaluation. Public and private funders of APC initiatives have played a critical role in expanding advocacy capacity, engaging in internal, national, regional, and local policy change, and serving as a political force in their own right. In their review of the literature on foundation support and engagement in advocacy, Jared Raynor and his colleagues (2013, 1) have identified three key reasons why funders are active in this arena: "1) To achieve a social mission through addressing root causes of a targeted issues; 2) To increase social return of investment (SOI) from their grant funding; and 3) To gain leverage from partnerships or cross-sector networks, thereby encouraging government or other investment." They have made a significant investment in scaling up the U.S. nonprofit sector and expanding the impact of high-performing organizations. Additionally, they are willing to do some of the heavy lifting that many solo advocates cannot do, such as targeting federal policy where they can achieve systems-level change, undertaking broad, lengthy initiatives, such as the Pew Foundation's multiyear International Land Conservation Initiative, and large public communication efforts to shape the debate, such as the Colorado Trust's Project Health Colorado. Other roles include issue framing, knowledge building, litigation, funder collaboration, supporting grantee communication networks, place-based changes or demonstration projects, and implementation monitoring (Raynor et al. 2013).

Targeting the grassroots and expanding local capacity to be heard in the policy debates has been a key focus of private foundations. Referred to as the "advocacy niche approach," funders usually provide two kinds of support to advocates: core support for administrative activities and capacity-building to help experienced advocates expand their advocacy activities, increase their effectiveness, and get new advocates up to speed; and project grants that focus on specific projects, advocacy or otherwise.

Funders also have many options for supporting policy change, or what is called a "policy target approach" (Beer, Ingargioloa, and Beer 2012). They have considerable latitude in supporting groups that influence specific policy goals, such as the Rockefeller Foundation's targeting of the reauthorization of the 2009 Federal Surface Transportation Bill and encouragement of commensurate state policies in key, influential states. Alternatively, they can pursue social policy goals that might not be as high on the public radar as other issues, such as health disparities of low-income populations, supporting a broad range of grantee activities with few limitations (Campbell and Coffman 2009). Last, they can provide support for social movements, including cultivating networks, leadership development, media work, and organizational capacity building around vision development and research, among many other functions. Many times funders combine these aims in an initiative. For example, the Ford Foundation supported a six-year initiative, Collaborations that Count, to create new models for inclusive collaboration and to develop equitable policies in eleven northwestern and southern states (Applied Research Center 2004).

There are some important limits to what funders can do that can constrain the evaluation design. Evaluators need to be knowledgeable of the types of advocacy that different funders are allowed and not allowed to support. In the United States, any foundation can support public charities that advocate and even lobby. All foundations can provide targeted support to grantees that work on specific policy actions including the enforcement of existing laws, regulatory efforts, executive orders, or litigation, and, with some restrictions, they can support groups that lobby (Alliance for Justice 2015). They can also pursue general policy goals, such as increased food security, and support a broad range of grantee activities with few limitations (Campbell and Coffman 2009).

Private foundations, such as corporate or family foundations, have to be careful not to instruct a public charity to use a grant specifically for lobbying (also known as "earmarking") or the private foundation will have to pay a tax on those activities. By contrast, public foundations (also referred to as "public charities," such as international NGOs and environmental conservation organizations) can make grants earmarked for lobbying and even engage in lobbying themselves without penalty, so long as they stay within their lobbying limit (Alliance for Justice 2015).[1]

These rules can pose unique challenges for evaluators. While funding may be targeted for specific activities that do not include lobbying, grantees may use other organizational resources for lobbying, potentially contributing to a successful outcome that is targeted by a funder. Evaluators may or may not be able to factor the role of lobbying into a contribution analysis, and some funders may not want to be credited with supporting lobbying. At a minimum, evaluators can clearly indicate what was funded under a grant and document the contribution of just those strategies and tactics, while acknowledging the role of other factors.

Addressing Funder Information Needs
Funder information needs are not radically different from those of their grantees, but they are more oriented to understanding the effectiveness

---

1. In the United States, public foundations can make donations to two types of organizations: 501(c)(3) public charities, or what is referred to as a "nonprofit"; and 501(c) (4) social welfare organizations, such as the Sierra Club and League of Conservation of Voters, which can engage in unlimited lobbying and a limited amount of work supporting or opposing candidates for public office. Private foundations can make donations to both types of organizations, but they cannot support lobbying and voter registration for either entity. However, 501(c)(3) organizations can partner with 501(c)(4) organizations to strengthen their advocacy activities (Alliance for Justice 2015).

of their funding, including the impacts more broadly and on advocates and their organizations, such as how advocates build upon their experiences to strengthen the types of strategies they pursue in their next wave of efforts. Both funders and grantees are interested in the findings from the advocacy capacity assessments and how they translate into targeted funder support. Funders and grantees benefit from analysis of advocacy strategy and tactics, providing front-line information to private funders that may be new to a policy arena. Funders are not alone in wanting to know whether their investment resulted in a financial or other gain; grantees can also leverage this outcome as an indicator of success. A key difference lies in the application of evaluation findings. Grantees value the real-time application of evaluation findings to their work, while funders often are interested in the evidence about the benefits of their support within a portfolio of initiatives. Funders also are under pressure to increase the accountability and effectiveness of their funding in an era where there is increased scrutiny of private sector funding. A word of caution here: funder and advocate needs continue to evolve as evidenced by recent funder support for advocacy field building, human rights, equity and social justice actions, and sustainability of coalitions and networks or standing capacity.

There are many ways that evaluators can partner with funders at all stages of the initiative. They can strengthen grant-making at the front end, in addition to assessing the progress and effectiveness of their initiatives during and at the end of the initiative. For example, a recent toolkit developed by APC evaluators Tanya Beer and Julia Coffman (2015) includes four tools to support grant-making as well as formative and summative evaluation activities: a Question Bank for proposal development and progress reports; Structure Grantee Reporting, an External Partner Interview Guide; and John Mayne's Contribution Analysis.

Evaluators are also working with funders to assess the success of their portfolio of advocacy grant-making, not just the success of an individual initiative. These initiatives include the Atlas Learning Project, a three-year effort by the Center for Evaluation Innovation to synthesize the learnings from the policy and change efforts supported by the Atlantic Philanthropies and other funders that is being used to advance philanthropy and advocacy more broadly. Innovation Network Inc. worked with the Atlantic Philanthropies to document and reflect on the foundation's ten years of grant-making (2004–14) to support U.S. federal immigration reform, including a comprehensive reform strategy (Morariu, Athanasiade, and Pankaj 2015). Last, MastersPolicyConsulting conducted a multipronged evaluation of the California Wellness Foundation's Responsive Grantmaking Program, which had public policy change as a crosscutting theme in nine of its portfolios. The program had reached its tenth year, and the foundation wanted to evaluate its contribution to grantee advocacy capacity building, building the policy and advocacy fields of each portfolio, and to achieving particular policy wins (Master, Barsoum, and Rounsaville 2014). These and other evaluations of foundation initiatives provide insights into the depth and breadth of funder involvement, as well as evaluation strategies that can bolster funder learning and leveraging of their resources.

Increasingly, evaluators are working with private and public funders to help them define and achieve their policy goals. Involvement in this arena requires new business models and considerable savoir-faire in navigating a fluid and uncertain environment. Private funders in the United States have had to give considerable thought to their role and the type of advocacy they will support, as well as clarify what they mean by "success." They need the political acumen to understand where they can intervene and how their support relates to that of other funders, including those that oppose their position. The APC evaluation community has been active in this arena and has developed two tools to assist funders in supporting strategy development—the *Visual Framework of Public Policy Strategies* and a *Foundation Engagement Tool*. The former tool, which was described in more detail in Chapter 5, aligns advocacy tactics with their anticipated outcomes (awareness, will, and action) and target audiences (public, influencers, and decision-makers). The second tool increases foundation board involvement in the strategy development and planning process and assists with the decision about whether or not to engage in a policy initiative (Campbell and Coffman 2009). The Alliance for Justice's *Investing in Change: A Funders Guide to Supporting Advocacy* and its *Philanthropy Advocacy Playbook: Leveraging Your Dollars* provide detailed advice on planning and evaluating an advocacy approach, including navigating the legal restrictions on lobbying, selecting the right advocacy approach, and advice and resources for evaluating an advocacy campaign.

More recently, evaluators are working with private foundations to assess field building and expanding the advocacy capacity of a collective or "field" of advocacy organizations that work together to influence a particular policy arena. Less targeted to a specific policy issue, this approach focuses on the relationships and connectivity among a group of advocates that may be diverse in their positions, perspectives, advocacy capacity, strategies, and tactics (Beer, Ingargiola, and Beer 2012). APC evaluators are also translating the learnings from field-building initiatives, such as the Colorado Trust's Project Health Colorado, and developing evaluation frameworks, outcomes, and indicators. For example, Jewlya Lynn (2014) and other APC evaluators have developed a core set of dimensions—field frame, field skills and resources, connectivity, composition, and adaptive capacity—to organize numerous conventional and unique evaluation methods for assessing capacities, relationships, power dynamics, and change across a field of advocates.

Evaluator Eleanor Chelimsky (2001) has identified other opportunities for partnering with funders and supporting evaluation capacity, including: conducting an evaluative assessment of prospective grantees; development of in-house data repository and monitoring system; provision of evaluation technical assistance to grantees and reviewing their evaluation systems and products; expanding the rigor of in-house evaluation practice; and advising on contracting with external evaluators. While the primary objective is to bring to bear evaluation expertise that supports advocacy and policy change grant-making, evaluators are also increasing the likelihood that funders and their grantees will use evaluation findings early and often.

EVALUATOR AS BRIDGE BUILDER AND PARTNER

Funders are already integral evaluation partners and have played a key role in advancing internal and external APC evaluation and supporting the development of several evaluation guides, tools, and field-building convenings. They have proactively responded to the gaps in advocate evaluation capacity, helping individual organizations and collections of organizations either develop their own evaluation capacity or invest in external evaluation. These funders have also brought to bear their own evaluation expertise and are integral members of the APC evaluation community and the dialogue to advance evaluation practice, including focusing on cultural competency, the development of new data collection instruments and metrics, as well as the vehicles to disseminate these tools more broadly.

Notwithstanding this ongoing involvement and commitment to APC evaluation, there are areas where advocates feel they require additional support from funders. The findings from Innovation Network's 2008 study, *Speaking for Themselves*, identifies challenges to the funder/grantee evaluation partnership: a top-down approach to determining evaluation goals and objectives; insufficient funding for evaluation; funder ambivalence about supporting advocacy because of concerns about the restrictions on funding lobbying; and unresponsive or onerous funder reporting systems. There are many points during the evaluation process that APC evaluators can address these obstacles and strengthen the partnership between funders and advocates while addressing their unique learning needs.

The evaluation plan design is critical for addressing varying stakeholder needs, particularly a flexible, mixed-method approach that focuses on questions of importance, but does not overlook other perspectives. The process of developing an evaluation plan can be used to create a dialogue with stakeholders about evaluation concepts and practices and managing expectations about the difficulties inherent in APC evaluation. Approaches used in the democracy and governance evaluation arena where the evaluator facilitates collaborative inquiry among evaluation stakeholders also work well in advocacy and policy change evaluations that aspire to mirror the democratic principles of the initiative itself (Cousins, Whitmore, and Shulha 2013). Evaluators must adroitly navigate the power differential that separates advocates from funders, which many times results in the evaluator being perceived as part of the privileged elite.

Evaluators also need to be sensitive to tensions that can undermine the advocate/funder relationship, such as a funder that is concerned more with outcomes than capacity development. The development of a theory of change can help build a bridge between the grantee and funder perspectives and identify what type of information is meaningful and to whom. For example, the *Impact, Influence, Leverage, and Learning I2L2 Outcomes Framework* focuses on bridge building and creating a shared understanding among stakeholders in more complex, systems change settings. While impact and changes in the lives of individuals, populations, communities or a geographic area is the primary focus, the framework is a means for surfacing assumptions on how impact will be achieved, as well as recognizing potential influencers on outcomes (such as change in public engagement) and leveraged outcomes (such as new public and/or private funding methods) (Reisman, Gienapp, and Kelly 2015).

Adopting a monitoring approach enables funders to get a detailed look at organizational capacity, successful advocacy tactics, and partnerships that might otherwise get overlooked by focusing only on goals that may or may not be achieved. Integrating grantee reporting with data from other sources, such as tracking social media coverage of the campaign, is enormously useful to all parties and can offset tensions that can arise with more hands-on funders. Grantees can reflect on their strategies and tactics, while communicating their progress to funders in real time. Evaluators can work with funders to develop their capacity as a critical friend and adjust their expectations accordingly, developing a deeper understanding of the advocate mind-set. Evaluators can reflect on the impact of their findings on grantees and funders while being sensitive to the risks of divulging information in a politically volatile space.

To be successful, the evaluator/advocate/funder partnership requires a multifaceted communications plan. Tailored evaluation products increase the utility of the findings and facilitate evaluative learning of all stakeholders, including short, descriptive best practice issue briefs, annual reporting of longitudinal data, accessible FAQ sheets, PowerPoint slides, and tailored briefs. With the availability of social media, additional dissemination can occur through interactive webinars, webpage stories, and through tweeting major results. Grantees are usually under pressure to secure grants and can include information about their strengths and accomplishments in their proposals, citing the evaluation results accomplished in previous advocacy campaigns. The human dimension should not be minimized, and we recommend in-person approaches to reflecting on evaluation findings, particularly convenings that facilitate a discussion among participants, not just a reporting of findings. Additionally, creation of a grantee evaluation work group and regular calls to vet instruments, review products in draft form, facilitate an in-person meeting, and discuss evaluation activities for the upcoming year will support process use and increased grantee engagement and learning.

All of these strategies support a partnership-based approach to evaluation, an organized yet organic learning community and vehicle for reflecting on and applying evaluation findings. Since the partnership depends in large part on relationships with people rather than organizations, evaluators need to be sensitive to people's positions, personalities, learning styles, and contextual factors that facilitate and limit people's actions. All evaluators are advised to take sufficient time early in the evaluation planning process to identify and understand the complicated web of key stakeholders, using tools like social-network analysis or developing an organizational chart that describes the influential stakeholders and their relationships. Time invested in cultivating and maintaining these relationships is time well spent and may provide the impetus for continued engagement and increased use of the evaluation results.

EXPANDING DECISION-MAKER KNOWLEDGE

While not necessarily the primary target of APC evaluation findings, APC evaluators should not discount or ignore the role of evaluation in educating decision-makers and influencing policy, particularly in the *policy proposal development* and *policy implementation* stages where decision-makers at all levels are keenly interested in the costs and early impacts of policy proposals and new programs. Public agencies are also supporting policy and advocacy initiatives and are commissioning evaluations. For example, in 2010, the Centers for Disease Control and Prevention (CDC) funded thirteen comprehensive cancer control (CCC) programs to increase their focus on Policy, System, and Environmental (PSE) change strategies in their state-level cancer control efforts.

APC evaluators will be hard pressed to separate themselves from the political culture and policy arena in which they are working. It is virtually impossible to prevent an evaluator's efforts from having a direct or indirect impact on decision-makers. Once an evaluator engages with policymakers or has evaluation findings that are released in a policy arena, an APC evaluator becomes part of the political context even if that is not his or her intention.

Some APC evaluators may struggle with having the skill set to be a competent advocate since it is not part of the traditional training of evaluators, such as being sensitive to ideological agendas and maintaining independence in the face of pressure to take sides or declare a position (Chelimsky 1995). These skills are not too different from communicating findings to other stakeholders, but they do require a high level of professionalism, discretion, and savoir-faire in maintaining one's credibility.

Additionally, playing an advocate role may be seen as contrary to the aim of many evaluators to be perceived as neutral, evidence-based social scientists. However, the work of evaluators is highly relevant to budget decisions, independent program evaluations, and strategic planning. The evaluation arena has wrestled with the issue of balancing responsiveness to stakeholders and maintaining the independence needed to produce credible findings. APC evaluators can turn to AEA's *Guiding Principles for Evaluators* and other evaluation standards specific to the government arena to achieve a balance. Here are five strategies recommended by evaluator Rakesh Mohan (2014) to maximize responsiveness and evaluator independence:

1. Understand the political context of the evaluation. Identify key stakeholders and know their relationships with each other, their values and competing, conflicting and complementing interests.

2. Establish trust with stakeholders. Involve them in the evaluation process, get their buy-in on scope and methodology, and keep the evaluation process transparent.

3. Disclose all conflicts of interest between evaluators and evaluation stakeholders and avoid the appearance of any conflicts.

4. Develop practical recommendations that are sensitive to sociopolitical and economic conditions.

5. Prepare evaluation reports that are balanced in both content and tone (Mohan 2014, 2).

Moreover, there are sectors of the evaluation community striving to increase evaluation use among policymakers. The work of evaluators is highly relevant to budget decisions, independent program evaluations, and strategic planning. The Government Performance and Results Act of 1993 requires federal agencies in the United States to conduct program evaluation, particularly performance measurement, to increase accountability and inform policymaking (Mohan and Sullivan 2006).

Term limits and the need to bring new policymakers up to speed as quickly as possible, as well as educate legislative and public agency staff, are fueling the demand for increased evaluation in the government arena. For example, presenting a policy problem from an advocate's perspective can carry considerable weight with decision-makers who are sensitive to marginalized voices. By contrast, there are situations where third-party, credible research and data can carry considerable weight. Two strategies to promote use of evaluation findings by state legislators are (1) establish strong networks with decision-makers, and (2) produce credible, accessible and timely evaluation products that can be acted on. It is also important to be mindful of the different perspectives at each level of government and their roles in implementing a policy, as well as budgetary constraints and opportunities. For example, local government has a lot of discretion in the execution of newly funded programs and is sensitive to community-level advocacy. Empowerment evaluation concepts can increase the relevance of an evaluation at the local level as well as facilitate learning beyond decision-makers.

Notwithstanding the value that an informed perspective brings to the table, evaluators need to recognize that APC evaluation use by decision-makers is likely to be extremely limited, similar to the limited use of social science research and evaluations of public programs in public policy. While there has been a shift toward evidence-based decision-making, as described by Carol Weiss and her colleagues (2008) and their experience with the Drug Abuse Resistance Education (D.A.R.E.) program, unless there is a requirement to include rational consideration of sound evidence, other interests and sources of less sound evidence will prevail. Recognizing that this problem has vexed the U.S. evaluation community for many years, evaluators Robert Granger and Rebecca Maynard (2015) provide some guidelines for increasing the use of program impact evaluations that can also be improved use of APC evaluations: (1) emphasize learning from all studies over sorting out winners and losers; (2) learn about contextual conditions that shape an initiative's success or failure, including the counterfactual condition; and (3) learn about the features of a program and policies that influence effectiveness or why programs succeed or fail. Evaluators can also play a few different types of advocacy roles to increase use of findings by decision-makers, including advocating for evaluation and its use, providing real-time, practical solutions to difficult problems, and facilitating a broader understanding of evaluation findings and solutions (Grob 2014).

EVALUATION PRACTICE: USES OF
EVALUATION FINDINGS

To better understand the role of APC evaluators in supporting advocate and funder evaluation capacity and learning, we asked evaluators how their evaluation findings were used. As reported in the Aspen/UCSF APC Evaluation Survey, evaluation findings are used for multiple purposes, though they are being used primarily by funders, namely:

- in communications and reports to stakeholders (77 percent);

- to report to funders on grants and/or contracts (77 percent);

- to plan/revise advocacy initiatives and strategies (75 percent);

- in proposals to funders (61 percent);

- to present at conferences or publish journals/articles (56 percent);

- to plan/revise advocacy tactics (53 percent); and

- to make resource allocation decisions, including staffing decisions (44 percent).

APC evaluators report that they are making inroads in informing future strategy and supporting iterative learning, but it is not clear that evaluation findings are being used to the extent that they could be by advocates to inform their advocacy tactics. Slightly over half of the survey respondents (53 percent) indicated their evaluations generally included assessments and recommendations related to their clients' *advocacy tactics*, as compared to 75 percent who said evaluation findings were used to plan/revise *advocacy initiatives and strategies*.

Linking evaluation findings to advocacy practice can be challenging for several reasons, including: difficulties in producing and disseminating findings when an advocacy initiative is underway, often exacerbated by the lengthy nature of producing advocacy outcomes; limited organizational capacity to reflect and integrate findings into advocacy strategy; and the development and sharing of evaluation findings that speak to advocates in their language. Some evaluators of the six evaluation cases used storytelling to describe and facilitate the use of their findings by advocates and/or used multiple strategies to disseminate evaluation findings.

EVALUATION PRACTICE: SIX EVALUATION CASES

The use of evaluation findings in the six cases corroborate our observation that APC evaluation findings are targeted primarily to funders and advocates, though only two evaluations had formal processes to share and reflect on the findings with advocates throughout the course of the evaluation: Project Health Colorado and the Tribal Tobacco Education and Policy Initiative. Conducting the evaluation at the mid- or end-point of the program may limit the extent to which evaluators can forge working relationships with advocates. Additionally, the type and scope of the advocacy and policy change initiatives may shape the evaluator/advocate relationship. Initiatives that are more diffuse and cut across multiple advocates in multiple geographic levels, such as the International Lands Conservation Program and Sustainable Transportation Initiative, may preclude an evaluation/advocate relationship that supports advocate learning.

Although the maturity of the initiative and timing of the evaluation varied among the six evaluations, the findings were consistently used to adjust the overarching strategy, refine individual tactics, and validate the program. Specifically the Tribal Tobacco Education and Policy Initiative evaluation findings were used to monitor grantee progress while being shared more broadly as an approach to addressing tobacco use; the Project Health Colorado evaluation findings were used to fine-tune the communications strategy and inform grantee evaluation technical assistance;

the GROW Campaign evaluation findings were used to inform Oxfam strategy and extending the reach of the campaign while assisting advocates in the field; the findings from the evaluation of the International Land Conservation Program were used to inform the Pew Foundation's decision-making and continued involvement in the initiative as well as strategy going forward; the Initiative Promoting Equitable and Sustainable Transportation evaluation findings were used by the Rockefeller Foundation to inform strategy on building and sustaining coalitions, as well as support state grantees and identify overarching outcomes; and the findings from the Let Girls Lead evaluation were used to disseminate the model more broadly, as well as facilitate sharing of lessons learned at the local level that might have saliency elsewhere.

There are some differences in the types of products developed by the evaluators and their dissemination. All evaluators produced formal evaluation reports, which have or are being disseminated more broadly, and three evaluation teams developed stand-alone cases and/or issue briefs (Tribal Tobacco Education and Policy Initiative, Project Health Colorado, and Let Girls Lead). Resources permitting, we have found that developing shorter, stand-alone case studies that reflect the advocate perspective and focus on discrete tactics or achievements is useful to advocates. They are accessible evidence of advocate role and achievements and can be disseminated by advocates and targeted to funders and other advocates.

In sum, the six case study evaluators are being "heard" by funders and advocates, but not always in the same way or using the same means of communication. While funder priorities and resources will dictate the size and scope of the development and dissemination of findings, there are multiple options for packaging and distributing the findings and for reflecting on them with stakeholders. (See Appendix A for descriptions of the use of findings in the six cases.)

CONCLUSION

In closing, the evaluator/stakeholder relationship is complicated and multiple stakeholders with diverse and potentially conflicting information needs require APC evaluators to wear different hats—researcher, educator, strategist, and influencer—skills that can be learned formerly and through experience. APC evaluators need to be transparent in their goals and ensure they align with those of their sponsor and advocates. The APC evaluator needs to clarify his or her role as a partner and be sensitive to the needs of different stakeholders, their diverse and changing information needs, and varying learning styles. Last, evaluators must be sensitive to their role as an advocate and the possibility of influencing the outcomes of an APC initiative. They must back up their findings with credible evidence and understand the political dimensions, particularly the constraints in use of evaluation findings by decision-makers.

The evaluation design can also strengthen stakeholder buy-in and use of evaluation findings. Adopting a mixed-method approach increases the likelihood that the APC evaluation plan will be responsive to diverse stakeholder information needs, as well as provide opportunities for educating stakeholders beyond traditional evaluation products. In particular, including ongoing monitoring and providing real-time, tailored reports to advocates can facilitate advocate learning while increasing their buy-in and involvement in the evaluation. However, evaluators may have to balance advocate information needs with funder needs to validate the program and prove its effectiveness, though in many cases these are shared information needs. A partnership-based approach, which builds on evaluator relationships with funders and grantees, can help facilitate learning for all stakeholders.

The six evaluation cases illustrate the diverse funder and advocate information needs and the variety of products that can be developed for different target audiences, including traditional reports and stand-alone cases that demonstrate contribution while giving voice to the advocate perspective. The two multiyear evaluations included more vehicles for sharing and learning among advocates and funders, as well as opportunities for evaluation capacity building. However, a short time horizon, such as six months, doesn't preclude development of products with high practical utility to all parties, such as detailed descriptions of a strategy or tactic and its effectiveness and impacts. For funders, the value added of the evaluation may be the advice proffered for continued involvement and adjustments to a strategy. Knowing and articulating these diverse needs and modes of communication in advance will put the evaluation design on stable footing.

CHAPTER 7

ADVANCING ADVOCACY AND POLICY
CHANGE EVALUATION PRACTICE

INTRODUCTION

Using a theory-to-practice approach, the aims of the first six chapters are primarily practical: to ground evaluators in existing scholarship, concepts, models, and evaluation design approaches so that they will be better able to navigate and evaluate diverse advocacy and policy change (APC) initiatives. We have compiled a repository of APC evaluation resources, as well as actual models of evaluation practice and lessons learned to inform individual practice and advance the field as a whole.

In this chapter, we tap into the wisdom of individual evaluators and the field to create a shared understanding of the strengths and weaknesses in advocacy and policy change evaluation practice that can be used to inform future practice. What seems like a gap now in all likelihood is an opportunity for the creative evaluator who has no compunctions about creating or retooling existing methods and forging new ground in partnering with advocates and funders and documenting the extent of their successes as well as limitations. APC evaluation has incorporated many of the same existing and emerging conceptual frameworks and methods as other types of evaluation, such as systems thinking and Social Network Analysis (SNA). The distinguishing feature is the evaluand—advocacy capacity and/or a policy change strategy—and a complicated and evolving APC context, which has been the impetus for using some methods over others, as well as breaking new methodological ground.

At one level, this chapter is an opportunity to step back and reflect on the implications of the theoretical and practical dimensions of advocacy and policy change evaluation for individual evaluation practice. Based on findings from the Aspen/UCSF APC Evaluation Survey that speak to the attributes of the APC evaluation field and the six evaluation cases on actual evaluation practice, we offer recommendations for reflecting on one's practice and integrating evaluation concepts and models that support the core principles of APC initiatives, particularly increased representation, empowerment, and civic engagement.

Next, we discuss advancing the field of APC evaluation or field building, such as supporting training in methods that are less often used by evaluators, but which hold promise for future evaluations. We assume advocacy and policy change will continue to be a potent force for social betterment and evaluation will continue to be an important and integral component. With input from other long-time advocacy and policy change evaluators and funders, we discuss some practical approaches for supporting a community of practice, such as resources to facilitate field building and strategies for building on the growing base of evaluation practice. The findings from the Aspen/UCSF Survey and six evaluation cases indicate that APC evaluators are well positioned to inform and support the many different ways that individuals, organizations, and communities "speak truth to power" as well as contribute to a growing knowledge base of successful forms of influence and improved policy solutions.

Last, APC evaluators are not alone in their quest to characterize and assess advocacy and policy change initiatives. They are fortunate to have multiple arenas—political science, nonprofit organizations, and advocacy capacity—from which they can draw and to which they can contribute. We highlight some of the more promising research areas and identify topics where evaluators may be able to contribute their findings and research acumen to the scholarship on influence, organizational or network capacity, civic renewal, and advocacy effectiveness.

ADVANCING INDIVIDUAL APC
EVALUATION PRACTICE

The 2014 Aspen/UCSF APC Evaluation Survey findings provide a pro-file of the typical APC evaluator and that profile is complex. An evaluator may be new to APC evaluation or seasoned with more than ten years of experience in conducting APC evaluations. They are independent consul-tants as well as employed by different types of organizations—universities, nonprofit organizations, foundations, for-profit corporations, advocacy organizations, and government. They are entrepreneurial in their focus and policy areas of expertise. While their areas of focus tilt to health and education policy, evaluators are active in diverse policy arenas that focus on social and environmental improvements. They do not focus solely on advocacy and policy change evaluation: approximately 95 percent of sur-vey respondents report that they conduct other types of evaluation, which includes close neighbors of APC initiatives, such as policy analysis, re-search, and budget monitoring. Alternatively, an APC evaluator may be a generalist and evaluate a variety of programs and services with no one topical area or methodological expertise guiding his or her practice. Last, APC evaluators do not necessarily limit their practice to one country or geographic area or a particular level of decision-making—an asset. In short, the APC evaluation community reflects significant diversity in ex-pertise, topical and geographic areas of focus, as well as broad experience with other types of evaluation.

This diversity enriches APC evaluation practice, but it raises serious questions about standards of practice and the need for greater uniformity in the APC field. At a minimum, the individual evaluator is responsible for referring back to conventional evaluation principles in designing his or her evaluation design and paying attention to changes in the advocacy and policy change evaluation arena. We liken this to "mindful" evalua-tion and provide some pointers for upping one's evaluation game in some specific areas.

Knowing What You Don't Know

How deep and broad is your knowledge of advocacy and policy change and the particular policy arena in which you may be working? Approximately 40 percent of the Aspen/UCSF APC Evaluation Survey respondents indicated that *limited expertise among evaluators in the policy or issue area of the advocacy initiative under evaluation* was a "somewhat significant gap," and 25 percent reported that it was a "very significant gap." Too little knowledge of advocacy practice, the policy change process, and stakeholders can compromise all aspects of an evaluation. While being a quick study is a common trait among evaluators, at some point there needs to be an honest appraisal and willingness to partner with others who are more knowledgeable about the APC initiative and the political context. Policy arenas vary in their transparency and complexity, with some arenas having a small number of political actors and others having too many actors to easily measure, such as health policy. For example, the evaluators of the Program for Equitable and Sustainable Transportation engaged an expert in state transportation policy in order to develop deeper contextual and content expertise.

As demonstrated by our six evaluation cases, critical to evaluator success is a deep knowledge of the evolving cultural and political contexts in which the initiative or strategy take place. Evaluators of all evaluations except Project Health Colorado partnered with experts in the geographic area, including language ability, working with indigenous peoples, and knowledge of the political context and access to local decision-makers. Culturally competent evaluation approaches are not new, but the call for their inclusion is only just reaching a crescendo.

We cannot emphasize enough the importance of having a high degree of familiarity of advocacy and policy change concepts, models, and definitions in working with advocates, funders, and decision-makers. That nearly half of the Aspen/UCSF Survey respondents (48 percent) thought *poor understanding of advocacy and policy change processes among funders and/or grantees (such as advocacy groups)* was a "very significant gap" means that APC evaluators need to make sure their expertise in advocacy strategy and policy change is as great, if not greater, than that of stakeholders. They cannot subscribe to just one model of policy change or have a narrow understanding of advocacy tactics. Advocacy initiatives usually include more than one type of tactic, many of which are areas of significant scholarship, such as the role of media in shaping policymaker and public opinion. Carving out time to avail oneself on the existing body of literature and/or consulting the experts in a policy arena is time well spent. And this expertise needs to continue to be built as most cultural and topic content is dynamic and changes over time. This gap also points to the necessity of achieving a shared understanding of an advocacy and policy change initiative among stakeholders early on. If not addressed, there is the potential for misalignment in stakeholder information needs and the purpose of the evaluation.

Evaluation Planning and Design

The Aspen/UCSF Survey results and comparison of the six evaluation cases indicate that APC evaluators are embracing new planning models, new partnership models, and new ways of addressing advocacy initiative complexity and uncertainty. The results also suggest new approaches to balancing the desire to prove with the need to improve, and the integration of processes and products that support strategic learning. Evaluators are well positioned to apply these approaches and find the sweet spot in aligning stakeholder learning needs. It is difficult, but it is the key to a successful evaluation. While a theory of change and/or logic model may not be an exact replica of the complicated reality that characterizes most advocacy initiatives, it helps to build clarity among stakeholders so that they are on the same page and understand the purpose of the evaluation. For example, a funder may have a narrow interpretation of advocacy and limited understanding about other forms of advocacy that are not lobbying, particularly education more broadly of policymakers and the public.

Expanding the Evaluator Gaze

The evaluation scenarios that evaluators are likely to encounter are diverse and not limited to specific policy issues or advocacy tactics, but also include democracy expansions in developing countries and an increased focus on human rights worldwide. This should not trouble APC evaluators, who are a creative group and continue to develop new data collection approaches, as well as tailor existing methods to an APC context. There are a few areas where evaluators are likely to increase activity, including focusing more APC evaluation on advocacy activities postpassage of a policy. While not always an obvious form of advocacy, participating in the development of rules and regulations, as well as informing budget allocation processes, are critical for achieving the desired policy objectives. This longitudinal perspective is resource intensive, but it is the missing link between a policy change and the desired improvements in people's lives.

Another area ripe for examination in an APC evaluation is the opposition, be it a political party or entrenched interest that is resistant to change, moneyed interests that have significant clout, or large membership organizations that have a worldwide presence and reach. While their tactics may not be readily observable, in all likelihood experienced advocates will be aware of their involvement in the past and the position they are taking in a current campaign.

Third, use of communications of all types is likely to be a growth area for some time and to be a component of many initiatives. Social media analysis is a promising approach and has great relevance to APC evaluation. Early research on use of social media by advocacy groups suggests that use of more popular social media, such as Facebook and Twitter, for advocacy is likely to grow. Social media are perceived to be an effective, less expensive approach to facilitating civic engagement and collective action (Obar, Zube, and Lampe 2012). Similarly, evaluators need to be knowledgeable about the information technologies that facilitate 24/7 sharing of information, some of which can also be useful sources of information, such as tracking the number of times a policy issue is mentioned in blogs or collecting survey data via cell phones.

Additionally, mapping software that allows for the visual representation of social characteristics (such as income levels or high school graduation rates) are potent tools for developing a baseline against which to assess systems change later on. Geographic analyses and Google Maps also have potential for characterizing the influence of an advocacy and policy change initiative on a census tract, neighborhood, city, region, community, or state(s).

Last, individual evaluators may want to take a second look at data collection activities that have traditionally been in the political science domain. The low participation of APC evaluators in assessing some conventional advocacy tactics, such as protests and marches and get-out-the vote campaigns may reflect funder priorities and/or evaluator expertise in examining these activities. However, protests and marches are still a potent form of advocacy as evidenced by the recent activities in U.S. cities in the wake of police treatment of African American males. Additionally, APC evaluators are reforming conventional data collection approaches. For example, the evaluators of Project Health Colorado combined polling with traditional interviews and surveys to evaluate changes in public will.

Responding to the Demand for Increased Rigor
The external pressures to increase rigor and demonstrate that a program plays an important role in producing its intended results means that APC evaluators need to consider approaches to increasing the validity in their design, methods, and instruments. While this may reflect the continuing tensions in the evaluation field about whether evaluation should emphasize proving program effectiveness over the desire to improve program functioning, it also speaks to a gap that evaluators need to factor into their self-appraisal.

At the design level, APC evaluators should include counterfactual thinking and rival explanations as well as assemble a collection of tested methods. Multimethod approaches are much needed in this arena as any one method may have its limitations in capturing all the potentially rich data that emerges as part of APC evaluations. Our six evaluation cases speak to two kinds of APC evaluation design: the multiyear, mixed-method enterprise that explores multiple aspects of a complex advocacy and policy change initiative and the smaller, targeted design that starts at the midpoint or toward the end of an APC initiative. While a multiyear, mixed-method evaluation can dive deep and surface findings that might otherwise be overlooked, a smaller, point-in-time evaluation can also inform strategic learning and the initiative going forward.

At the methods level, evaluators need to be brutally honest about their capacity to develop or adopt instruments that are valid, reliable, and possibly generalizable, and to undertake statistical and financial analyses.

In addition to framing the design and methods in social science research terms, they should consider partnering with those who have the appropriate methodological expertise. For example, a survey methodologist can advise on instrument design and align the questions with the purpose of the survey, develop appropriate response categories and scales, determine the optimal response rate, and identify the types of statistical analyses that are possible and under what circumstances.

There should also be an examination of alternative and emerging statistical approaches, such as Survey with Placebo (SwP), when randomization or a comparison group is not feasible. Additionally, the areas where more than 50 percent of Aspen/UCSF Survey respondents said they had not used a method or *outcome mapping*, *Most Significant Change (MSC) technique*, *systems mapping*, *policymaker ratings*, *policymaker surveys*, *public opinion polling*, and *story collection and journals*, may be areas where evaluators might benefit from additional training.

Furthering Advocate and Funder Learning

The relationships among the evaluator, advocate, and funder are a work in progress, reflecting larger trends in the evaluation arena, such as increased emphasis on strategic learning and proliferation of different models of participatory, partnership-based evaluation. The Aspen/UCSF APC Survey findings about the role of evaluation in informing advocacy capacity suggest that evaluators are translating their results into useful and actionable products that can address funder information needs, with many survey respondents reporting that their evaluations generally included assessments of APC initiatives and recommendations on strategy. However, more can be done to increase the utility of evaluation findings for advocates, particularly to help plan and/or revise advocacy tactics. The six evaluation cases provide some examples to bolster advocate learning, such as including advocates and affected communities in the presentation and dissemination of evaluation findings and finding new and inventive ways to empower advocates to use APC toolkits and tools.

We suggest a stay-the-course strategy here, with greater attention to the evaluator/advocate partnership and identification of real-time opportunities to communicate evaluation findings, particularly providing interim findings in different formats that can inform organizational capacity and tactics. The increased emphasis on learning-focused evaluation more broadly holds promise for APC evaluators working with funders to understand their contribution to a single initiative or a multiyear campaign of policy and advocacy grant making.

The challenge is to have the resources to create an ongoing and meaningful relationship with advocates broadly defined, whose partnership universe may be very complicated, including coalitions and individual citizens, numerous advocacy allies, and episodic partnerships that may be in conflict at times, all occurring concurrently within a changing context. And this universe may expand as advocates and funders see the value of working with or supporting 501(c)(4) organizations, which have more flexibility in the advocacy tactics they can undertake.

Last, the primary gap identified by Aspen/UCSF Survey respondents, *insufficient funding for advocacy and policy change evaluations*, means that individual evaluators need to know how to be efficient in their designs, while maximizing learning and the assessment of program effectiveness. The reality is that while potentially useful new evaluation methods are emerging, such as systems thinking, and APC evaluators have developed many useful unique approaches, evaluators in most cases do not have the luxury of using many of them in their designs. They have to balance budgetary considerations, as well as the priorities established by the funder, with the type of design that they can pursue successfully. In some situations, it is better for the evaluator to do a thorough and high-quality job with a less rigorous design that can offer the needed answers.

In sum, there are many ways that new and seasoned evaluators of APC initiatives can continue to expand their evaluation practice. Feedback from the APC field suggests the prospects for continued expansions in individual APC evaluation practice are good in the areas of designs, methods, products, use of findings, and partnerships. The six evaluation cases and Aspen/UCSF Survey results indicate that APC evaluators are embracing new planning models, new partnership models, and new ways of characterizing and integrating complexity. The results also suggest new approaches to balancing the desire to prove with the need to improve. But they need to up their game in other areas. Not surprisingly, evaluators continue to struggle with context—geographic, political, cultural, and topical—and its impact upon the APC strategies adopted. Last, APC evaluators need to assess the level of rigor in their designs and methods and identify and address gaps, as well as communicate the limitations to stakeholders.

ADVANCING THE ADVOCACY AND POLICY CHANGE EVALUATION FIELD

Field building has been a focus of evaluators and funders of APC evaluation since the early 2000s. A core of committed APC evaluators have carried the torch for the field as a whole, providing wisdom and developing and/or disseminating planning tools, instruments, and examples of successful evaluations. The results have been impressive: a substantial knowledge base, new technical resources, new networking opportunities, and new tools targeted to evaluators, advocates, and funders. We offer some suggestions for supporting this emerging community of practice[1], particularly supporting increased rigor in evaluation practice, increased visibility and partnership within the evaluation arena, expanding the focus of APC evaluation, and proactive sharing of models, methods, and findings.

APC Evaluator Diversity: Asset, Liability, or Both?

The APC evaluation community is diverse, which can be a positive attribute if it results in creation of new approaches and supports diffusion of evaluation practice into new policy arenas. For example, the findings from the Aspen/UCSF APC Evaluation Survey speak to a range of evaluator expertise, from having two to five years of experience in evaluating advocacy and policy change programs (35 percent), five to ten years of experience (28 percent), and ten or more years of experience (27 percent). A relatively small percent of respondents (8 percent) had less than two years of experience. While we do not know how much experience is required, we assume that an unevenness in experience will persist as

---

1. By "community of practice," we mean a network of evaluators that directly and indirectly learn from each other in a variety of settings, advancing individual evaluation practice (Lave and Wegner 1991).

evaluators new to the advocacy and policy change arena continue to enter the field and experienced evaluators exit the arena. However, this range of experience raises nagging questions about differences in competency and experience that may compromise quality. More concretely, 23 percent thought that *having no standard nomenclature in the advocacy and policy change evaluation field* was a "very significant gap." Different understandings of "advocacy," "advocates," and "policymaking" are to be expected as the community becomes more international and diverse in composition, but these differences should be modest. Establishing rigorous but flexible standards has been proposed by some in the APC community to strengthen utility, propriety, cultural competency, and adequate understanding of policy and politics and accuracy (Aspen State of the Field Meeting, September 18, 2015).

Making the Case for Increased Rigor in Evaluation Design and Methods

This may be the time for the APC evaluation community to take steps to address the issue of rigor and the field's shortcomings in design and methods. Many survey respondents (43 percent) thought *lack of rigor in advocacy and policy change evaluations* was a "somewhat significant gap," and 28 percent thought it was a "very significant gap." In addition to supporting self-assessment by individual evaluators, the APC evaluation community can develop guidelines and trainings to address this gap, such as training in statistical approaches for working with small sample sizes and use of inter-rater reliability approaches in working with qualitative data. Additionally, it may want to consider a system for peer-review of designs targeted to evaluators new to APC evaluation as well as compiling a repository of quasi-experimental evaluations. Last, the field could take the lead in reviewing instruments for validity, disclosing their strengths and limitations.

The external pressures to address the question of rigor will continue, fueled by the demand for data-driven, evidence-based evaluation in the public sector and use of performance measurement in program evaluation more broadly. Advances in theory-based evaluation and approaches to characterize and assess complex, developmental, or adaptive initiatives, such as realist evaluation, systems thinking, and network analyses, may provide the means for APC evaluation to advance to the next level and not rely so heavily on a mixed-method approach to establish credibility. However, even these approaches are still a work in progress and adoption could be slow if not supported by the field.

Whether rigor will be overshadowed by other gaps is an important question. Not surprisingly, the primary gaps identified by APC evaluators as "very significant" are external to evaluation practice, namely *insufficient funding for advocacy and policy change evaluations* (50 percent). Despite the pronounced role of funders in building the APC evaluation field, there continues to be limited or uneven funding for APC evaluation that may be due to funder unwillingness to dedicate sufficient funds to build measurement into the design, in the face of other priorities, as well as funder prioritization of overall program evaluation over APC evaluation. The field will have to continue to make the case for a more robust approach to APC evaluation, including documenting the difference that evaluation findings make to funders, grantees and even to the desired policy change and its outcomes.

Expanding the Field's Gaze
Historically, the APC evaluation field has focused more on upstream advocacy, such as community organizing and expanding organizational advocacy capacity building. As our six cases demonstrate, evaluators are focusing on upstream and downstream advocacy, including documenting policy gains that can follow quickly on the heels of or coincide with expanded capacity of individuals and organizations. We anticipate the field will focus more attention on advocacy activities postpassage of a policy, strengthening assessment of policy implementation and documenting achievement of longer-term outcomes and systems-level change. While not always an obvious form of advocacy, participating in the development of rules and regulations, as well as informing budget allocation processes are critical for achieving the desired policy objectives. Specifically, without attention to the operationalization and implementation of policy, the law or regulation may only exist on the books, rather than being implemented with fidelity to the original intent of the advocacy action. Additionally, the field is extending its gaze to other forms of advocacy, such as litigation advocacy, which may be beyond the reach of nonprofits and

other individual organizations, but is a type of advocacy that funders can undertake. Less visible forms of advocacy are gaining more recognition, such as the donation of "dark money" or funding that does not have to be disclosed to election campaigns in the United States and the emergence of a "shadow elite" or top power brokers—consultants, advisors, and think tanks—that operate under the radar to protect their business interests at the expense of democracy (Wedel 2009).

Education advocacy during the *problem recognition* stage is also coming into fore, such as producing research briefs targeted to the public and/or decision-makers that describe a problem more generally and do not take a position on a particular policy proposal. The advocate is perceived as an expert and reliable source of information and who can be consulted at later stages, such as providing testimony. This and other less-known policy stages require closer examination by the field to determine whether or not they are increasingly useful stages for exerting influence.

Second, evaluators are increasingly documenting a policy change throughout its life course to demonstrate program effectiveness and the contributions of funders and advocates. This longitudinal perspective is resource intensive, but we have found that it surfaces important information on the links among advocacy capacity, policy change, and the desired improvements in people's lives, as well as validate the theory of change.

Last, there needs to be more collective action to synthesize and disseminate lessons learned across different policy content areas and advocacy strategies. This book is one approach, but it cannot document the entirety of evaluation practice and share this learning in real time. Structuring professional forums and virtual learning networks to cross geographic and content boundaries and quickly surface tested models and methods would expose new frontiers and propel the field forward.

Strengthening the Crosswalk Between APC Evaluation with Other Types of Evaluation

Though there is some synergy between APC evaluation and other types of evaluation, APC evaluation has not yet achieved its full potential in shaping evaluation practice more broadly. The perception by the APC evaluation community is that APC evaluation is sufficiently different that it requires different evaluation models and approaches from other types of program and intervention evaluations. Consequently, the APC field has forged its own path, developing definitions, toolkits, and instruments from scratch. The results have been impressive: it has been one of the fastest-growing areas in the American Evaluation Association (AEA). However, only 51 percent of survey respondents reported that they were actual members of the AEA Advocacy and Policy Change Topical Interest Group (TIG).

A strength of the APC evaluation arena is that it has porous boundaries and it overlaps with several other evaluation areas, including most of the topical areas of the American Evaluation Association, such as health, education, and the environment. APC evaluation also touches on areas that focus on the role of stakeholders, such as empowerment evaluation, nonprofits and foundations evaluation, and all of the methods-specific arenas. In all likelihood, APC evaluators already identify with one or more of these areas and are not solely APC evaluators. Most of the Aspen/UCSF Survey respondents (95 percent) reported that their organizations conducted other types of evaluation in addition to advocacy and policy change evaluation.

These synergies speak to a variety of ways in which the APC field could grow as well as inform other arenas, and there needs to be more intentional forging and nurturing of these relationships and professional networks to assure that they are sustained and enhanced over time. Professional meetings and conferences that intentionally build bridges between evaluation arenas would pave the way to broader use of tools and findings, while also providing networking opportunities for evaluators who work in the same topical area.

Additionally, like the rest of the evaluation community, the APC field is expanding its ranks of evaluators who conduct APC evaluations outside of the United States and Europe. A little over one-third of survey respondents reported that they focus on the Global South in their advocacy and policy change evaluations. Latin America is experiencing growth in the evaluation of social programs, including formation of a professional evaluation organization and increase in evaluation resources and training, which may reflect the expansion in civil society (Kushner and Rotondo

2012). Fewer respondents (22 percent) said their APC evaluations focused on the Global North or OECD countries not including the United States. The United Nations Resolution A69237 and declaration of 2015 as the Year of International Evaluation (EvalYear) may provide the boost the field needs to expand its ranks, as well as reduce the barriers to participation at national and international meetings, such as providing scholarship assistance to APC evaluators who reside in developing countries and who have much to share on the evaluation of democracy and civil society building projects, social justice movements, and initiatives to strengthen human rights.

New Approaches to Communicating Evaluation
Designs, Methods, and Findings
APC evaluators have not hesitated to use a variety of vehicles to showcase their activities, including: AEA's annual meetings and electronic venues, such as the aea365 blog; publically available resources from the Alliance for Justice's Bolder Advocacy initiative, Innovation Network's online Point K Learning Center, the Sparks Institute, and the Center for Evaluation Innovation; and the Aspen Institute's evaluation breakfast series and online blog, *So What? Your Weekly Guide to Advocacy Impact*. But given the global nature of APC evaluation work, there needs to be additional vehicles that address geographic and language barriers, such as YouTube videos that showcase evaluations from around the world and that are translated into multiple languages. The recent focus on identifying exemplary evaluations by the American Evaluation Association supports sharing among evaluators and contributes to strengthening individual practice and supporting field building. Perhaps, though, we should also consider the less successful evaluations and better understand the weaknesses, as well as the challenges that exist in other evaluation contexts.

However, these efforts are likely to be hampered by three significant barriers to disseminating evaluations and their findings or the proprietary nature of some evaluations, concerns about disclosing detailed information about a specific advocacy tactic that could benefit the opposition, and the slow nature of publishing in the peer review literature. *The Foundation Review* did the field a great service when it produced a themed issue on advocacy and policy change evaluation in 2009. The field is ready for another comprehensive review of current practice, and such reviews ideally would occur every three to five years. It is also ready to contribute to a themed issue of a mainstream evaluation journal, such as *New Directions in Evaluation* and the *American Journal of Evaluation,* surfacing and sharing evaluations, which have sound designs and credible findings.

Networking, Partnering with Other Evaluators and Researchers
The AEA Annual Meeting has been a very useful vehicle for hosting these conversations and exposing evaluators to APC concepts and tools, as well as solidifying the identity of the APC field as distinct from other evaluation arenas. However, a significant portion of the field may not affiliate with the APC topical interest group and/or attend the annual meeting on a regular basis. Thanks to a dedicated core group of APC evaluators and funders of advocacy and policy evaluation, the APC field has had a few in-person professional meetings outside the AEA annual meeting. There is no question that individual evaluators and the field have benefited greatly from these opportunities to discuss strengths and gaps in evaluation practice, understand the advocate and funder perspectives, as well as inform toolkit and tool development. It is clear that the field would like and would benefit from more of these meetings. Upwards of 42 percent of survey respondents indicated that *few conferences or meetings to discuss advocacy and policy change evaluation approaches and advance the field* was a "somewhat significant gap." The networking and potential for partnership development are greater when people have a chance to come together to share as well as have a meeting that focuses exclusively on APC evaluation.

Second, the extent that the attendees at these meetings reflect on the APC field as a whole is unclear since they are convened primarily in the United States. More consideration should be given to hosting international meetings, rotating among developed and developing countries, and increasing the inclusivity of the agenda and discussion points. The growth in the number of Voluntary Organization for Professional Evaluation (VOPE) organizations around the world could greatly facilitate sharing and cross-border pollination. Supported by the EvalPartners Initiative, which was launched in 2012 by the International Organization for Co-operation in Evaluation and UNICEF, the networking of VOPEs could result in a more potent evaluation community overall, while promoting equity-focused and gender-focused evaluation—values that are shared by the APC community (Kosheleva and Segone 2013).

Developing, Using Appropriate Resources

There is no shortage of resources, including published articles, books, guidelines, blogs, conferences, and listservs. This is particularly true for *APC evaluation planning tools* where nearly 60 percent of Aspen/UCSF Survey respondents thought this was "not a gap" or "not a very significant gap." Whether or not there are enough technical resources is an open question. While rated lower than other gaps, almost 20 percent of Survey respondents thought that *few conferences or meetings to discuss advocacy and policy change evaluation approaches and advance the field* was a "very significant gap."

This veritable cornucopia of planning tools, capacity assessments, and new methods can only benefit APC evaluation capacity among advocates, funders, and evaluators, but they need to avail themselves of these resources. Regarding fifteen better-known tools or toolkits, a large percentage of survey respondents (60 to 94 percent) indicated that they had not used many of these resources in evaluating advocacy and policy change efforts. We can only speculate about the barriers to using these resources.

The field's work is not done in this area. Tailored trainings at the Evaluator's Institute and inclusion of courses in graduate-level training programs could bring less-experienced evaluators up to speed while standardizing evaluation practice. We are hopeful that new field-building resources (such as trainings, tested instruments, and toolkits) and the technical reports being developed by the Center for Evaluation Innovation and others that reflect on what has been learned over the last twenty years will close this gap once and for all in the near future.

APPLYING EVALUATION PRACTICE TO THEORY

We come full circle and end this chapter where we started: with a discussion of theory and how APC evaluation can contribute to the scholarship in multiple arenas. While many times disconnected from

the theoretical underpinnings of much advocacy and policy evaluation, APC evaluators are part of a large community comprised of public policy scholars who seek an explanation of how the policymaking
process works, political scientists who conduct research on politics and
policymaking, as well as policy analysts who use primarily cost-analyses
to identify and compare the best policy options to address a problem.
Though there are differences in foci, questions, and methods, the context remains the same. In Table 7.1, we describe some areas where there
is a ready crosswalk between evaluation practice and the policy sciences.
For example, evaluators who focus on the passage of a specific policy
may be able to inform scholarship in the areas of policy design and
educate policymakers early in the policy process. The opportunities for
the APC evaluation community to contribute to the knowledge base
are discussed below.

Taking the Policy Stage Model to the Next Level
Evaluators are fundamentally concerned with assessing the impacts of
advocacy initiatives that may target some or all stages and aspects of a
policy change process. Each stage of the policy stage model described in
Chapter 1 is a rich vein of scholarship that can both guide and be guided
by evaluation inquiry. In particular, evaluators can assist with documenting advocacy tactics throughout the policy cycle. To what extent do specific tactics wax and wane and why? Given limited resources, is it better
to engage in targeted advocacy during one stage of the policymaking process? Maintenance of effort pre- and postpassage may give advocates the
advantage, particularly into the implementation stage where the real deals
are struck. The preponderance of advocacy and policy change evaluations
focus on advocacy during the early stages of the policymaking process.
Evaluators would do well to work with funders and advocates to consider
extending the time horizon postpassage, if a policy is passed.

Second, evaluators can drill down into a stage and situate specific advocacy tactics in that body of literature. John Kingdon's (1995) policy
windows model is a good example of a well-articulated, conceptually co-
herent understanding of the complex interplay of actors, issues, and timing during the agenda-setting stage. Evaluators should seek other equally

Table 7.1. Guiding Policy Research Questions and Evaluation Methods

Field of Study	Research Questions	Methods and Examples
Policy analysis	What actions should we take? What options exist to address a particular problem? What policy option should be chosen?	Cost analyses Forecasting Risk assessment
Policy design	How do people perceive problems and policies? How do policies distribute power, and why? Whose values are represented by policy?	Qualitative analysis Content analysis
Policymakers and policymaking institutions	Who makes policy decisions? How do policymakers decide what to do? Why do they make the decisions they do?	Quantitative analysis Qualitative analysis
Interest groups	How do groups exert influence? What impact do groups have on public policy? Are groups changing?	Quantitative analysis
Policy process	Why does government pay attention to some problems and not others? How are policy options developed? Why does policy change?	Quantitative analysis
Policy implementation	Why did a policy fail or succeed? How was a policy decision translated into action?	Quantitative analysis Qualitative analysis
Policy evaluation	What have we done? What impact did a particular program or policy have?	Quantitative analysis Qualitative analysis Statistics Expert judgment

Source: Smith and Larimer 2013.

sound and tested frameworks. If one is lacking or requires further testing, evaluators should see this as an opportunity for advancing scholarship.

Advocacy and Policy Change Evaluation Contextual Analysis
Political science comparisons of democratic systems and political cultures can benefit from evaluation experience of diverse policymaking contexts, such as the differences and similarities between international, national, state, and local policymaking models. The roles of social, economic, political, and cultural contexts in the policymaking process are acknowledged but not always well understood. Evaluators, by virtue of their diverse backgrounds and expertise in different topical evaluation arenas, are well equipped to navigate these complicated arenas, drawing on sociology, government evaluation, nonprofit organizations, organizational development, and media studies. Evaluators can contribute to characterizing the roles and relationships of advocates and decision-makers who work together to craft and/or implement policy. Advocates are not limited to exerting pressure and can play an integral role in the formulation, support, passage, and implementation of specific policies, such as providing data on the use of existing health care services. Understanding the different ways that advocates relate to decision-makers is a well-established line of inquiry. Advocates may use formal and informal targeting of decision-makers, such as conversing during a social event or participating on an agency committee to craft rules and regulations. A perennial research question is: Is it "Who you know" or "What you know?" Or is it both? Given their vantage point, evaluators have an opportunity to contribute to the knowledge base.

Assessing Advocacy Effectiveness
Large-scale surveys of interest groups and lobbyists date back to the 1950s and provide an in-depth understanding of group tactics and composition of the interest group population. While a repository of instruments exists that can be adapted to diverse policy settings and organizations, scholars have struggled with questions about individual and collective influence of tactics. Additionally, the survey approach has some drawbacks, including insensitivity to the policy context, the issue, actor,

and constituents (Baumgartner and Leech 1998). For example, key informants may hesitate to share the primary tactics that they use to advance their cause. However, some advocates have been forthcoming, and in 2010 they reported that their most effective strategies were community or grassroots organizing, coalition building, educating the public, and legislative advocacy (Innovation Network 2008).

By virtue of their close proximity to advocates and their decision-makers, evaluators are well positioned to provide qualitative and quantitative information on advocacy group tactics and the extent of their influence, such as findings from policymaker surveys that inquire about their awareness of and relationship with a specific advocate and perceptions of specific advocacy tactics. Additionally, the focus on contextual factors can advance our understanding of the circumstances when advocacy is successful and when it is not.

Measuring Civil Society and Civic Renewal
The decline in traditional group membership, such as political parties, and dissatisfaction with government in the United States and other democracies in the 1990s resulted in a reexamination of civil society and the extent to which civic engagement is being undermined. The depletion of social capital or the "features of social life—networks, norms, and trust—that enable participants to act together more effectively to pursue shared objectives" was hypothesized to have eroded civic engagement in public sphere activities (Putnam 1995, 664–65). While a contested proposition, it focused attention on the role of civil society and its attributes, such as trust, diversity, and economic security (Bennet 1998). These questions persist today and are an important part of the discussion about new and different types of advocacy. APC evaluators that focus on grassroots, community-based advocacy campaigns have a front-row seat to assessing the effectiveness and impacts of these initiatives and their potential for laying the groundwork for achieving systems change.

New Voices in the Policy Process
Interest group surveys have been helpful for describing the composition of the advocacy community and how it has changed over the decades.

Recent scholarship has focused on the entry of new types of organizations, including nonprofit service providers, for-profit business organizations, and think tanks, such as the Rand Corporation. There is increasing interest in less well-defined entities, such as Super PACs and the "shadow elite," a network of power brokers that go beyond national borders and act as potent behind-the-scenes players (Wedel 2009). Other emerging voices are disadvantaged and underrepresented populations in the policy process—racial minorities, low-income people, undocumented immigrants, and youth. While the number of organizations representing these populations has proliferated, the research suggests that they do not enjoy a level playing field and the same policy gains as entrenched, wealthier interests (Schlozman, Verba, and Brady 2012). Still, the literature on social movements and nonprofit organizations emphasize the potential for increased voice by these populations through a variety of means, including grassroots mobilization, connecting clients and providers directly with the media and decision-makers, and voter outreach. The 2008 Great Recession saw the meteoric rise of the Occupy Wall Street movement and foregrounding of income inequality as a hot policy issue.

Foundation interest in cultivating and empowering these new voices has afforded evaluators an opportunity to inform the scholarship on the formation, capacity building, and potential influence of many of these less well-known individuals and entities. Evaluators have a long track record of focusing on advocacy capacity development of all types of organizations as well as mapping the advocate universe for a particular policy or policy issue. Additionally, APC evaluators have not shied away from identifying new voices or recognizing existing voices whose influence has gone unnoticed, such as bellwethers, who are influential experts in a particular policy arena.

New Forms of Participation

There is no better place to learn about new advocacy strategies and tactics than speaking to advocates. In all likelihood, they will have leveraged new forms of communication, such as text messaging, well before researchers have begun studying it. Increased use of new technology—electronic data systems, social media, digital cameras, and phones—is clearly an important trend that has influenced a variety of outcomes, including national political elections. But new technology does not necessarily imply new strategies or tactics. The reality is that much of advocacy—groups and tactics—has stayed the same (Schlozman and Tierney 1986). However, with new, cheaper, and faster forms of communications and social media, such as Twitter, there is increased potential for more people to be engaged far more quickly. In addition, the spread of information supports democratization and enables greater numbers of the public to be involved, as seen in the 2010 Arab Spring in the Middle East. This is making the landscape increasingly diverse in who might be engaged in advocacy although issues remain regarding the depth and longevity of commitment to an issue.

Another way to look at new forms of participation is to focus on the policy issue and whether or not it has expanded to include new political players. For example, the Clinton administration's health care reform proposal resulted in a significant increase in the number and type of advocates in the 1990s, but the policy itself took another two decades to achieve.

APC evaluators have been very active in this area, documenting and informing our thinking of new types of tactics or existing tactics that may be more important in achieving a policy change than previously thought. Flexibility in using a stage model or social network analysis of a policy arena may help to reveal new forms of influence or heretofore, unrecognized influence. For example, the APC evaluation community is documenting the role of interim outcomes that result from increased advocacy capacity but are not the final outcome itself, such as developing a working relationship with media and/or decision-makers (Gill and Freedman, 2014).

CONCLUSION

Feedback from the APC field suggests the prospects are good for continued expansions in APC evaluation practice in the areas of models, methods, resources, dissemination, and learning. The APC evaluation community has built a strong base of practitioners and a broad and deep body of work. The arena is no longer the uncharted territory it used to be, and there is now the infrastructure to capture and share the wisdom of the individual evaluation, as well as seasoned APC evaluators who have a decade or more of experience. But challenges remain—financial, conceptual, and technical. They are not insurmountable but they do require ongoing attention to field building and educating funders, advocates, and other evaluators.

It is easy to suggest new and different ways to grow the APC field. It is not so easy to act on any or all of these suggestions. Competing priorities, insufficient funding, and a transient community of evaluators who may only self-identify as being an APC evaluator when he or she is evaluating an APC initiative, are significant constraints. However, we do not think they will stop individual evaluators and the field from advancing. A core of dedicated APC evaluators and funders continues to gently nudge the field forward, and new leaders from inside and outside the APC evaluation community will continue to emerge. Building on this base and being open to new partnerships, as well as developing new areas of foci and new ways of thinking about APC evaluation, are some of the means for solidifying and sustaining this evolving community of practice. Commitment by funders to continue to support and expand their focus on APC issues, as well as invest in external and internal evaluations are also key for growth in this field.

Given the significant policy and political issues of our day and the need to learn from them, there is no reason why APC evaluators should not strive to be an integral partner in the evaluation arena and beyond. There are new and emerging ways to partner with advocates, funders, and decision-makers. There are also opportunities to contribute back to the scholarship that serves as the theoretical underpinnings of APC evaluation, such as the policy sciences, the nonprofit literature, and the growing body of research on advocacy and advocates. This is also a time in which APC as a field continues to be recognized as important in assuring that the voices of the marginalized are heard and that they have a place at the table. If we are to continue to make societal progress in achieving social justice, we must ensure the significant disparities in resources available in communities receive the public attention they deserve. We hope this book helps pave the way toward realizing these opportunities and partnerships, bringing to bear scholarship, models, resources, and examples of useful evaluation designs and tools so that advocacy can fulfill its vision more effectively.

SIX EVALUATION CASES

LET GIRLS LEAD'S ADOLESCENT GIRLS' ADVOCACY AND LEADERSHIP INITIATIVE (AGALI)

Initiative Description

Created by the United Nations Foundation (UNF) and the Public Health Institute (PHI), Let Girls Lead is building a global movement of champions to ensure that girls can attend school, stay healthy, escape poverty, and overcome violence. Since 2009, Let Girls Lead's model—endorsed, validated, and supported by leading foundations—has contributed to better health, education, livelihoods, and rights for more than seven million girls globally. It catalyzes scalable change for girls by investing in visionary leaders and local organizations through leadership development, organizational strengthening, grant making, and advocacy. This initiative was intended to strengthen the capacity of civil society leaders, girl advocates, and local organizations to promote girl-friendly laws, policies, programs, and funding in Guatemala, Honduras, Liberia, Malawi, and Ethiopia.

ADVOCACY STRATEGY AND TACTICS

Let Girls Lead uses a holistic approach to advocacy capacity building, offering intensive workshops, seed grant funding, and ongoing technical assistance and engagement to its Fellows. Let Girls Lead Fellows have undertaken a range of advocacy tactics that varies by country. These tactics have included (1) experts communicating with policymakers, weighing in on the development of policy; (2) experts focusing on implementation, and determining whether a policy was implemented, and if not, why not, and bringing this to the correct people; (3) adolescent girls and boys meeting with local officials to explain why a policy change was necessary; (4) broad public education; and (5) marches and reading of materials. It also focused on media as part of training and used radio in two countries. As of 2013, it had developed a global network of 110 leaders advocating for adolescent girls' rights.

Evaluation Purpose, Design, and Instruments

In 2013, toward the end of the initiative's first five years, the UNF commissioned an external evaluation to assess the program's effectiveness, capture part of the Let Girls Lead story, and provide guidance to other groups. It was a four-country, mixed-methods evaluation with four evaluation questions: (1) What evidence is there to demonstrate Let Girls Lead's contribution to key advocacy and policy results aimed at improving adolescent girls' health, education, livelihoods, and human rights? (2) What differences have Let Girls Lead made in the lives of adolescent girls who have been involved in the initiative? (3) What evidence is there to demonstrate Let Girls Lead's contribution to advocacy capacity building for Fellows, their organizations, and the Let Girls Lead supported networks? and (4) Has the Let Girls Lead model catalyzed advocacy efforts and policy change? If so, how has this been achieved?

There was a theory of change: "Adolescent girls (10 to 24 years of age) are empowered to realize their full potential through the creation and implementation of programs and policies that ensure their health, education, human rights, and socio-economic well-being." A logic model was developed by the PHI to guide the program. The evaluation team used it from the beginning and focused on the links between the outcomes as well as the four pieces of the model (advocacy training workshops, technical assistance and coaching, seed grants, and outreach with adolescent girls). Evaluators also looked at what made a difference: the package as a whole, or individual pieces? Also, they looked at what changes the girls were able to make and changes in their tactics.

Data Collection and Analysis Activities

To assess the Let Girls Lead model, the evaluation team surveyed the eighty Let Girls Lead Fellows who at the time of the evaluation had participated in Let Girls Lead in the four focus countries and then interviewed thirty-two key stakeholders, including Fellows, staff, trainers, and representatives of the UN Foundation. To validate Let Girls Lead's contribution to key advocacy and policy results, the evaluation team used a contribution analysis to assess six illustrative case studies, examining policy changes and the roles of Let Girls Lead and its Fellows in influencing them. Four cases were related to national-level advocacy, such as passage of the national Children's Law in Liberia, and two cases were examples of local-level advocacy, such as enactment of bylaws to eliminate the practice of child marriage in Malawi. To gather early information about changes in adolescent girls' lives resulting from the policy changes that Let Girls Lead Fellows influenced with Let Girls Lead's support, the evaluation team collected Most Significant Change (MSC) stories from thirty-five adolescent girls and boys and conducted a meta-analysis of them.

Challenges Addressed

The evaluation team had to contend with time and budget constraints. The time frame for the evaluation limited the changes in adolescent girls lives affected by the influenced policy changes that could be captured. Both time and budget constraints limited the evaluation team's ability to thoroughly triangulate some of the data collected related to the contribution analysis processes. Last, working with a team of national evaluators in two different languages reduced the ability of the evaluation team to share findings and learn from each other internally, but it increased the team's access to policymakers, adolescent girls and other stakeholders, as well as deepened the team's understanding of contextual factors.

Use of Evaluation Findings

The findings of the evaluation indicated the Let Girls Lead model was effective at increasing individual leadership, organizational effectiveness, and advocacy capacity and impacts. There were several recommendations for fine-tuning model components, such as including adolescent boys as advocates and replication in other countries. Evaluation products included a four-pager and two-pager issue briefs, external evaluation executive summary, and an article in the *Guardian* on cases in Honduras, in addition to the internal evaluation report. Evaluators also compiled the Most Significant Change stories, shared lessons learned, and disseminated the Let Girls Lead model. Contribution analysis reports and Most Significant Change stories went back to NGOs. At the program level, there may have been some changes, such as increasing the roles of the country-level partners. They reinforced the validation of the model. The findings may have also influenced the design of programs going forward.

Evaluators: BLE Solutions, LLC

THE INITIATIVE TO PROMOTE EQUITABLE AND SUSTAINABLE TRANSPORTATION

Initiative Description

Launched in 2008 by the Rockefeller Foundation Board, the Initiative to Promote Equitable and Sustainable Transportation was based on the premise that informing the adoption of new federal incentives and policies for equitable and sustainable transportation options would initiate a systemic shift in investment choices and policies surrounding transportation. The Initiative had three intended outcomes: (1) to inform transportation policy through actionable research, analytical support, and practical examples; (2) to strengthen capacity and leadership in strategically diverse organizations and create an enduring constituency for change and reform toward a new transportation paradigm; and (3) to expand partnerships of new and diverse philanthropic and donor partners to collaborate in support of federal efforts and in sustaining regional ones. The initiative ended in 2013.

ADVOCACY STRATEGY AND TACTICS

The Initiative had three levels of activity: (1) the federal level that was primarily focused on informing the Surface Transportation Reauthorization Bill but also included some communication activities; (2) the state level to improve state and regional decision-making; and (3) demonstration projects to showcase innovative models of transportation infrastructure. Strategies and tactics included research and policy analysis and new vision development, communications and framing the debate, organizational capacity building, program/project support, coalition and diverse partner development, and funder-to-funder meetings.

Evaluation Purpose, Design, and Instruments

The purpose of the evaluation was a combination of learning and improvement throughout the life of the initiative to support achievement of initiative outcomes, accountability to the Rockefeller Foundation for funds invested in the initiative, and contribution to knowledge in transportation policy, advocacy, and philanthropy and the field of evaluation as a public good. The federal and state components were evaluated separately, using mixed-method but different approaches. The evaluation was conducted between 2011 and 2013 and was implemented in two phases: the first phase of the Monitoring and Evaluation (M&E) work included a retrospective summative evaluation of the federal policy reform initiative. The campaign was at a transition point at the time of the evaluation, but the Reauthorization Bill had been delayed substantially and was still under a tenuous consideration. It was passed while the evaluators were finishing the data collection. For the second phase, evaluators conducted a formative evaluation design for the state-level work since it was more in its infancy. A third methodology based on appreciative inquiry (relying on perceptions of most significant changes) was used to evaluate the communications portfolio of grants, which had a broader and less defined set of outcomes. There were eighteen evaluation questions broken into five criteria: relevance, effectiveness, influence/impact, efficiency, and sustainability.

The theory of change was that the foundation needed to be involved in state-level policy work so that when federal reauthorization occurred, it would initiate a systemic shift in investment choices and policies surrounding transportation. A logic model for the initiative was developed by the evaluators and vetted by an evaluation advisory group. Its components included inputs, strategies, short-term outcomes, interim outcomes, long-term outcomes, and external forces. Long-term outcomes included increased conversation about smart transportation alternatives and increased ability to target key policymakers. There was a direct relationship between the logic model and evaluation plan, with evaluation questions derived from the logic model. The qualitative data was analyzed using a coding rubric based on the logic model. The goal was to correctly capture the strategy and activities that were being conceived through the campaign as well as make sure they had the big picture buckets in which to code or categorize findings. There was an effort to explore causal relationships between the logic model components through the data analysis. Additionally, the evaluators sought to get stakeholder buy-in to the data collection strategy.

Data Collection and Analysis Activities

The evaluation of the federal component consisted of fifty-five interviews of foundation staff, policymakers, media, and of advocates/grantees as well as other foundation leaders that had been funding in similar areas. Questionnaires varied by informant type and focused on perceptions of role of the grant, achievement of outcomes, capacity, and benefits. Evaluators also surveyed grantees and collected quantitative data about progress, coalition and organizational capacity, and perceived future needs. Last, they analyzed secondary data such as initiative records or proposal and grantee reports, as well as publicly available data or press releases on reports, drafts of bill text, and some bill monitoring. For the state component, the evaluators used a similar set of instruments: grantee survey, grant analysis and coding, interviews with grantees, funders, and observers, as well as discussions with initiative staff.

Challenges Addressed

A point-in-time evaluation that took place in a dynamic, complex environment, the evaluation was challenged with collecting data from all of the relevant sources, including some decision-makers. The evaluation team contracted with a transportation expert and included an evaluation reference group to provide content expertise in federal transportation policy. Last, informants sometimes provided conflicting reports, which were reported or analyzed further to determine validity.

Use of Evaluation Findings

The evaluation findings were used by the foundation to inform how they proceeded with the initiative. The Reauthorization Bill passed as the evaluation findings were being developed for the federal component. The findings raised a number of issues that spoke to the broader field. For example, the evaluation team found that the dismantling of the advocacy infrastructure in the wake of the last major transportation overhaul left the field weak, and there were some difficulties in mobilizing around the current reauthorization. The field had to build a new coalition with Rockefeller support. There were some lessons learned in the wake of a "win" and thinking about the capacity infrastructure over time, as well as the costs in terms of time, effort, and money in bringing together a broad-based coalition in the transportation arena. The advocates, particularly the primary coalition, used the evaluation findings in developing a new strategic plan. The formative evaluation of the state-level work provided more information about state strategies and practices.

Evaluators: TCC Group

OXFAM GROW CAMPAIGN

Initiative Description

On June 1, 2011, Oxfam launched the GROW Campaign to tackle food injustice and build a better food system that sustainably feeds a growing population. Targeted to more than forty countries, the GROW Campaign operates at national, regional, and international levels across four thematic areas: land, investment in small-scale agriculture, climate change, and food price volatility. As part of this four-year initiative, Oxfam launched a six-month campaign targeting the World Bank in October 2012. The Land Freeze Campaign had two aims: a six-month freeze on large-scale land acquisition led by the World Bank; and a review and improvement of the World Bank policies and regulations in relation to free, prior and informed consent, transparency, and governance of land. The World Bank provides financial support in the billions for land acquisition in developing countries where the land rights of small-scale farmers and indigenous persons have been violated with some of them being pushed off their land. The World Bank Campaign was intended to be a unifying element within Oxfam in which all affiliates could participate.

ADVOCACY STRATEGY AND TACTICS

Oxfam undertook a broad range of activities including: lobbying and direct advocacy to decision-makers in the public and private sectors and on policy reforms; public mobilization through online and offline activities; generating media coverage with a range of media outreach strategies; and research and development of policy briefs. Oxfam led the campaign, but in many national contexts it was run by coalitions of allies and partner groups. In addition, for the World Bank campaign, there was a video project with the rock group Coldplay as well as social media actions and stunts.

Evaluation Purpose, Design, and Instruments

Evaluators conducted a mixed-method, midpoint evaluation of the GROW Campaign that covered the twenty-one-month period from the campaign launch in 2011 to 2013 that had broad implications. The evaluation focused on four main areas for which a series of questions were developed and which were matched to indicators and data collection tools, or assessing progress to date, the Campaign model, recommendations for future work, and specific projects (achievement, role of Oxfam). The evaluation design combined research and analysis of international strategies with deep dives into specific national and team campaigns and projects. There was a theory of change and an Impact Chain (logic model) for the overarching GROW Campaign, which was used as part of a progress review. The data collection instruments were matched to the model indicators and outcomes.

Data Collection and Analysis Activities

For the GROW Campaign as a whole, evaluators conducted a document review, a cross-campaign survey, semistructured interviews with Oxfam staff, external interviews with stakeholders and informants, and developed five case studies of international and country-level activities. They also analyzed social media, focusing on reach and where Oxfam had exposure. Oxfam had a target, and the evaluators could determine the progress in reaching it, such as the number of signatures received on an online petition. For the World Bank case study, the evaluators conducted interviews with Oxfam, the World Bank, academics, and NGOs working on land issues. The latter two could provide a third-party view and were more observers rather than targets of the campaign. They also had sufficient documentation that they could conduct a policy analysis, which focused on whether or not the policy change happened and estimating the influence of Oxfam on the change seen. This involved looking at when change happened (pre/post), specifically what was changed in the policy and then comparing the language of Oxfam's "ask" with what was in the policy. Last, this was validated inside and outside of Oxfam through a simplified contribution analysis.

Challenges Addressed

Due to the broad scope of the GROW Campaign, the evaluation team could not assess all the campaign activities and had to focus on key objectives and actionable findings, such as selecting cases that were diverse, targeted to different levels of involvement, contained a mix of GROW objectives, and would inform understanding of the broader campaign. It was unable to focus on gender to the extent that was hoped. The team relied on internal documentation and Oxfam staff opinions but tried to offset the potential for bias with interviews of upwards of ninety external persons. Documenting contribution can be challenging since targets of advocacy will not necessarily reveal to what extent they were influenced (or not), and this requires triangulation with other sources and the documentation of the policy processes to assess the level of contribution. The evaluation was conducted in a relatively short time—six months—and the evaluation team included expertise in managing multicounty evaluations, working with clients to develop an evaluation framework, expertise in assessing policy/advocacy strategies, including communications, and international evaluation experience, particularly in southern contexts.

Use of Evaluation Findings

Oxfam staff primarily used the evaluation findings internally along with lessons learned concerning the various tactics deployed. Within Oxfam, at the midpoint of the GROW Campaign, the findings revealed a focus and provided some insights as to how and where they should go forward. The findings were also intended to assist advocacy practitioners and evaluators in the field, and this is why Oxfam made the report public. The targeted World Bank campaign resulted in significant media coverage although social media actions achieved 10–25 percent of its exposure/action targets. It raised awareness of the land grab issue within the World Bank and externally. While the World Bank rejected the six-month freeze, there were changes in World Bank policies and regulations, with inclusions of land rights in the World Bank safeguards review. The World Bank campaign was limited to six months, but Oxfam still has an ongoing relationship with the World Bank and considers itself a critical friend with a constant dialogue about land and other development issues. It was felt that the campaign strategies that included a combination of public pressure and targeted policy influence worked in accelerating policy change within the World Bank even if the main goal (the land freeze) was not taken up.

Evaluators: Owl RE

INTERNATIONAL LAND CONSERVATION PROGRAM

Initiative Description

In 1991, the Pew Charitable Trusts began a series of campaigns to conserve old-growth forests and wilderness areas in the United States and British Columbia. In 1999, it developed a new strategy that would extend its land protection work into Canada's boreal forest, and it created the International Boreal Conservation Campaign to manage these efforts. In mid-2008, Pew launched the conservation campaign, Outback Australia. In 2011, Pew's new long-term goal for these campaigns was to protect one billion acres in Canada and 500 million acres in Australia by 2022, half with formal protection and the other half through sustainable development rules.

ADVOCACY STRATEGY AND TACTICS
Similar campaigns took place in Canada and Australia, including: leveraging science-based arguments for the value of land conversation; empowering Indigenous communities to assert their rights over native lands; and cultivating strong relationships with key decision-makers from across the political spectrum. In Canada, the campaign and its partner organizations developed the Boreal Forest Conservation Framework, a game-changing document calling for 50 percent of the boreal to be placed in permanent protection with the remaining 50 percent open to commercial activities, but subject to strict sustainable development rules. The Canada campaign inspired the campaign in Australia where it supported funding for an Indigenous ranger program, *Working on County*, to provide employment opportunities for Aboriginal Australians while ensuring ongoing land stewardship that is essential for maintaining biodiversity.

Evaluation Purpose, Design, and Instruments
In 2013, the evaluators undertook a six-month midcourse cluster review that included a mixed-method, retrospective assessment of the effectiveness of the two campaigns and a prospective analysis of how strategy might be refined going forward. The evaluation team was tasked with addressing six evaluation questions and assessing the campaign's success in protecting lands during the 2007 and 2012 period in Canada and Australia, including overall progress in achieving strategy objectives, understanding Pew project's contributions, identifying factors that have challenged progress, and lessons learned that can be applied to the two initiatives as well as land protection and advocacy more broadly. Since Australia and Canada pursued different objectives and used different strategies (and because the Canadian effort was more mature than Australia), the evaluation team conducted separate analyses in the two countries. Because of the complexity (such as number of advocates and their roles) and the fluid nature of campaigns that operated opportunistically

in response to changing circumstances, a logic model was not deemed appropriate. Outcomes and indicators of effectiveness were used to identify progress toward the stated goals as well as the contribution of Pew's projects.

DATA COLLECTION AND ANALYSIS ACTIVITIES

A mix of data collection and analysis activities were used: (1) in-depth interviews representing diverse perspectives, including 119 partners and stakeholders who were involved in the two campaigns, plus "informed observers" who were not involved in the campaign but were knowledgeable. Evaluators also spoke to a few representatives of groups that were politically opposed to Pew's objectives; (2) development of regional case studies that focused on select regions in the two countries (three in Canada and six in Australia) to assess the campaigns at the regional level and to complement the research at the national level; (3) a quantitative analysis of land protection outcomes, namely, a GIS analysis of the amount and type of conserved and protected land; and (4) a contribution analysis with documents, media coverage, and interviews to piece together the sequence of events that led to the outcomes.

Challenges Addressed

The two campaigns pursued different objectives, requiring the evaluation team to conduct separate analyses of the data for both the retrospective and prospective evaluation activities. Additionally, different contextual factors, such as ecological differences in the forest distribution in the two countries and different policy contexts, meant that the Canada strategy had to be reconfigured somewhat and evaluators had to develop an evaluation approach that was consistent and allowed for comparisons between the two countries. Second, the evaluation team partnered with experts in the two countries to lead the country-level components as well as an expert in working with indigenous peoples. Last, some of the sites were very remote and weather conditions impeded access.

Use of Evaluation Findings

In Canada, nearly 99 million acres were placed in protected status, and two landmark provincial agreements to protect or sustainably develop another 400 million acres were adopted during the evaluation period (bringing the total amount of lands protected since Pew began work in Canada to approximately 158 million acres). In Australia, Pew's efforts contributed to protecting about 75 million acres in the Outback, and $482 million was secured to support Indigenous conservation programs in the Outback. The evaluation findings indicate Pew's work in both countries was decisive or important in achieving a number of key outcomes in both countries. In addition to producing a description of the lessons learned, the findings were used to inform a revised five-year strategy for the International Lands Protection program. The findings were well received and validated Pew's decision to continue this line of work. The report helped educate Pew about the difficulties of applying 50/50 to the Australian effort and the extreme diversity of the Australian landscape.

Evaluators: Community Solutions
Stratcom
Edward W. Wilson Consulting

TRIBAL TOBACCO EDUCATION AND POLICY (TTEP) INITIATIVE

Initiative Description

In 2008, ClearWay Minnesota launched the Tribal Tobacco Education and Policy (TTEP) Initiative to provide resources and assistance to five tribal communities (four Anishinaabe [Objiwe] and one Dakota tribe) in order to address commercial tobacco through policy and advocacy approaches. The smoking rate of tribal populations is high (59 percent) compared to other populations. The goals of the initiative were: (1) support American Indian efforts to educate tribal government leaders, community members, traditional and spiritual leaders, and elders about the dangers of commercial tobacco use and secondhand smoke, and support community-level policy advocacy activities to advance comprehensive smoke-free policies on tribal lands; and (2) provide resources to make available training and technical assistance to the grant recipients in order to carry out efforts to support comprehensive, effective policies and strategies in Minnesota's Tribal Nations. TTEP was originally a five-year initiative, but it may continue another five-year cycle.

ADVOCACY STRATEGY AND TACTICS

The strategy is comprised of five core elements that together achieve healthy goals regarding tobacco use. Initiated by the TTEP staff members, who were employees of the tribes, strategies included research and planning, education, organizing and building support, and policy. Activities varied somewhat by the five tribes and included adopting smoke-free policies in public buildings and educating decision-makers, elected leaders, commissioners, and department heads. Messaging, coalition building, and community ownership of change were targeted at the community. There was also an effort to resurrect "Indigenous Tobacco Control" protocol, which is tied to spiritual ceremonies.

Evaluation Purpose, Design, and Instruments

In 2008, the evaluators employed a utilization-focused, mixed-method framework that included qualitative and quantitative data. It collaborated with TTEP teams and ClearWay staff to develop process and outcome evaluation questions and indicators for each of the five core elements. As part of their multiyear framework, they drew on empowerment evaluation strategies (building capacity and reflection), and developmental evaluation, trying and revising (or dropping) methods as they went along. They also tried to ensure that grantees and funders were working from the five core elements framework and learning the same thing, such as a sharing session and cross-site indicators. The five core elements are: (1) tribal communities acknowledge and restore traditional/sacred tobacco traditions; (2) tribal communities address and reduce tobacco industry marketing and influence; (3) tribal communities create formal and informal smoke-free politics and systems changes; (4) businesses and casinos in tribal communities are smoke-free; and (5) TTEP teams will have the staff capacity and resources for ongoing sustained efforts. The evaluators developed a logic model based on a CDC model. However, placing the five core elements into a circular framework proved more useful and was something to which stakeholders could relate.

Data Collection and Analysis Activities

Data collection activities commenced in 2009 and were completed in 2012. In the beginning, the core evaluation methods included: (1) Tribal Tobacco Story (TTS), a web-based monthly data collection/reflection systems structured as a program log to document major actions taken during the last month in the areas of community, staff capacity building and media; (2) media analysis using a nineteen-item instrument; (3) Technical Assistance & Training (TAT) Survey to assess satisfaction with TTEP capacity-building activities; (4) dialoguing or four interactive sessions with sites per year with a focus on listening and learning; (5) Tobacco Experience Inventory to assess TTEP staff advocacy experience and expertise; (6) Support Spider diagram, which provided a visual representation of community support from various sectors; (7) observations at TTEP communities, including powwows, tribal headquarters, and community service centers; and (8) Community Change Stories, a structured storytelling method that focused on a specific change process from the community point of view. Later, they added Policy Mapping, which is similar to the Advocacy Planning Tool and used the tactics section of the tool, dropping and adding some tactics, such as a focus on restoring traditional use of tobacco. The evaluators used the Tobacco Experience Inventory (TEI) survey for two years but dropped it after they had collected enough information about capacity. They also dropped the Support Spider diagram, which was helpful for learning about support early on and instead focused on assessing support for specific policies in the grantee work plan objectives.

Challenges Addressed

Launched early in the program, the evaluation team had to anticipate continued refinement throughout the project. Because American Indians have experienced traumatic colonization and continued attacks on cultural and political integrity, the evaluation needed to explicitly take the time to learn about and find ways to acknowledge these historical conditions. This included providing opportunities for tribal coordinators to conduct member checks and review results as well as education of the funders on the context of the project, with special attention to previous attacks on tribal sovereignty and cultural autonomy, which directly relate to work on policy issues within the tribal nation context. The evaluation team developed a participatory framework, which included a biennial group meeting of grantees or Sharing Sessions and were responsive to tribe-specific issues. To strengthen validity, they used triangulation and longitudinal data collection from multiple sources to ensure accuracy of the findings and to check for inconsistencies. They also applied complementarity principles or the synthesis of data from multiple sources to develop a more robust understanding of community action and community change. Inter-rater reliability assessment and statistical analyses were used to strengthen the findings from individual methods.

Use of Evaluation Findings

The evaluation findings indicate the TTEP Initiative supported four sites to pass formal smoke-free policies and all sites to expand informal smoke-free policies. The TTEP sites also increased community awareness of secondhand smoke. The findings have been disseminated multiple ways. The evaluators had an annual meeting at each site and generated the site TTS report. They performed what is called a "Target Practice" to describe progress for each of the objectives. Findings were discussed as a group to surface everybody's opinion. It was a period of reflection and celebration in which funders attended. Also, the TTEP group within the funder presented findings to the ClearWay Board. This was a small part of ClearWay's work, but it is a community that is experiencing huge disparities. This program has been discussed with the CDC and may get more visibility now that they are at the five-year mark of the program. Evaluators are moving to disseminate the results more aggressively, such as writing a formal paper, which will be done by TTEP coordinators. This will be disseminated to tribal communities as well as the public health community at large. Tribal policy gains have been reported in two-page Community Change stories and distributed nationally, including establishment of smoke-free rules targeted to facilities for children and elders, smoke-free buffer zones, and casino restrictions on employee smoking.

Evaluators: Scott Consulting Partners LLC

PROJECT HEALTH COLORADO
Initiative Description
Funded by the Colorado Trust, Project Heath Colorado (PHC) took place from 2011 to 2013. It was a public-will-building campaign designed to engage individuals and organizations in a statewide discussion about health care and how it can be improved. By asking questions, getting straight answers, and encouraging people across the state to be part of the solution, Project Health Colorado sought to activate the public to have a voice in the decisions being made about the healthcare system.

Advocacy Strategy and Tactics
The strategy was comprised of a communications campaign, on the ground organizing and community and leadership engagement, and building a network of organizations with the capacity and commitment to build will. Fourteen grantees, some new to advocacy and some veteran advocates, used a common message framework while engaging in diverse activities such as storytelling, leadership development, neighborhood mobilization, service-learning projects, and community and congregation forums. Grantees represented multiple sectors, including nonprofit advocates, nonprofit service providers, a hospital system, local government, and a faith-based organization. The initiatives had its own social media strategy that included a PHC interactive website, Facebook page, Twitter account, paid media campaign, and street teams at major festivals/events. More than twenty-five thousand people were reached in-person by street teams, community members and grantee staff, with some participating in volunteer trainings, community forums, and sharing their stories. Grantee social media and the overall communications campaign reached hundreds of thousands more.

Evaluation Purpose, Design, and Instruments

The evaluation deployed a multisource, mixed-method design that used a variety of approaches, including those intended to surface emergent outcomes that were unpredictable before the initiative was implemented. The design drew on a complex, adaptive system evaluation since the initiative had many interrelated parts with a variety of feedback loops. In addition, the evaluators integrated a public-will-building framework from the Metropolitan Group to develop a rubric with five levels of change that was used to create a common evaluation story across many different sources of data and types of audiences. The evaluation process began with each grantee developing a theory of change that aligned with the five outcomes included in the overall initiative theory of change. Then the evaluators worked with each grantee and the Colorado Trust to engage in real-time, data-driven strategic learning to steadily improve their strategies and outcomes. This was ongoing throughout the three years of the strategy. In addition to in-the-moment learning, every six months the funder and grantees engaged in learning debriefs, separately and together, identifying specific opportunities to improve their strategies and the initiative overall. The evaluation team developed the overall summative evaluation design one year into the strategy, giving time for a robust design that could respond to the shifting strategies and environment. It included: (1) spatial analysis of messenger distribution based on grantee reports and GIS techniques; (2) analysis of messengers' ability to use the message, their actions, and their reach; (3) network analysis of organizational partners; (4) fieldwork to identify emergent outcomes; and (5) in-depth case studies about strategies and their outcomes. While the overall evaluation strategy did not change once designed, the evaluators responded to the adaptive environment by changing how the evaluation strategies were deployed.

Data Collection and Analysis Activities

The data collection instruments included in the evaluation were: (1) analysis of grantee learning reports; (2) cross-survey analysis of grantee feedback; (3) organizational survey of grantees and their partner organizations; (4) case studies about messenger development, community forums and story collection (which included interviews, focus groups, ob-servations); (5) a story survey using a control group and five intervention groups to test the impact of stories; (6) survey of individual messengers; (7) analysis of message use by grantees and their audiences in their writ-ten, audio and video materials; (8) analysis of communications campaign tracking data; (9) GIS analysis of messenger distribution combined with field work in intensity areas; (10) time trend analysis for tracking polling results and external environment influencers; and (11) choice modeling (not in the original evaluation plan), which is a marketing research tech-nique focused on surfacing which combination of messages will reach the highest percentage of audience members.

Challenges Addressed

The evaluators developed an adaptive design that anticipated changes in the initiative that proved to be very complex. While evaluators reported limitations for many of the methods, they addressed these by using mul-tiple tools to strengthen the findings. Additionally, some of the data collection activities proved to be methodologically very rigorous. The qualitative data from the 110 interviews that were part of the fieldwork was deep enough to surface unexpected and emergent outcomes, infor-mation they couldn't get from a smaller sample size or survey data alone. The storytelling survey had a control group and the findings were action-able. They also integrated a field building assessment into the final round of the organizational network survey to meet the emerging needs of the Colorado Trust.

Use of Evaluation Findings

The ongoing analysis of grantee and nongrantee messaging resulted in shifts in the deployment of resources including how technical assistance for communications was delivered across grantees and the content and format of grantee convenings (an opportunity to do skill-building with peer-to-peer networking and sharing). Learning about the overall com-munications campaign informed a shift in the training, message use, and use of technology by the street teams. Grantee shifts largely came from their own deployment of real-time, data-driven strategic learning.

Grantees built this capacity as a result of the evaluation team coaching and facilitating twice yearly debriefs. They also received tailored reports about what the evaluators had learned, such as the level of commitment of messengers. Evaluation products included twice yearly presentations and facilitated dialogues with the grantees and the funder. There also were individual memos for grantees with findings related to their specific work, two interim evaluation reports and a final report, a pending public version of the final report, a Foundation Review article, and four issue briefs. The issue briefs described different advocacy strategies, including social media, communicating about health reform, storytelling, and working with faith leaders. These briefs were electronically disseminated to stakeholders in 2014.

Evaluators: Spark Policy Institute

ADVOCACY AND POLICY CHANGE
EVALUATION RESOURCES

ADVOCACY AND POLICY CHANGE
EVALUATION FRAMEWORKS

A Guide to Measuring Advocacy and Policy Change by Organizational Research Services for the Annie E. Casey Foundation. 2007.

A User's Guide to Advocacy Evaluation Planning by Julia Coffman for the Harvard Family Research Project. 2009.

Advocacy Assessment Framework by Redstone Strategy Group. 2013.

Advocacy Progress Planner by Aspen Planning and Evaluation Program at the Aspen Institute.

Advocacy Impact Assessment Guidelines prepared by Megan Lloyd Laney for CIMRC. 2003.

Advocacy and Policy Change Composite Model by Julia Coffman and representatives from the California Endowment, the Atlantic Philanthropies, and the Annie E. Casey Foundation. 2007.

Getting Equity Advocacy Results (GEAR) PolicyLink.

Framework for Policy and Advocacy Outcomes by Center for Evaluation Innovation.

Smart Chart for Communication Strategies by Spitfire Strategies.

The Advocacy Strategy Framework prepared by Julia Coffman and Tanya Beer, Center for Evaluation Innovation. 2015.

The Challenge of Assessing Policy and Advocacy Initiatives: Strategies for a Prospective Evaluation Approach by Blueprint Research & Design for the California Endowment. 2005.

The Challenges of Assessing Policy and Advocacy Initiatives: Part II—Moving from Theory to Practice prepared by Kendall Guthrie, Justin Louie, and Catherine Crystal Foster for the California Endowment. 2006.

Monitoring, Evaluation and Learning in NGO Advocacy prepared by Jim Coe and Juliette Majot for Overseas Development Institute (ODI). 2013.

Pathfinder: A Practical Guide to Advocacy Evaluation by Innovation Network for the Atlantic Philanthropies. 2009.

What Makes an Effective Advocacy Organization: A Framework for Determining Advocacy Capacity by TCC Group for the California Endowment. 2009.

What Makes an Effective Coalition: Evidence-based Indicators of Success by TCC Group for the California Endowment. 2011.

RAPID Outcome Assessment by Overseas Development Institute (ODI). 2013.

ADVOCACY AND POLICY CHANGE
EVALUATION TOOL-KITS

A Handbook of Data Collection Tools: Companion to A Guide to Measuring Advocacy and Policy prepared by Jane Resiman, Anne Gienapp, and Sarah Stachowiak, Organizational Research Services for the Annie E. Casey Foundation. 2007.

A Practical Guide to Documenting Influence and Leverage in Making Connections Communities prepared by Organizational Research Services for the Annie E. Casey Foundation. 2004.

An Advocacy Evaluation Mini-Toolkit: Tips and Tools for Busy Organizations by LFA Group. 2013.

Assessing and Evaluating Change in Advocacy Fields prepared by Jewyla Lynn. Center for Evaluation Innovation. 2014.

Assessing the Impact of Research on Policy: A Review of the Literature for a Project on Bridging Research on Policy Through Outcome Evaluation prepared by Annette Boaz, Siobhan Fitzpatrick, and Ben Shaw. Kings College London and Policy Studies Institute. 2008.

Consumer Voices for Coverage: Advocacy Evaluation Toolkit prepared by Debra Strong, Todd Honeycutt, and Judith Wooldridge, Mathematica Policy Research. 2011.

EAA Advocacy Evaluation Guide prepared by Christina Mansfield for the Ecumenical Advocacy Alliance. 2010.

Four Tools for Assessing Grantee Contribution to Advocacy Efforts prepared by Tanya Beer and Julia Coffman for the Center for Evaluation Innovation. 2015.

Monitoring & Evaluation of Advocacy Campaigns: Literature Review prepared by Christina Mansfield for the Ecumenical Advocacy Alliance. 2010.

Monitoring and Evaluation of Policy Influence and Advocacy prepared by Overseas Development Institute (ODI). 2014.

Monitoring and Evaluating Advocacy: A Companion to the Advocacy Toolkit prepared by Julia Coffman for UNICEF. 2010.

Monitoring and Evaluating Advocacy: A Scoping Study prepared by Jennifer Chapman and Amboka Wameyo for ActionAid. 2001.

Saving Newborn Lives: Champions Toolkit prepared by Sarah Roma and Carlisle Levine for Save the Children. 2016

The CARE International Advocacy Handbook published by CARE International. 2014.

Tools for Policy Impact: A Handbook for Researchers by Daniel Start and Ingie Hovland for ODI. 2004.

UNIQUE ADVOCACY AND POLICY CHANGE
EVALUATION TOOLS

Advocacy Index by USAID.

Advocacy Capacity Tool and the *International Advocacy Capacity Tool* by Alliance for Justice.

Advocacy Core Capacity Assessment Tool by TCC Group.

Alignment Index by ORS and the Bill and Melinda Gates Foundation Education Pathways team.

Bellwether Methodology by the Harvard Family Research Project.

Champion Scorecard by the Aspen Institute.

Intense-Period Debrief Protocol by Innovation Network.

Policymaker Ratings Scale by The Harvard Family Research Program.

Power Check: Community Organizing Capacity Assessment Tool by Alliance for Justice.

Powercube.net, an Online Resource for Thinking About Power Relations. Developed by the Participation, Power and Social Change team at the Institute of Development Studies, University of Sussex. http://www.powercube.net.

ADVOCACY AND POLICY CHANGE
EVALUATION ELECTRONIC REPOSITORIES

Center for Evaluation Innovation
http://www.evaluationinnovation.org
Innovation Network Point K Learning Center
http://www.innonet.org

REFERENCES

Alinsky, Saul, D. 1970. *Rules for Radicals: A Practical Primer for Realistic Radicals.* New York: Vintage Books.

Alliance for Justice. 2015. *Philanthropy Advocacy Playbook: Leveraging Your Dollars.*

Andrews, Kenneth T., and Bob Edwards. 2004. "Advocacy Organizations in the U.S. Political Process." *Annual Review of Sociology 30*: 479–506.

Bamberger, Michael, Jim Rugh, Mary Church, and Lucia Fort. 2004. "Shoestring Evaluation: Designing Impact Evaluations Under Budget, Time and Data Constraints." *American Journal of Evaluation* 25(1): 5–37.

Bamberger, Michael, Jim Rugh, and Linda Mabry. 2012. *RealWorld Evaluation: Working Under Budget, Time, Data, and Political Constraints.* 2d ed. Thousand Oaks, CA: SAGE Publications, Inc.

Bardach, Eugene. 2012. *A Practical Guide for Policy Analysis.* 4th ed. Thousand Oaks, CA: CQ Press, an Imprint of SAGE Publications.

Barkhorn, Ivan, Nathen Hunter, and Jason Blau. 2013. "Assessing Advocacy." *Stanford Social Science Innovation Review.*

Baron, Michelle E. 2011. "Designing Internal Evaluation for a Small Organization With Limited Resources." *New Directions for Evaluation* 132: 87–100.

Baumgartner, Frank R., Bryan Jones, and Peter B. Mortenson. 2014. "Punctuated Equilibrium Theory: Explaining Stability and Change in Public Policymaking." In *Theories of the Policy Process.* P. Sabatier and C. Weible, eds. Boulder, CO: Westview Press.

Baumgartner, Frank R., and Beth L. Leech. 1998. *Basic Interests: The Importance of Groups in Politics and Political Science.* Princeton, NJ: Princeton University Press.

Beer, Tanya, Pilar Stella Ingargiola, and Meghann Flynn Beer. 2012. *Advocacy & Public Policy Grantmaking: Matching Process to Purpose.* The Colorado Trust.

Bickman, Leonard, and Stephanie M. Reich. 2015. "Randomized Controlled Trials: A Gold Standard or Gold Plated? In *Credible and Actionable Evidence: The Foundations for Rigorous and Influential Evaluations.* 2d ed. S. Donaldson, C. Christie, and M. Mark, eds. Thousand Oaks, CA: SAGE Publications, Inc.

Birkland, Thomas A. 2001. *An Introduction to the Policy Process: Theories, Concepts and Models of Public Policy.* Armonk, NY: M.E. Sharpe, Inc.

Boaz, Annette, Siobhan Fitzpatrick, and Ben Shaw. 2008. *Assessing the Impact of Research on Policy: A Review of the Literature for a Project on Bridging Research and Policy Through Outcome Evaluation.* Centre for Evidence & Policy at King's College London and the Policy Studies Institute.

Boehmeke, Frederick J., Sean Gailmard, and John W. Patty. 2013. "Business as Usual:

Interest Group Access and Representation Across Policy-making Venues." *Journal of Public Policy* 33(1): 3–33.

Brindis, Claire D., Sara P. Geierstanger, and Adrienne Faxio. 2009. "The Role of Advocacy in Assuring Comprehensive Family Life Education in California." *Health Education & Behavior* 36(6):1095–108.

Carden, Fred. 2004. "Issues in Assessing the Policy Influence of Research." In *UNESCO 2004*. Published by Blackwell Publishing Ltd. Oxford UK. 135–51.

Chapman, Jennifer, and Amboka Wameyo. 2001. *Monitoring and Evaluating Advocacy: A Scoping Study*. ActionAid.

Charney, Craig. 2009. "Political Will: What is It? How is it Measured?" (Charney Research). http://www.charneyresearch.com/resources/political-will-what-is-it-how-is-it-measured/

Chelimsky, Eleanor. 1995. "The Political Environment of Evaluation and What it Means for the Development of the Field." *Evaluation Practice* 16(3): 215–25.

———. 2001. "What Evaluation Could Do to Support Foundations: A Framework with Nine Component Parts." *American Journal of Evaluation* 22(1): 13–28.

———. 2007. "Factors Influencing the Choice of Methods in Federal Evaluation Practice." *New Directions for Evaluation* 113: 13–33.

———. 2014. "Public-Interest Values and Program Sustainability: Some Implications for Evaluation Practice." *American Journal of Evaluation* 35(4): 527–42.

Chen, Huey T., Stewart I. Donaldson, and Melvin M. Mark. 2011. "Validity Frameworks for Outcome Evaluation. *New Directors for Evaluation* 130: 5–16.

Chen, Huey T., and Nanette C. Turner. 2012. "Formal Theory Versus Stakeholder Theory: New Insights From a Tobacco Prevention Program Evaluation." *American Journal of Evaluation* 33(3): 395–413.

Christie, Christina A. and Dreolin Fleischer. 2015. "Social Inquiry Paradigms as a Frame for the Debate on Credible Evidence." In *Credible and Actionable Evidence: The Foundation for Rigorous and Influential Evaluations*. Stewart I. Donaldson, Christina A. Christie, and Melvin M. Mark Editors. Thousand Oaks, CA: SAGE Publications.

Coe, Jim, and Juliette Majot. 2013. *Monitoring, Evaluation and Learning in NGO Advocacy*. London: Overseas Development Institute.

Coffman, Julia. 2009. *Overview of Current Advocacy Evaluation Practice*. Center for Evaluation Innovation.

———. 2008. *A User's Guide to Advocacy and Evaluation Planning*. Harvard Family Research Project.

———. 2014. "Evaluation Designs for Advocacy." Unpublished.

———and Tanya Beer. 2015. *The Advocacy Strategy Framework*. Center for Evaluation Innovation.

———and Ehren Reed. 2009. *Unique Methods in Advocacy Evaluation*. Innovation Associates.

Cousins, J. Bradley, Elizabeth Whitmore, and Lyn Shulha. 2013. "Arguments for a Common Set of Principles for Collaborative Inquiry in Evaluation." *American Journal of Evaluation* 34(1): 7–22.

Coghlan, Anne T., Halie Preskill, and Tessie Tzavaras Catsambas. 2003. "An Overview of Appreciative Inquiry in Evaluation." *New Directions for Evaluation* 100: 5–22.

Costa, Arthur L., and Bena Kallick. 1993. "Through the Lens of a Critical Friend." *Educational Leadership* 51(2): 49–51.

Dahl, Robert A. 1991. *Modern Political Analysis.* 5th Ed. Englewood Cliffs, NJ: Prentice Hall, Inc.

Dart, Jessica J. 2000. *Stories for Change: A Systematic Approach to Participatory Monitoring.* Latrobe University.

Devlin-Foltz, David, and Lisa Molinaro. 2010. *Champions and "Champion-ness": Measuring Efforts to Create Champions for Policy Change.* Continuous Progress Strategic Services Center for Evaluation Innovation.

Devlin-Foltz, David, Michael E. Fagen, Ehren Reed, Robert Medina, and Brad L. Neiger. 2012. "Advocacy Evaluation: Challenges and Emerging Trends." *Health Promotion Practice*, 13(5): 581–86.

Dryzek, John S. 1996. "Political Inclusion and the Dynamics of Democratization." *American Political Science Review* 90(1): 475–87.

Dynaway, Krystal E., Jennifer A. Morrow, and Bryan E. Porter. 2012. "Development and Validation of the Cultural Competence of Program Evaluators (CCPE) Self-Report Scale." *American Journal of Evaluation* 33(4): 496–514.

Dye, Thomas R. 2002. *Understanding Public Policy.* Upper Saddle River, NJ: Prentice Hall.

Ecumenical Advocacy Alliance. *EAA Advocacy Evaluation Guide* and *Monitoring & Evaluation of Advocacy Campaigns: Literature Review.* September 2010.

Evaluating Community Change: A Framework for Grantmakers. 2014. Grantmakers for Effective Organizations (GEO)

Ezell, Mark. 2001. *Advocacy in the Human Services.* Belmond, CA: Brooks/Cole, Cengage Learning.

Fetterman, David M. 2005. "A Window into the Heart and Soul of Empowerment Evaluation." In *Evaluation Principles in Practice.* D. Fetterman, and A. Wandersman, eds. New York: The Guilford Press.

Feinstein, Clare, and Claire O'Kane. 2005. *The Spider Tool: A Self-Assessment and Planning Tool for Child Led Initiatives and Organizations.* International Save the Children. Sweden.

Foster, Catherine C., and Justin Louie. 2010. *Grassroots Action and Learning for Social Change: Evaluating Community Organizing.* Center for Evaluation Innovation and Blueprint Research & Design, Inc.

Foster-Fishman, Pennie, G., Brenda Nowell, and Huilan Yang. 2007. "Putting the System Back into Systems Change: A Framework for Understanding and Changing Organizational and Community Systems." *American Journal of Community Psychology* 39: 197–215.

Freeman, Melissa, and Erika Franca Vasconcelos. 2010. "Critical Social Theory: Core Tenets, Inherent Issues." *New Directions for Evaluation* 127: 7–19.

Friere, Paulo. 2000. *Pedagogy of the Oppressed: 30th Edition.* New York: Bloomsbury Press.

Funnell, Sue C., and Patricia J. Rogers. 2011. *Purposeful Program Theory: Effective Use of Theories of Change and Logic Models*. San Francisco, CA: John Wiley & Sons, Inc.

Gardner, Annette, Sara Geierstanger, Claire D. Brindis, and Coline McConnel. 2010. "Clinic Consortia Media Advocacy Capacity: Partnering With the Media and Increasing Policymaker Awareness." *Journal of Health Communication* 15: 293–306.

Gardner, Annette, Sara Geierstanger, Lori Nascimento, and Claire Brindis. 2011. "Expanding Organizational Capacity: Lessons From the Field." *The Foundation Review* 3 (1&2): 23–42.

Gaventa, John. 2006. "Finding the Space for Change: A Power Analysis." In Exploring Power for Change, *IDS Bulletin* 37(6): 23–33.

Gill, Sam, and Tom Freedman. 2014. "Climbing the Mountain: An Approach to Planning and Evaluating Public-Policy Advocacy." *The Foundation Review* 6(3): 48–59.

Granger, Robert C., and Rebecca Maynard. 2015. "Unlocking the Potential of the 'What Works' Approach to Policymaking and Practice: Improving Impact Evaluations." *American Journal of Evaluation* 36(4): 558–69.

Grob, George F. "How to Become an Effective Advocate Without Selling Your Soul." *American Journal of Evaluation*, online 22 April 2014: 1–7.

Guthrie, Kendall, Justin Louie, Tom David, and Catherine Crystal Foster. 2005. *The Challenge of Assessing Policy and Advocacy Activities: Strategies for a Prospective Evaluation Approach*. Commissioned by the California Endowment.

Hargreaves, Margaret B. 2010. *Evaluating System Change: A Planning Guide*. Mathematica Policy Research, Inc.

Harner, Michael A., and Hallie Preskill. 2007. "Evaluators' Descriptions of Process Use: An Exploratory Study." *New Directions for Evaluation* 116: 27–44.

Heinz, John P., Edward O. Laumann, Robert L. Nelson, and Robert H. Salisbury. 1993. *The Hollow Core*. Cambridge, MA: Harvard University Press.

Henry, Gary T., Adriaenne A. Smith, David C. Kershaw, and Rebecca A. Zulli. 2013. "Formative Evaluation: Estimating Preliminary Outcomes and Testing Rival Explanations." *American Journal of Evaluation* 34(4): 465–85.

Hesse-Biber, Sharlene. 2013. "Thinking Outside the Randomized Controlled Trials Experimental Box: Strategies for Enhancing Credibility and Social Justice." *New Directions for Evaluation* 138: 49–60.

Hilt, Lisa. 2014. *Yes, it can be that simple! Value for Money Analyses in Policy Advocacy and Campaigns*. American Evaluation Association APC TIG Week.

Hoeffer, Richard. 2012. *Advocacy Practice for Social Justice*. Chicago, IL: Lyceum Books, Inc.

Holley, Marc J., Cheri A. Reccia, and Valarie Bocksette. 2016. "Measuring What Matters: Five Grant Performance Measurement Traps and How to Avoid Them." *Stanford Social Innovation Review*. Retrieved online October 13, 2016 at https://ssir.org/articles/entry/measuring_what_matters.

Honeycutt, Todd C., and Debra A. Strong. 2012. "Using Social Network Analysis to Predict Early Collaboration Within Health Advocacy Coalitions." *American Journal of Evaluation* 33(2) 221–39.

Huitema, Dave, Andrew Jordon, Eric Massey, Tim Raynor, Harro van Asselt, Constanze Haug, Roger Hildingsson, Suvi Monni, and Johannes Stripple. 2011. "The Evaluation of Climate Policy: Theory and Emerging Practice in Europe." *Policy Sciences* 44: 179–98.

Innovation Network. 2008. *Speaking for Themselves: Advocates' Perspectives on Evaluation.* Washington, D.C.

———. 2012. *State of Evaluation 2012: Evaluation Practice and Capacity in the Nonprofit Sector.* Washington, DC.

I-TECH. 2008. *Rapid Evaluation.* I-TECH Technical Implementation Guide #6. Seattle: University of Washington.

Jenkins-Smith, Hank C., and Paul A. Sabatier. 1994. "Evaluating the Advocacy Coalition Framework." *Journal of Public Policy 14*: 175–203.

Jones, Harry. 2011. *A Guide to Monitoring and Evaluating Policy Influence.* Background Note. Overseas Development Institute.

Kelly, Linda. 2002. "International Advocacy: Measuring Performance and Effectiveness." Paper presented to the 2002 Australasian Evaluation Society International Conference. Wollongong, Australia.

Kimberlin, Sara E. 2010. "Advocacy by Nonprofits: Roles and Practices of Core Advocacy Organizations and Direct Service Agencies." *Journal of Policy Practice* (9)3–4:164–82.

Kingdon, John W. 1995. *Agendas, Alternatives, and Public Policies.* 2d ed. New York: HarperCollins College Publishers.

Klugman, Barbara. 2010. *Evaluating Social Justice Advocacy: A Values Based Approach.* Center for Evaluation Innovation.

Kosheleva, Natalia, and Marco Segone. 2013. "EvalPartners: Facilitating the Development of a New Model of Voluntary Organization for Professional Evaluation to Support the Development of National Evaluation Capacities." *American Journal of Evaluation* 34(4): 568–72.

Kraft, Michael E., and Scott R. Furlong. 2010. *Public Policy: Politics, Analysis, and Alternatives.* Washington, DC: CQ Press.

Kushner, Saville, and Emma Rotondo. 2012. "Editors' Notes." *New Directions for Evaluation* 134: 1–4.

Laney, Megan Lloyed. 2003. *Advocacy Impact Assessment Guidelines.* Communications and Information Management Resource Center (CIMRC). Walingford, UK.

Latham, Nancy. 2014. *A Practical Guide to Evaluating Systems Change in a Human Services System Context.* Center for Evaluation Innovation and Learning for Action.

Lave, Jean, and Etienne Wegner. 1991. *Situated Learning: Legitimate Peripheral Participation.* New York: Cambridge University Press.

Lindblom, Charles E. 1979. "Still Muddling, Not Yet Through." *Public Administration Review* 39(6): 517–26.

Lipsky, Michael. 2011. *Street-level Democracy: Dilemmas of the Individual in Public Services.* New York: Russell Sage Foundation.

Loomis, Burdette A., and Allan J. Cigler. 2007. "Introduction: The Changing Nature of

Interest Group Politics." In *Interest Group Politics*. B. Loomis and A. Cigler, eds. Washington, DC: CQ Press.

Lowe, Theodore J. 1964. "American Business, Public Policy Case Studies and Political Theory." *World Politics* 16: 677–715.

Lowery, David, and Holly Brasher. 2004. *Organized Interests and American Government*. New York: McGraw-Hill.

Lynn, Jewlya. 2014. *Assessing and Evaluating Change in Advocacy Fields*. Center for Evaluation Innovation.

Mahoney, Christine, and Frank R. Baumgartner. 2015. "Partners in Advocacy: Lobbyists and Government Officials in Washington." *The Journal of Politics* 77(1): 202–15.

Mansfield, Cristina. 2010. *EAA Advocacy Evaluation Guide*. Ecumenical Advocacy Alliance, Geneva.

———. 2010. *Monitoring & Evaluation of Advocacy Campaigns Literature Review*. Ecumenical Advocacy Alliance, Geneva.

Masters, Barbara, Gigi Barsoum, and Amanda Rounsaville. In collaboration with Fenton Communications and the Center for Evaluation Collaboration. 2014. *Policy Change Ten Years in the Making: Evaluation of The California Wellness Foundation's Decade of Public Policy Grantmaking*.

Masters, Barbara, and Torie Osborn. 2010. "Social Movements and Philanthropy: How Foundations Can Support Movement Building." *The Foundation Review* 2(2): 12–27.

Mayne, John. 2012. "Contribution Analysis: Coming of Age?" *Evaluation* 18: 270–80.

McClure, Mary, William Renderos, with Sue Hoechstetter and Abby Levine. 2015. *ACT Data and Analysis: The First 280 Advocacy Capacity Tool Users*. Alliance for Justice.

Mertens, Donna M., and Sharlene Hesse-Biber. 2013. "Mixed Methods and Credibility of Evidence in Evaluation." *New Directions for Evaluation* 138: 5–13.

Mintron, Michael, and Sandra Vergari. 1998. "Policy Networks and Innovation Diffusion: The Case of State Education Reforms." *The Journal of Politics* 60(1): 126–48.

Mohan, Rakesh. 2014. "Evaluator Advocacy: It Is All in a Day's Work." *American Journal of Evaluation*, online 22 April 2014: 1–7.

Mohan, Rakesh, and Kathleen Sullivan. 2006. "Managing the Politics of Evaluation to Achieve Impact." *New Directions for Evaluation* 112: 7–23.

Morariu, Johanna, and Kathleen Brennan. 2009. "Effective Advocacy Evaluation: The Role of Funders.' *The Foundation Review*, 1(3): 100–108.

Morariu, Johanna, Katherine Athanasiades, and Veena Pankai. 2015. *Advocacy, Politics and Philanthropy: A Reflection on a Decade of Immigration Report and Advocacy 2004—2014*. Innovation Network.

Nowlin, Mathew, C. 2011. "Theories in the Policy Process: State of the Research and Emerging Trends." *Policy Studies Journal* 39(S1): 41–60.

Mossberter, Karen, and Harold Wolman. 2003. "Policy Transfer as a Form of Prospective Policy Evaluation: Challenges and Recommendations." *Public Administration Review* 63(4): 428–40.

Network Impact and Center for Evaluation Innovation. 2014. *Framing Paper: The State of Network Evaluation*.

O'Flynn, Maureen. 2009. *Tracking Progress in Advocacy: Why and How to Monitor and Evaluate Advocacy Projects and Programmes.* International NGO Training and Research Centre (INTRAC).

Obar, Jonathan A., Paul Zube, and Clifford Lampe. 2012. "Advocacy 2.0: An Analysis of How Advocacy Groups in the United States Perceive and Use Social Media as Tools for Facilitating Civic Engagement and Collective Action." *Journal of Information Policy* 2: 1–25.

ORS Impact. 2010. *Evaluation of Networks.* Seattle, WA.

Parrish, Simone. 2008. *Measuring Influence: Advocacy Evaluation Challenges and Successes.* Innovation Network, Inc.

Pasanen, Tina, and Louise Shaxson. 2016. *How to Design a Monitoring and Evaluation Framework for a Policy Research Project.* A Methods Lab Publication. ODI, London, UK.

Patton, Michael Q. 2008. "Advocacy Impact Evaluation." *Journal of MultiDisciplinary Evaluation* 5(9): 1–9.

———. 2011. *Developmental Evaluation: Applying Complexity Concepts to Enhance Innovation and Use.* New York: Guilford Press.

———. 2012. *Essentials of Utilization-Focused Evaluation.* Thousand Oaks, CA: SAGE Publications.

Post, Lori Ann, Amber N. W. Raile, and Eric D. Raile. 2010. "Defining Political Will." *Politics & Policy* 38 (4): 653–76.

Preskill, Haillie, and Srik Gopal. 2014. *Evaluating Complexity: Propositions for Improving Progress.* New York: Farrar Straus & Giroux.

Putnam, Robert. 1996. "The Strange Disappearance of Civic America." *The American Prospect* 24: 34–48.

Ranghelli, Lisa. 2008. *Strengthening Democracy, Increasing Opportunities: Impacts of Advocacy, Organizing, and Civic Engagement in New Mexico.* National Committee for Responsive Philanthropy.

Raynor, Jared, Locke, Nadia Gomes, and Chen, PeiYao. 2013. *A Study to Support the Evaluation of the Rockefeller Foundation's Promoting Equitable and Sustainable Transportation Initiative.* TCC Group.

Reisman, Jane, Kasey Langley, Sarah Stachowiak, and Anne Gienapp. 2007. *A Guide to Measuring Advocacy and Policy.* Organizational Research Services.

———. 2007. *A Handbook of Data Collection Tools: Companion to "A Guide to Measuring Advocacy and Policy."* Organizational Research Services.

Reisman, Jane, Anne Gienapp, and Sarah Stachowiak. 2004. *A Practical Guide to Documenting Influence and Leverage in Making Connections Communities.* Organizational Research Services.

Reisman, Jane, Anne Gienapp, and Tom Kelly. 2015. *I2L2: Impact = Influence+ Leverage+Learning.* ORS Impact and Hawaii Community Foundation.

Rog, Debra J. 2012. "When Background Becomes Foreground: Toward Context-Sensitive Evaluation Practice." *New Directions for Evaluation* 135: 25–40.

Rogers, Everett M. 1995. *Diffusion of Innovations.* 4th Edition. New York: The Free Press.

Roma, Sarah, and Carlisle Levine. 2016. *Saving Newborn Lives: Champions Toolkit.* Save the Children.

Rossi, Peter H., Mark W. Lipsey, and Howard E. Freeman. 2004. *Evaluation: A Systematic Approach 7th Edition.* Thousand Oaks, CA: SAGE Publications.

Schlager, Edella, and William Blomquist. 1996. "A Comparison of Three Emerging Theories of the Policy Process." *Political Research Quarterly* 49 (3): 651–72.

Schlangen, Rhonda. 2014. *Monitoring and Evaluation for Human Rights Organizations: Three Case Studies.* Center for Evaluation Innovation.

Schlozman, Kay L., and John T. Tierney. 1986. *Organized Interests and American Democracy.* New York: Harper & Row Publishers.

Schlozman, Kay L., Sidney Verba, and Henry E. Brady. 2012. *The Unheavenly Chorus: Unequal Political Voice and the Broken Promises of American Democracy.* Princeton, NJ: Princeton University Press.

Sherman, John, and Gayle Peterson. 2009. "Finding the Win in Wicked Problems: Lessons from Evaluating Public Policy Advocacy." *The Foundation Review* 1(3): 87–99.

Smith, Kevin B., and Christopher W. Larimer. 2013. *The Public Policy Theory Primer.* 2d ed. Boulder, CO: Westview Press.

Smith, Stephen R. 2010. "Nonprofit Organizations and Government: Implications for Policy and Practice." *Journal of Policy Analysis and Management* 29(3): 621–44.

Spark Policy Institute. 2011. *Constituency Tracking Tool.* Denver, CO.

Stachowiak, Sarah. 2013. *Pathways for Change: 10 Theories to Inform Advocacy and Policy Change Efforts.* ORS Impact and the Center for Evaluation Innovation.

Stachowiak, Sarah, Sara Afflerback, and Melissa Howlett. 2016. *Measuring Political Will: Lessons from Modifying the Policymaker Ratings Method.* ORS Impact.

Stachowiak, Sarah, Jane Reisman, and Emily Boardman. 2013. *Getting More From Measurement.* ORS Impact.

Stachowiak, Sarah, Leonor Robles, Eritrea Habtermariam, and Melanie Malty. 2016. *Beyond the Win: Pathways for Policy Implementation.* ORS Impact.

Stewart, Joseph, Jr., David M. Hedge, and James P. Lester. 2008. *Public Policy: An Evolutionary Approach.* Boston, MA: Thomson Higher Education.

Stroh, David P. 2009. "Leveraging Grantmaking: Understanding the Dynamics of Complex Social Systems." *Foundation Review* 1(3): 109–22.

Strong, Debra, Todd Honeycutt, and Judith Woolridge. 2011. *Consumer Voices for Coverage: Advocacy Evaluation Toolkit.* Mathematica Policy Research.

Teles, Steven, and Mark Schmitt. 2011. "The Elusive Craft of Evaluating Advocacy." *Stanford Social Innovation Review* 39–43.

Theodoulu, Stella Z., and Mathew A. Cahn. 1995. *Public Policy: The Essential Readings.* Englewood Cliffs, NJ: Prentice-Hall.

Theodoulu, Stella Z., and Chris Kofinis. 2004. *The Art of the Game: Understanding American Public Policy Making.* Belmont, CA: Thomson/Wadsworth.

Tsui, Josehphine. 2013. *The Effectiveness of Measuring Influence.* GSDRC Applied Knowledge Services.

———, Simon Hearn, and John Young. 2014. *Monitoring and Evaluating Policy Influence and Advocacy*. Working Paper. London: Overseas Development Institute.

Verba, Sidney, Kay Lehman Schlozman, and Henry Brady. 1995. *Voice and Equality: Civic Voluntarism in American Politics*. Cambridge, MA: Harvard University Press.

Volkov, Boris B. 2011. "Beyond Being an Evaluator: the Multiplicity of Roles of the Internal Evaluator." *New Directions for Evaluation* 132: 25–42.

Walker, Jack L. 1983. "The Origins and Maintenance of Interest Groups in America." *The American Political Science Review* 77(2): 390–406.

Wedel, Janine R. 2009. *Shadow Elite: How the World's New Power Brokers Undermine Democracy, Government, and the Free Market*. Philadelphia, PA: Basic Books.

Weiss, Carol H. 1999. "The Interface Between Evaluation and Public Policy." *Evaluation* 5(4): 468–86.

———, Erin Murphy-Graham, Anthony Petrosino, and Allison G. Gandhi. 2008. "The Fairy Godmother—and Her Warts: Making the Dream of Evidence-based Policy Come True." *American Journal of Evaluation* 29(1): 29–47.

Weissert, Carol S., and William G. Weissert. 1996. *Governing Health*. Baltimore, MD: Johns Hopkins University Press.

White, Howard. 2013. "The Use of Mixed Methods in Randomized Control Trials." *New Directions for Evaluation* 138: 61–73.

Whitehurst, Grover J., and David Stuit. 2014. *Survey with Placebo: A Method for Evaluating the Influence of Advocacy*. Presentation to the Aspen Institute.

Wilson-Grau, Ricardo, and Heather Britt. 2013. *Outcome Harvesting*. Ford Foundation.

Wolfson, Sara, and Cameron Lefevre. 2012. *2012 eNonprofit Benchmarks Study*. M&R Strategic Services and Nonprofit Technology Networks (N TEN).

Yin, Robert K. 2014. *Case Study Research; Design and Methods*. 5th ed. Thousand Oaks, CA: SAGE Publications.